WITHDRAWN

The Lives of Women

A New History
of Inquisitional Spain

THE LIVES
of WOMEN

A New History
of Inquisitional Spain

Lisa Vollendorf

Vanderbilt University Press

NASHVILLE

© 2005 Vanderbilt University Press
All rights reserved
First Edition 2005

This book is printed on acid-free paper.
Manufactured in the United States of America

Publication of this book has been supported by a generous subsidy
from the Program for Cultural Cooperation between Spain's
Ministry of Culture and United States Universities.

Library of Congress Cataloging-in-Publication Data

Vollendorf, Lisa.
  The lives of women : a new history of Inquisitional Spain /
Lisa Vollendorf.—1st ed., 2005.
    p. cm.
  Includes bibliographical references and index.
ISBN 0-8265-1481-2 (cloth : alk. paper)
1. Women—Spain—History. 2. Women—Spain—Social
conditions. 3. Women authors, Spanish. 4. Feminism—Spain—
History. 5. Inquisition—Spain.
I. Title.
HQ1693.V65 2005
305.4'0946'0903—dc22

2005007619

In honor of Mary Elizabeth Perry,
an exemplary scholar and friend

CONTENTS

PART III
Women's Worlds
Convent Culture

PART IV
Women's Networks
Leadership and Community

ACKNOWLEDGMENTS

R esearch support for this book was provided by many sources, including postdoctoral fellowships from the Monticello College Foundation at the Newberry Library and an Ahmanson-Getty Postdoctoral Fellowship from UCLA's William Andrews Clark Memorial Library and the Center for Seventeenth and Eighteenth Century Studies. Wayne State University gave me several research leaves, which allowed me to finish the book. Numerous grants from the university's general research funds and the Humanities Center provided funding for archival research during three summers in Madrid. In 2003, an Andrew W. Mellon grant at the Huntington Library afforded me the opportunity to consult Inquisition cases at that institution, and a research grant from the Program for Cultural Cooperation between Spain's Ministry of Culture, Education, and Sports and United States Universities funded a trip to Spanish archives.

Archivists in the United States and in Spain gave of their time and knowledge to help bring the project to completion. The following people guided my research: John Aubry and John Powell, of the Newberry Library; Jennifer Schaffner and Bruce Whiteman, of UCLA's William Andrews Clark Memorial Library; and the librarians and reader services personnel at the Huntington Library. In Spain, the fine staff at the Biblioteca Nacional and at the Archivo Histórico Nacional, particularly Pilar Bravo Lledó and José Luis Clares, and at the Biblioteca Nacional assisted me in my research. Finally, the Humanities Center at Wayne State University and the Asociación de Escritoras de España y las Américas (1300–1800) provided invaluable scholarly support.

The editors at the *Arizona Journal for Hispanic Cultural Studies* and the University Press of Florida generously gave permission to reprint revised versions of "The Future of Early Modern Women's Studies: The Case of Same-Sex Friendship and Desire in Zayas and Carvajal" (*Arizona Journal of Hispanic Cultural Studies* 4 [2000]: 265–84) and of "Desire Unbound: Women's Theater of Spain's Golden Age," in Joan Cammarata, ed., *Women's Discourse in Early Modern Spain* (University Press of Florida, 2003). Barbara Simerka and Christopher Weimer, editors of *Laberinto*, also supported and published my work.

The Lives of Women: A New History of Inquisitional Spain has benefited from the fine research of countless scholars of early modern Europe and the Hispanic world. In Spain, Isabel Barbeito Carneiro has brought numerous texts to light through her impeccable archival work. In North America, I have been guided and inspired by a cohort of impressive scholars, including Anne J. Cruz, Amy Katz Kaminsky, Mary Elizabeth Perry, Stacey Schlau, Teresa Soufas, and Alison Weber. This book could not have been written without the consummate scholarship and tireless support of these women.

A number of other colleagues have been extraordinarily generous of time and spirit. I thank Electa Arenal, Joan Cammarata, Renato Barahona, Jodi Bilinkoff, Marina Brownlee, Gwyn Campbell, Frances Dolan, Walter Edwards, James Farr, Charles Ganelin, Mitchell Greenberg, Stephen Haliczer, Richard Kagan, Suzanne Kessler, Peggy McCracken, Helen Nader, David Nirenberg, María Helena Sánchez Ortega, Barbara Simerka, Charles Stivale, Valerie Traub, Sandra VanBurkleo, Elissa Weaver, Judith Whitenack, and Amy Williamsen. I am grateful for these individuals' encouragement and for their willingness to write more letters of recommendation for me than most people require in an entire career.

I am further indebted to Stacey Schlau and Reyes Coll-Tellechea for reviewing the manuscript and making invaluable suggestions for improvement. Michael Ames, Betsy Phillips, Dariel Mayer, Bobbe Needham, and the staff at Vanderbilt University Press have nurtured this project through the editorial process with enthusiasm and professionalism. For demonstrating that publishing can be a pleasurable, rewarding enterprise, I applaud and thank them.

Akin to some early modern nuns who practiced bilocation, I lived in two places during the preparation of the manuscript. Friends, colleagues, and students provided professional and personal support for my scholarly activities. In conjunction with the Northwest Airlines flight attendants, my friends John Corvino and Kate Paesani always took good care of me in the Motor City. My parents and my brothers have been strong allies, and I thank them for the fun and friendship they bring to my life. In Southern California, my friends, family, and, seemingly, the weather continue to make special efforts to welcome me. Sam barks and Max smiles. When my partner, Scott, walks in the door, the sun shines and I know I am home.

I dedicate this book to Mary Elizabeth Perry, a model scholar, colleague, and friend whose generosity knows no bounds.

PREFACE

The *Lives of Women: A New History of Inquisitional Spain* begins with the most basic of questions. What did it mean to be a woman in Spain's early modern period? Part I, "Defining Gender: The Inquisition," examines two Inquisition cases that share a fundamental concern with the definitions of gender and femininity.[1] Chapter 1, "'I am a man *and* a woman': Eleno/a de Céspedes Faces the Inquisition," discusses the remarkable Inquisition trial of a Moorish hermaphrodite. The trial record highlights anxieties that surrounded lesbianism, ethnicity, and gender nonconformity. Chapter 2, "Bernarda Manuel: Defending Femininity to the Holy Office," examines the case of a merchant-class immigrant who wrote her own defense to charges of Judaizing. The histories of madness, domestic violence, and religious intolerance converge in Manuel's 1650 trial record.

Part II, "Imagining Gender: Women and Their Readers," explores female authors' representations of women in literary texts written for the public in the seventeenth century. For the first time, the Spanish public read fiction written by women about women. In a fascinating point of convergence, almost every fictional text written by women for the public deals with what today we would consider women's issues. Chapter 3 examines the focus on women in prose fiction by María de Zayas y Sotomayor and Mariana de Carvajal, as well as the implications of women writing for the Spanish reading public. Chapter 4 examines the representation of desire in the dramatic texts of three of the half dozen known playwrights from the seventeenth century: Angela de Azevedo, María de Zayas, and Ana Caro Mallén de Soto. The discussions of literature in Chapters 3 and 4 examine the sustained attention to women's friendship, sexuality, and intimacy in the female canon of Spain's Golden Age. This analysis puts into relief the expectations of the Spanish public, as well as the role of women authors vis-à-vis that public.

Part III turns to the convent, examining representations of gender and religion in literature produced by and about female religious. The importance of convents in the history of women in Catholic countries cannot be overstated. Convents nurtured both mind and spirit, providing an opportunity for community and education not found in the outside world. It follows that literature produced in religious houses represents most of the texts produced by pre-twentieth-century women in the Catholic world. Convents provide the perfect backdrop for the consideration of women's relationships with the broader Catholic culture and with each other.

Chapter 5, "Nuns as Writers: The Cloister and Beyond," examines the representation of gender and religious life in the texts of three nuns. Women religious wrote for each other, for their confessors, and for readers beyond convent walls. The writings of Sor Marcela de San Félix, Sor Violante do Ceo, and Ana Abarca de Bolea exemplify this diversity of readership and purpose, and thus provide a useful triad for considering religious women and their readers. Each of these women cultivated a different genre, and each wrote for a different audience. Contrary to what we might expect, women religious raise many of the same issues regarding gender that non-convent writers raise. As evidenced by Abarca de Bolea's parodic text, they also took part in the debate on the worth of women, known as the *querelle des femmes*, that was the venue for feminist and antifeminist posturing throughout the early modern period.[2] The analysis of the three nuns' texts in Chapter 5 allows us to glimpse gender relations as seen from inside the cloister.

Spiritual auto/biographies, known as *vidas*, also gave expression to the complex rules that governed gender behavior and spirituality. Chapter 6 examines the representation of motherhood and sexuality in the *vida* of Sor Catalina de Jesús y San Francisco, a widow who became a nun. In this instance, a priest wrote his mother's biography using excerpts from her own writing. The text provides the opportunity to consider the conflicting expectations faced by women in Spanish society and in the culture of women religious.

The literary texts and Inquisition records examined throughout the first three sections of the book provide ample evidence for the existence of strong, intelligent women who manipulated dominant gender ideologies to their advantage. The dispersion of these women across class lines, as well as over space and time, makes us question the extent to which educated women knew, supported, and helped each other. In what contexts did they position themselves as educators of other women? The extent to which women sought each other out, knew of each other's intellectual work, and built networks of support has not been studied in depth. The commonalities among women's discursive strategies and thematic concerns suggest that networks of education and support existed among various communities of women.

Part IV, "Women's Networks: Leadership and Community," identifies the leadership and support roles that women occupied in inquisitional Spain.

No systematic study has yet been done on women's advisory, religious, or even business networks in this era. Indeed, a complete history of female education—including formal and informal educational mechanisms—has yet to be written. The final section of *The Lives of Women* begins to write that history, delineating a methodology for studying the foundations of female education. In combination with inquisitorial trials of businesswomen, abbesses, and other defendants, numerous texts document women's roles as leaders, advisors, and educators. These records suggest that women of all classes advised and assisted each other in more organized ways than we previously were able to determine.

Drawing from a variety of sources, Chapters 7 and 8 reconstruct the means by which women supported themselves and each other during the period. Focusing on sorcery and heresy, Chapter 7, "Single Women: The Price of Independence," analyzes the survival strategies used by four controversial women—María de Orozco, Teresa Valle de la Cerda, Lucrecia de León, and María Romero—whose stories come down to us through letters, biographies, and Inquisition records. The chapter reconstructs the roles that unorthodox women forged for themselves and, in the process, the means by which they created and supported entire networks of women.

Chapter 8 proposes a new model for recovering the heretofore invisible history of Hispanic women's education. The chapter reads advice manuals, legal reform tracts, and convent instructional documents as key texts for understanding women's educational history. Building on the methodology employed throughout the book, Part IV argues that the history of women's education can be recovered only if we broaden our definitions of education to take into account the formal and informal mechanisms by which women and other nondominant groups have supported and instructed each other through the centuries. Analyzing those mechanisms, Chapter 8 presents evidence for the early modern period as a key moment in the foundation of women's educational history in the West.

Like many countries around the world, the emerging Spanish nation sought to silence women. The textual record confirms that this goal was met with frustration, as women of different class and ethnic backgrounds ignored dicta on their silence. Women weighed in on public and private matters. They competently ran households, businesses, and convents. They advised and educated on matters ranging from the quotidian to the highest realms of culture. Women acted as advisors to kings and healers of the poor. Legal, church, fictional, and nonfictional texts give us access to the roles women played and the lives they led. The richly layered documents studied throughout *The Lives of Women* confirm that individual stories have much to teach us about surviving and thriving in societies that seek to oppress women and minorities.

SELECTING THE STORIES

I chose the texts in this book to represent aspects of the full spectrum of early modern Spanish women's lives. From the hundreds of possible sources, I wrote about those that spoke to the diverse choices made by women—both in their daily lives and in the representation of those lives to tribunals, religious communities, and readers. The fascinating stories about early modern Spanish women provide a point of departure for considering the interworkings of gender, class, and ethnicity in the West. They open up a world in which women interacted as friends, mothers, sisters, wives, workers, and leaders. Finally, they allow us to consider many facets of women's existence and to revisit our assumptions about the role of gender in European and Hispanic history.

Texts that record women's words provide us with a way to reconstruct the lives of those whose voices have not formed part of the historical record. We need to look at all available kinds of documentation if we are to effectively integrate these unheard voices into history. With literature, we must examine the filters of readership, genre, and fiction. Inquisition records present the problem of formulaic discourse, making it even more difficult to untangle factual information from the defense strategies. Similarly, religious writing was produced in environments in which orthodoxy and conformity were the guiding forces for authors who narrated life stories and provided instruction for their spiritual families.

By introducing and interpreting stories from Hispanic women's pasts, I hope to convince readers that, unless we listen to the voices of women and minorities, we cannot expect to write accurate history. Prohibitions on women's speech and liberties not withstanding, literary, convent, and Inquisition records from the early modern period confirm that women enjoyed certain freedoms of action and choice, and that they found ways to express their opinions and cultivate their talents. These records hold the key to the strategies used by individuals and groups in their struggle to cope with the policies of exclusion and persecution adopted by the emerging Spanish nation. *The Lives of Women: A New History of Inquisitional Spain* provides a model for incorporating these and other stories into our understanding of the complex lives of women and men in the past and in the present.

INTRODUCTION

¡Somos mujeres! Pregunto:
¿Cómo seremos oídas?

We are but women! So I ask:
How then shall we be heard?
— María de San José (Salazar), 1602

I n the late sixteenth century, Spanish inquisitors asked María del Caño if she knew the true sex of her husband. Suspecting that the husband was a woman in disguise, they asked the young wife whether she had ever seen or touched his penis. Caño insisted that her husband made love to her like a man. She could not describe his genitalia, however, because he had not allowed her to touch him:

> [Caño said that] she had heard other women say that they enjoyed a certain liberty with their husbands, [and] she had the desire to do so too, so she tried to carefully touch his male parts in order to see what exactly he had down there.[1]

To the end, Caño claimed that she never managed to see or touch her husband's "shameful parts." The husband eventually was convicted for scorning the sacrament of matrimony. He was sentenced to ten years' service in a hospital. María del Caño was set free.

If we move ahead fifty years, the trial of a woman convicted of unorthodox religious practices gives us similarly intimate information about women's lives in the early modern period. In a 1629 communication with the Inquisition, the aristocratic nun Teresa Valle de la Cerda defended the custom of letting confessors caress her face and hold her hands:

> I believe that [holding hands] is an action that, done without warning and with sincerity, I do not take as anything bad, and it is something that all of us do. Indeed, the more saintly the person, the better.[2]

Valle's convent had come under suspicion because many of her sisters spoke in strange voices, sermonized, and had ecstatic visions. The question of holding hands was damaging to her case, yet the nun insisted on justifying her views on the matter even after her initial conviction.[3]

Finally, a fictional story about similar issues: A 1647 collection of novellas published by the best-selling author María de Zayas included a story about same-sex love between women. In "Love for the Sake of Conquest" ("Amar sólo por vencer"), a man poses as a handmaid in order to woo a young girl. The disguise provides a front for an exchange that culminates in an overt defense of same-sex alliances. Much to the surprise of modern readers, the young man argues that gender bears no weight on desire:

> [S]ince the soul is the same in male and female, it matters not whether I'm a man or a woman. Souls aren't male or female and true love dwells in the soul, not in the body.[4]

This bucolic depiction of same-sex desire is disrupted by the dangers of male-female relations when the man reveals his true identity later in the story. The two have consensual sex, after which the girl's family kills her for being sexually corrupt.

These declarations about sex and love in Spain seem more in keeping with our own times than with the period in which they were recorded. The statements contain an element of surprise, perhaps because they reveal that women felt sexual desire or because they expressed opinions about everyday issues that continue to interest us hundreds of years later. Our reaction to recorded references to intimacy and sexuality also suggests that we are surprised because we do not expect the full spectrum of women's lives that such historical documents reflect.

The Lives of Women: A New History of Inquisitional Spain demonstrates that our expectations are out of sync with the textual record because we still have limited knowledge about women of the past. It is generally believed that women in early modern Spain were given few options in a culture that sought to control them. The current understanding of those controlled lives suggests that women's primary duties involved guarding their chastity and demonstrating obedience to men. Yet women's lives were far more complex than this representation suggests. Women had responsibilities and obligations, with which came influence and control. They expressed preferences and, at times, gave voice to their desire.

Much of the textual history that captures the complexity of women's experiences dates to the seventeenth century. In addition to calling for a revision of our understanding of early modern Europe, *The Lives of Women* argues that Spain's long seventeenth century (1580–1700) should be recognized as a foundational period for women's intellectual and educational history. A heretofore unrecognized momentous shift in women's lives occurred during the period. As of approximately 1580, women's writing in the Iberian Peninsula experienced a boom that lasted through the 1600s. During this time, more women wrote for the public book market and participated in literary culture than ever before. The rise in convents and female education contributed to a marked increase in texts produced by and about women religious. In conjunction with Inquisition records, legal documents, and individuals' correspondence, such texts offer us access to women's perspectives on life in early modern Spain. In turn, this access should teach us to reconceptualize history by taking into account a large sector of the population whose voices have been relegated to dusty archives.

Women formed an important part of life in early modern Spain, an age that has been heralded as the nation's Golden Age of letters and empire, a time of expansion, wealth, and artistic achievement. From the time of Queen Isabella and King Ferdinand in the late fifteenth century through the decline of the empire in the 1600s, Spain was the imperial power of the West. Modern formulations of citizenship and leadership began to emerge throughout Europe, providing the basis for the modern nation-state. The Inquisition served as the keeper of orthodoxy and order at home and across the Atlantic. Cervantes's *Don Quixote* and Velázquez's *Las meninas* epitomize the artistic triumph of the era. Ideologically, structurally, and ethnically, society changed. When the last Habsburg king died in 1700, Hispanic culture spanned two continents, and the foundations of modern Western society had been built.

Spain's period of imperialism and nation building has had lasting repercussions in the Western world. Ramifications of the tumultuous era continue to be felt today. Gender, race, religion, and ethnicity in the Hispanic world are imbricated with complex and sometimes conflicting ideologies that have as much to do with Catholic culture as with the seeds of colonialism and imperialism sown centuries ago. The presence of Jews and Moslems remains controversial, as seen in the rise in anti-Semitism and anti-Moslem sentiments at the turn of the twenty-first century. The impact also is apparent in the legacy of colonialism that has contributed to the instability of Latin American nations and to the vexed relationship between the church and the peoples of the Hispanic diaspora.

The formation of the modern nation-state came at a cost. In particular, the first two centuries of inquisitional Spain were remarkable for the degree of social control imposed on the populace. The Inquisition was approved in 1476. By 1492, edicts of expulsion were declared in an attempt to erase all signs of ethnic and religious difference. The Counter-Reformation of the mid–sixteenth century brought further restrictions on individual beliefs and behavior. In the 1600s, a declining empire tightened its attempts at social control. As often is the case in times of uncertainty, the disempowered felt the brunt of the heightened anxiety. Women, ethnic minorities, and the poor were targets of the backlash. While ethnic groups faced prohibitions on their public and private activities, the laws and conduct books directed at women focused on the need to maintain sexual purity. Humanists exhorted chastity and piety, demanding that women remain in the home except to attend mass. Plays depicted the consequences of sexual impurity: More than three dozen wife-murder plays written by male dramatists bespeak a generalized anxiety about women and sexuality.

Many scholars have analyzed the political, economic, and social fallout of the impulse to create a homogeneous Spanish state, specifying the gains and losses in the Americas and the long-lasting effects of imperialism and contact.[5] Yet individual experiences of life in inquisitional Spain have been difficult to decipher. Most studies focus on the macrocosmic view of the Inquisition, politics, and the church, or on influential men of letters, the cloth, or the aristocracy. Even in the twenty-first century, our understanding of the period remains compromised by a reliance on male-authored texts. By and large, the stories of women, minorities, and the poor who experienced life in this transformative historical moment are absent. The failure to include the stories of second-class citizens is principally due to the practice of writing history based almost exclusively on texts (including laws, edicts, letters, and fiction) penned by upper-class Christian men.

Even research on gender in sixteenth- and seventeenth-century Spain continues to concentrate on men's depictions and treatment of women. The majority of scholarship explores how social practices, institutions, and laws defined women's roles. Based primarily on male-dominated institutions and male-authored texts, this work has led to lamentations about women's inferior position in a time in which the church and the legal system insisted on women's secondary status.[6] It generally has been believed that women had few options beyond the convent or marriage. Public life was virtually closed to them, as they could not conduct business or seek legal recourse without the permission of their fathers or husbands. They had little access to education, as evidenced by estimates that fix men's literacy at 40 percent and women's at 25 percent. Literacy varied by class and urban versus rural living, yet most studies suggest that women's literacy lagged considerably behind men's.[7]

Women—particularly poor, minority, and single women—seem to have been disadvantaged in every way imaginable. Yet the emphasis on oppression and discrimination fails to tell the whole story. Scholars of the past decade have returned to the archives and uncovered pockets of resistance, independence, and relative liberalism in the lives and cultural production of women and minorities during the period. Recent research suggests that, rather than merely pity women their lack of options, their relegation to the home, and their subordinate position, we need to recognize that women had more options than previously believed. Convent life offered a positive alternative for many. Port cities such as Seville offered business opportunities for women whose husbands left for the Americas. Aristocratic women exercised control over social and political affairs. Contrary to the traditional depiction of Spanish women as sheltered and disadvantaged, we now know that they enjoyed better legal protection than many of their contemporaries in western Europe.[8]

The argument is frequently made that we have few traces of women's own voices from this period, but a steady stream of scholarship tells us otherwise. Scholars have recovered dozens, if not hundreds, of texts written by women; an unprecedented number of studies and edited works have opened our eyes to the opinions and perspectives of women who exerted agency at home and in the public sphere.[9] Recent publications on noblewomen, prophets, Moriscos (Moslem converts to Christianity), and nuns richly exemplify the possibilities for rescuing stories from the archives.[10]

The Lives of Women: A New History of Inquisitional Spain deciphers the responses of women to the seventeenth century's culture of control by recovering a textual history that has not been integrated into early modern histories. The book illustrates that the archives hold hundreds, if not thousands, of untold stories of women of all classes and ethnic backgrounds. The stories illustrate that we need to revisit history and incorporate the perspectives of women, minorities, and the underclasses into our understanding of this key period in the development of Hispanic culture.[11]

As I have suggested, many of those untold stories date from 1580 to 1700. A confluence of changes in the late 1500s created new opportunities for women. Humanist writers Fray Luis de León and Juan Luis Vives advocated limited educational programs for women that would create better wives, household managers, and mothers of future heirs. This emphasis on basic education in the Renaissance found its baroque counterpart in changes that resulted from the Council of Trent (1545–63). The church's response to the Protestant Reformation resulted in a boom in convent foundations in Catholic Europe. For most women, the best chance for an education lay within the walls of those convents; the increase in foundations led to a marked rise in the numbers of educated women in Iberia.

The Counter-Reformation also brought renewed emphasis on the practice of confession, which in turn led to more spiritual autobiographies and biographies that detailed the intimate details of religious women's lives. One of the most high-profile women in the period was Teresa of Avila (1515–82), whose writings and religious reform offered a model of spirituality and activism for subsequent generations of Catholic women. Encouraged by Saint Teresa's writings and success, women often turned to the written word at the mandate of confessors and as a means of expression. Indeed, hundreds of nuns' texts are available today, most not yet studied in depth. Outside the convent, the phenomenon also took hold. For countless secular and religious women, Saint Teresa's dogged dedication to writing paved the way for women's legitimate participation in writing culture. As a result of this confluence of factors, Spain saw in the seventeenth century its first cohort of women who wrote plays, stories, and poetry for literary salons and the general public.[12]

The chapters that follow examine representations of gender in a broad range of texts produced during the boom in women's writing in the long seventeenth century. Building on the work of scholars of gender in Europe and the Americas, the book analyzes women's fictional prose, drama, poetry, biography, and Inquisition trial records. Some of the texts were written by women; others—such as depositions and biographies—were produced by men who claimed to faithfully quote or represent their female subjects. Some texts were written for publication or for the public stage. Others were written for convent audiences, confessors, or friends. The question of authenticity—of whose voice is heard in each text—becomes complicated by the imperatives of the various venues in which women wrote and spoke. Every text requires a different reading, as we must take into account the intended audience and the mediating factors—such as censorship and anticipated readership—that may have shaped the way the stories were crafted and told.

While differing in form and function, the texts detail the attitudes, beliefs, and customs of women of various class and ethnic backgrounds. Many of the documents touch on issues of sex and intimacy; others provide a road map for understanding religious practice. All allow us an opportunity to understand women's relationships and communities and give us access to women's reactions to the dominant culture's attempts to define, limit, and contain femininity.

By interpreting stories through the lens of gender, this book forges a new line of inquiry into the rich tradition of scholarship on Golden Age Spain. The chapters are devoted to texts produced in different arenas—Inquisition tribunals, convents, and the book market—but all analyses explore the relationship between the dominant culture and individual interpretations of femininity, masculinity, sexuality, and spirituality. The texts also allow give us the opportunity to consider the interplay of gender with questions of class, religion, and ethnicity.[13]

Single women, widows, wives, daughters, and mothers figure as authors and subjects here. The differences among the individuals and their texts are striking. Class, marital status, ethnic background, and life choices influenced their experiences, yet their texts reflect a shared preoccupation with redefining gender and creating legitimate spaces for women.

At the most basic level, *The Lives of Women* is about the stories women told and how they chose to tell them. Taken from archival and literary sources, these stories vary as much as those that any group of women might tell today. The book rests on the premise that only through an examination of women in various spheres—public, private, religious, and legal—can we understand the history of gender and gender relations. By looking at the stories women told—to each other, to readers, to inquisitors—we can come to understand the commonalities among their experiences and the ways they chose to present those experiences to the world. At the very least, we can come to understand how women expected others to judge them. We can identify the ways women interacted with and informed a culture in which the Inquisition loomed large in the life of every citizen.

The texts reveal that many women developed similar strategies to discuss issues they perceived as central to their existence. Women frequently drew on the dominant culture's views of femininity, depicting themselves as weak, ignorant, or intellectually inadequate. These and other commonalities suggest that women had particular means of interacting with each other and the world—that early modern women shared, to varying degrees, similar priorities and similar strategies for survival and self-presentation.

PART I

Defining Gender
The Inquisition

1

*"I am a man **and** a woman"*

Eleno/a de Céspedes Faces the Inquisition

In 1605, doña Magdalena Muñoz entered a convent in the town of Ubeda, in southern Spain. Muñoz was put there by her father, who deemed her unfit for marriage because she was a manly woman (*mujer varonil*) who could handle weapons and perform heavy manual labor with ease. Twelve years later, Muñoz experienced a bodily transformation: While transporting a load of grain, she felt a great pain in her groin. After three days, a penis emerged from her body. Muñoz feared that if she told the nuns about her genital swelling, they would think she had lost her virginity. At the very least, they would summon a doctor. Instead of telling her sisters, she called in a priest, Fray Agustín de Torres, to counsel her. When Torres examined Muñoz, he found her to be "as much of a man as any other."[1]

Even before the appearance of the phallus, Muñoz's manliness had been the cause of much curiosity over the years. The prioress had examined Muñoz once, and on several other occasions, the nuns had looked in vain for physical signs of masculinity on Muñoz's body while she slept, because her "strength, energy, characteristics, and general condition were those of a man."[2]

Muñoz described her situation to Torres with candor: She never had menstruated, but "when she disciplined herself, in order to keep the nuns from calling her a tomboy [*marimochacho*], she put blood on her nightshirts, saying that she had her period."[3] When the priest saw she had grown a penis and a beard and heard the change in the register of her voice, he immediately requested that Muñoz be locked in a cell and told her to maintain her silence. When Torres returned later with another priest, both clergymen "saw with their eyes and touched with their hands and found [Muñoz] to be a perfect man with the nature (*naturaleza*) of a man."[4] With a male member

intact and secondary sex characteristics that bolstered a finding of masculinity, Magdalena Muñoz was proclaimed a man.

As Fray Torres tells it in the letter that is our only source for these hap-
penings, Muñoz's father "thought he might die from shock" when the news
arrived in his town, Sabiote.[5] Soon thereafter, the priest escorted father and
son away from the convent and then informed the nuns of the strange turn
of events. While Torres offers no details on the nuns' reaction, he describes
the men's feelings:

> [T]he father is very happy because he is a rich man and he didn't have
> any heirs and now he finds himself with *a very manly son* and one who
> can marry, and *she*, too, is happy because after twelve years in jail [the
> convent], she knows liberty well, and *she was a woman and now a man*,
> which out of all things and timely events no better favor could have been
> paid her by nature itself.[6]

If Muñoz had become a man, why did the priest refer to the ex-nun as a man
and a woman in the same sentence? The mix of nouns calls attention to the
discomfort with gender instability that infuses his letter, and the triumph
of manliness emerges as the moral of the story. The father had a "manly son"
to inherit his wealth and carry on his line, and Muñoz was sprung from the
convent after twelve years of confinement. At the end of the letter, this triumphant attitude prevails—a man was liberated from his womanly body
and happily welcomed by men into their fold.

We know nothing more about Muñoz's life, and nothing else in Fray
Torres's letter indicates what Muñoz might have felt about becoming a man
at the age of thirty-four. The simplicity and brevity of the letter impose
order on the chaos. A nun who acts like a man but has no physical signs of
being one suddenly grows a penis, and two priests vouch for the legitimacy
of the change. The nun returns home as a man, ready to marry and step
into his father's shoes. A "strange case," in Torres's words, but not one that
provoked him to detail Muñoz's feelings or to write about the implications
of such a radical transformation.[7] Nor do we hear what the nuns thought
about having had a man living in their midst, or what the people of Sabiote
might think about having a woman-turned-man as a neighbor.

Documented examples of hermaphroditism—one of the phenomena
known collectively today as intersexuality—are rare for the early modern
period.[8] Muñoz's scenario conforms to a pattern validated by some medical
treatises, which postulated that women might become men through a burst
of heat that caused their interior, manlike genitals to be expelled. It followed
that men, on the other hand, would not devolve into the lesser female form.

The lack of agreement on this theory has been well documented, however. The oft-cited case of the young French girl Marie le Marcis exemplifies the debate that hermaphroditic bodies provoked in the period.[9] According to contemporary accounts, Marie generated enough heat while jumping over a fence to sprout male genitalia. She then lived as a man, changing her name to Marin and having a relationship with a woman. Marin's gender came under suspicion, however, and he was arrested for sodomy and then condemned to death by hanging. Le Marcis was exonerated only after a thorough examination by Jacques Duval, a medical authority who found that le Marcis had a male member that emerged when excited. As Duval explains in his *Treatise on Hermaphrodites* (1612), le Marcis' physiology made him capable of having sex as a man.[10]

The most famous Spanish case of intersexuality from the era is linked to Muñoz and le Marcis in that it also involved a woman whose body reportedly changed into a man's. In 1587, local authorities of the royal court in Ocaña referred their investigation of Eleno/a de Céspedes, a hermaphrodite, to the Inquisition of Toledo. Compared to the uncomplicated presentation of Muñoz's apparent sex change, the Céspedes trial offers a complex and devastating example of the early modern world's discomfort with gender instability. The Ocaña investigation and Inquisition trial involved accusations of sodomy, bigamy, impersonating a man, mocking matrimony, and having a pact with the devil.[11] Although convicted for scorning matrimony and having a pact with the devil, in reality Céspedes was arrested because he was rumored to have two sexes—to be both a man (Eleno) and a woman (Elena).

As a surgeon and a married man, Céspedes enjoyed a relatively secure position in the town of Ciempozuelos in central Spain, but rumors of his intersexuality brought him to the attention of local officials concerned about the legitimacy (and possible homosexuality) of his marriage to María del Caño. Once it was determined that the primary offense was mocking matrimony, it was only a matter of time before the case was referred to the Inquisition. Like Muñoz and le Marcis, Céspedes referred to himself as a man throughout his trial.[12] Unlike other cases, Céspedes's included extensive depositions that detailed the transformation from female to male and recorded various medical opinions about such bodily change. From a twenty-first-century perspective, Céspedes's trial seems to have been motivated by the threat that unconventional sexuality and nondominant ethnicity posed to the status quo.[13] Most immediately, the case provides us with unique commentary on what it meant to be both male and female in a society that strictly defined proper gender roles.

Céspedes's story is both a woman's and a man's. He identified as a man, but the Inquisition insisted on classifying him as a woman. It is crucial to bear in mind the filters that separate us from individuals tried and questioned by the Inquisition, as their "voices" come to us through third-person depositions and are recorded primarily in their responses to others' questions. The formulaic nature of the records makes it difficult to reconstruct individual responses—and impossible to know the exact words uttered by any defendant—particularly since evidence from other cases demonstrates conclusively that the scribes often summarized responses rather than writing the defendants' words verbatim.[14] With regard to Céspedes, this filter means that we cannot grasp the defendant's real viewpoint regarding life as a woman and a man. However, we can reconstruct the strategies he used to explain his unusual body and experience to the Holy Office. The strategies suggest that Céspedes put forth a defense of the flexible nature of sex and gender.

The trial of this Moorish defendant who had achieved a high degree of assimilation into the dominant culture played on both the sexual and ethnic anxieties of that culture. In its essence, the trial of Eleno de Céspedes documents a battle over identity and self-representation. Céspedes had been living as a man for more than twenty years when the authorities began to pry into his life. He had married María del Caño just a year before his arrest and supported her from his earnings as a licensed surgeon. In spite of the defendant's marriage to a woman, his self-identification as a man, and his success in a male profession, the Inquisition authorities referred to Céspedes as a woman throughout the ordeal. The first folio of the trial record reflects this schism, as it identifies the defendant as a woman (Elena), a man (Eleno), a male surgeon (*cirujano*), and a hermaphrodite.[15]

The defendant identified himself as a hermaphrodite to the inquisitors, saying that "in reality the truth is that [she] is and was a hermaphrodite and [she] had and has two natures, one of a man and the other of a woman."[16] The tension between Céspedes's acceptance of his intersexed body and the Inquisition's anxieties over such a body provides the focal point for the trial. The summary of the case given on the trial transcript's cover page captures the Inquisition's view of Céspedes's identity and the priorities of the case:

> Céspedes, Elena and Eleno de, born in Alhama, a slave and later free, married a man and had a son after, and once her husband was dead she dressed as a man and was in the War against the Moriscos of Granada, got licensed as a surgeon and married a woman.[17]

From our standpoint as well as the Inquisition's, the issues of dual identity, slavery, motherhood, and multiple professional activities stand out as salient characteristics of Céspedes's life. The summary slights one of the most gripping elements of the case: the tension between the defendant's claim to masculinity (with all its social benefits) and the Inquisition's insistence on his femininity.[18] Seen through this lens, the case offers many details about definitions of masculinity and femininity. The cultural implications of gender were profound. By belonging to neither gender, Céspedes challenged the limitations of gender definitions. In the end, the Inquisition contained this threat by forcing Céspedes to end his career, leave his wife, and live as a woman forever.

FROM WOMAN TO MAN

This fascinating story takes us into the depths of ethnic, racial, and gender politics of early modern Spain. Of mulatto stock, Elena de Céspedes was born a slave in Alhama, Spain, in 1545 or 1546. Branded, then eventually set free by her master, she moved away, became a weaver, and married Cristóbal de Lombardo around the age of sixteen. Neither Lombardo nor the child she had by him formed part of Elena's life for very long. Indeed, according to Céspedes, Lombardo left her and later died. Something of great consequence occurred during the marriage, however: Childbirth gave Céspedes male physical characteristics that he previously had not had.[19] The trial record describes this alteration:

> [W]hen she gave birth, as she said, with the force that she put into the labor a piece of skin that she had over the urinary canal broke and a small head of about half a thumb's length came out.[20]

Afterwards, when Céspedes became excited, the phallus would appear, but at other times it simply curled back into his body, presumably into the vaginal opening.

Intersexuality involves many chromosomal, hormonal, and physical phenomena. This complexity, in combination with the limitations of our knowledge of Céspedes's body, allows us only to guess at the physiological explanation for Céspedes's bodily change. Suzanne Kessler, author of *Lessons from the Intersexed*, has suggested that Céspedes likely was a female pseudohermaphrodite who had "a common form of intersexuality or another condition that 'masculinized' the clitoris prenatally," such as CAH (congenital adrenal hyperplasia). Kessler explains that female pseudohermaphroditism, in which two ovaries are present yet the person has visible male characteristics, is "the only kind of intersexuality that would explain how Céspedes could have been reproductive." Furthermore, current research suggests that females who develop a full phallic structure cannot reproduce. It is likely, then, that Céspedes had signs of a variant of a phallic structure previous to puberty, and that these became more evident after childbirth.[21]

In terms of what really happened to the body of Eleno/a de Céspedes, we have only the information provided in the case by Céspedes, physicians, and witnesses. From what can be gathered from the defendant's depositions, the appearance of the phallus did not immediately alter Céspedes's life. Living as a woman in Granada and San Lúcar de Barrameda after her mother's death, she practiced the trades of hosemaker (*calcetera*) and tailor. While in San Lúcar, Céspedes was in the company of Ana de Albánchez when, one day, Céspedes "felt the desire to kiss her and without saying a thing to her, she kissed her and the frightened Ana let her, and she told her that she could lie with her like a man."[22] When the two tried to make love, however, Céspedes was unable to perform sexually as a man. This failure, as Céspedes viewed it, led the defendant to seek medical advice from a local surgeon, who apparently gave a diagnosis of hermaphroditism.

It is interesting to imagine this scene playing out in front of the Inquisition, particularly since Céspedes was the one who introduced the term "hermaphrodite" into the trial. In doing so, he identified his body as different, yet he sought legitimacy for that difference by naming the phenomenon and labeling it a medical condition diagnosed by a reputable member of the community. Describing the surgeon's role in treating the newly developed condition, Céspedes explained that a small cut was made just above the protrusion. Subsequently a curved phallus approximately three or four inches long appeared. The surgeon finished his work by making another incision to straighten the penis and then prescribed a remedy that would allow the "penis" to grow harder. These procedures were a success. After fifteen days, Céspedes "returned to the said Ana de Albánchez and lay with her many times and performed many manly acts and was in her house for four or five months without her husband finding anything out."[23] Whether the events transpired as Céspedes presented them, it is important to note that, from the perspective of the inquisitors, the narrative raised questions about female-female sexual activity; indeed, the defendant specifically stated that the acts took place before he outwardly changed to a male appearance.

Céspedes indicated that he waited some time before donning men's clothing. He presented the sartorial change as one triggered by a fight with a man named Heredia in Jérez de la Frontera. Apparently Heredia initiated the altercation, accusing Céspedes of looking like a Moorish bandit, or *monfí*. From the description, it seems that Céspedes cut an odd figure, probably dressed as a woman yet appearing masculine:

[B]ecause of the threats that the said Heredia and his other ruffian com-
panions [made] on account of her disguise, she determined to go around
in men's clothes and she left behind the women's clothes that she had
always worn up to that point.[24]

This incident raises the issue of how others saw Céspedes before she
stopped wearing women's clothes. It seems that, at the very least, Céspedes
had an androgynous physical appearance (and perhaps was not wearing
many female accoutrements). Why else would others take a woman for a
bandit and take offense at this disguise? Céspedes's subsequent decision to
change his appearance communicates an awareness of the benefits of being a
man in a society that emphasized women's enclosure.[25] Although Céspedes
moved around, practiced different trades, and even "performed many manly
acts" before crossing over to full male dress, his subsequent adoption of male
clothing allowed him to take on manual labor as a farm worker and then as
a shepherd.

At one point, local authorities who had known Céspedes as a woman
identified him and forced him to dress in female attire. After seven months
in women's clothes, Céspedes abandoned this female appearance and left to
fight in the Alpujarras war. Over the next several years, Céspedes showed
tremendous industry and opportunism. He worked as a soldier and a tailor
before learning to perform surgery from a Valencian surgeon. Later, to avoid
prosecution for lack of certification, he got licensed for surgery, curing, and
purging. He then moved to the town of Ocaña, where there were no other
surgeons, and set up his trade.

Rumors of Céspedes's intersexuality plagued him throughout his adult
life. When he decided to marry María del Caño in Ocaña, the pressure of
these rumors led him to seek a special license from the vicar certifying that
he was a man. Nine doctors and midwives examined him and unanimously
declared him a man, upon which Céspedes received permission to marry. In
1586, Céspedes and Caño celebrated their nuptials, but their conjugal life
soon would be interrupted. Gossip caught up with Céspedes within a year
of the marriage when an ex-soldier, Ortega Velázquez, wrote to the gover-
nor indicating that during the war it had been rumored "that Céspedes was
a woman and there were others who said he was both man and woman."[26]
Velázquez's letter prompted the royal court to arrest Céspedes.

When he was arrested, Céspedes had no phallic structure. What happened between the time of his marriage and the Inquisition trial is probably
the most obscure aspect of the case. Céspedes claimed he had contracted
a disease—which he called cancer—four months earlier, in February or
March of 1587. His genital area was affected to the point that his penis

began to atrophy. He applied various cures to it, but nothing helped. Eventually, he began to clip his penis and testicles off little by little each day.[27] If Céspedes did not have a penis but did have a wife who said she had penetrative sex with him, the authorities would likely conclude that Elena had used a sexual implement (i.e., a dildo fashioned from wood) to penetrate María del Caño. At the time, female sodomy was defined as women using implements to impersonate men during sex.

The sodomy issue relates to the procedural problem that faced the tribunal from the start: How could they legitimately prosecute Céspedes? The defendant had been indicted in July 1587 for sodomy. Yet this was a crime that, as of 1509, could not be tried by the Castilian tribunal.[28] While this was fortunate for Caño and Céspedes, it probably heightened the frustration of the authorities, who found that Céspedes's case presented unanswerable questions. Finally, a priest decided that the primary offense was one that fell under the jurisdiction of the Inquisition. Charged with scorn for matrimony, the defendant was referred by the royal court to the Inquisition.

Inquisitors responded with disbelief to the claim that Céspedes had male genitalia until only twelve days before the interview. Whether or not Céspedes's descriptions of his body reflected the "truth," the normative discourse of sexuality and medicine simply did not account for a body such as the one he described. His testimonies suggest he was aware of this problem, as he reiterated the story of sexual change, stating that "he did have a member then and this is the truth."[29] As if in defiance of the attempts to pin a feminine identity on him, Céspedes identified himself as a man and signed his signature as Eleno throughout the documents.

Perhaps the inquisitors were not sure what to charge him with, for they set out to demonstrate that Céspedes was a woman who had tricked others (including her wife) into believing she was a man. They charged him with bigamy and impersonating a man, but convicted him for his "scorn for the sacrament of marriage." The concerns about sodomy—for the defendant having used implements to have sex with another woman—slipped into the background.[30] The bigamy charge also was dropped, probably because it was based on little more than a technicality. Although Céspedes claimed to have a letter that reported the death of Cristóbal Lombardo (Elena's husband), the death-of-spouse papers had never been filed officially. In the strictest interpretation of the law, Céspedes could be considered a bigamist.[31] In the end, the Inquisition convicted Céspedes of scorning matrimony and having a pact with the devil.

The range of charges explored during the case indicates the intensity with which officials sought to convict Céspedes under the auspices of the Holy Office. After all, it was no crime to be a hermaphrodite. Or was it?

Lorraine Daston and Katherine Park have shown that, in this period, the intersexed were increasingly policed by legal and medical authorities, who sought to determine whether a hermaphrodite was female or male. Once sex was assigned, the person could enjoy "all of the prerogatives of that sex."[32] With sodomy's criminalization, which dates to before the Renaissance in Europe and appears in a number of Inquisition cases, hermaphroditism moved from the arena of unusual *physiology* into that of unnatural or transgressive *behavior.*

The threat of the hermaphroditic body lay in its capacity to perform acts deemed nefarious: A woman with an enlarged clitoris, for example, might be accused of using her clitoris to impersonate a man sexually, and thus be considered a sodomite. This potential for transgression effected a shift in the ways ambiguous genitalia were understood. Since individuals might use their abnormal bodies to perform nefarious acts, they could not be relied on to identify their sex truthfully. Thus, legal apparati, medical testimony, and outside witnesses became increasingly important in the sex-assignment process. Hermaphrodites, according to Daston and Park, ran the risk of being deemed unnatural as opposed to merely preternatural. Being a spectacle of nature would spare the individual punishment, while being an aberration might come with an indictment for a crime such as sodomy.[33] Within this framework, the body was the battleground for legitimacy. In the case of Céspedes, the defendant's claim to male identity was undermined by his lack of a penis.

Céspedes's ethnicity further complicated the case. As a mulatto and ex-slave who had created a professional life for himself, Céspedes posed many threats to a society in the grip of ethnic and religious purges. As Israel Burshatin has pointed out, Céspedes's ethnicity, made visible by a slave brand and brown skin, played a significant role in people's perceptions of him. Burshatin adds a celebratory note to this, suggesting that Céspedes's "stigmatized body" was transformed "from domestic slave to soldier and surgeon, from subservient female to proud transgendered subject."[34] Whether or not one agrees with this interpretation, self-transformation and social mobility certainly played a role in the case. Céspedes's ethnicity and class compounded the importance of these issues.

Questions and answers about Céspedes's physical functions and actions comprise most of the testimony in the case. The topics raised include menstruation, urination, and ejaculation. Céspedes admitted that he always had an infrequent menstrual cycle (fol. III.8). His wife explained that, at the times that Céspedes had blood on his nightshirt, he told her it was from a wound caused by horseback riding (fol. III.74). Responding to questions about his sexual history and capacities, Céspedes did more than just mention some of his sex partners by name. To questions aimed at determining the normality of his penis, he answered that he urinated through it and that "whenever he lay with a woman he always followed through and left seed [semen] in her vessel."[35] As to the contradictory accusations about his sexual performance, Céspedes stated that he ejaculated "more than enough." He also explained that if he did not ejaculate, "it was not for the fault of not being a man" but something that affected "men like him," presumably referring to hermaphrodites.[36]

The obsession with Eleno's physical difference occasionally involved overtones of racial difference. After María del Caño testified several times that she had no firsthand knowledge of her husband's hermaphroditism and repeatedly swore that she thought she had married a man and had what she thought were normal (hetero)sexual relations with him, the inquisitors still insisted on her complicity in a cover-up. Focusing on Eleno's body—including his confession of menstruating irregularly—they initially rejected Caño's declarations of innocence:

> [I]t is to be assumed that she could not help but seeing how the said Eleno de Céspedes was not a man, and moreover seeing him without facial hair and with his ears pierced like a woman and having a period and so it is to be assumed that since she said that she had relations with him before getting married, that knowing this she married the said Elena de Céspedes knowing she was a woman like her.[37]

From the Inquisition's perspective, the oddities of the case included the issues of menstruation, pierced ears, and body hair. The latter two fail to take into account Céspedes's ethnic background, putting forth instead a normative male body that would have an appropriate amount of body hair and would not have pierced ears. For her part, María del Caño never mentioned whether she thought Eleno's ethnic background could explain such markers of difference. She did not speculate on whether mulattos might have less facial hair than other Mediterranean ethnic groups or mention that those born into slavery often pierced their ears, for example. Instead, Caño simply refused to admit any wrongdoing, explaining that she always thought her husband was a man, that the vicar gave them license to marry based on this assessment, and that she never touched Eleno's genitals to verify that he had a real penis.

As Caño's responses suggest, questions about the failure of Céspedes's body to conform to a normative physical appearance were at the center of the trial. This anxiety about non-Christian, nonnormative bodies had a precedent in medical sources that accused Jewish men of bleeding in the genital area due either to excessive hemorrhoids or to male menstruation. The notion that non-Christian men were effeminate and emasculated likely would have informed the inquisitors' reaction to Céspedes's pierced, branded, and nearly hairless body, and it probably did not help when the defendant mentioned his bleeding hemorrhoids.[38] In addition to confirming the importance of ethnicity in the trial, then, the attention given to the defendant's body and the weight attached to medical authority highlight one of the fundamental conceptual schisms between Céspedes and the Inquisition. The inquisitors remained in the realm of the physical, insisting the case turned on the mutually exclusive terms of femininity and masculinity. Even when medical doctors provided contradictory evidence, the Inquisition maintained that sex was an indisputable material fact.

For his part, Céspedes did more than merely describe his physiology. He also offered behavioral and psychological explanations for his masculinity, defending the gender he chose to embody two decades before the trial. The divide between the rhetoric used by inquisitors and by the defendant can be understood as one of sex versus gender, of biology versus behavior. In sharp contrast to the authorities' insistence on biological sex as clear-cut and indisputable, Céspedes's lived experience led him to enact and defend flexible notions about physiology and gender, and the relationship between the two.[39]

The Inquisition's focus on physical evidence emerges in the questions about Céspedes's body, and the repetition and sheer quantity of such testimony suggest an almost fetishistic interest in Céspedes's genitalia.[40] Although Céspedes and his wife described his body, the Inquisition turned elsewhere for what it saw as untainted, reliable information. The inquiry into the sex of the defendant thus relied on two sources of information: medical expertise and personal testimony. As a well-read surgeon whose belongings included several medical texts, Céspedes invoked medical authority, citing examples from Aristotle, Augustine, and Pliny to show that he did not have an unnatural or unprecedented case, but rather one that fit a pattern of dually sexed bodies known throughout history.[41]

Several times during questioning Céspedes described himself as a hermaphrodite, trying to legitimize his identity change and his marriage to María del Caño. Giving historical examples of the phenomenon, Céspedes stated that

> many times in this world there have been androgynous people who have both sexes and who by another name are called hermaphrodites. I, too, have been one of them.[42]

While he used hermaphroditism to rationalize his change from female to male, Céspedes focused most of his energy on defending the multifaceted male identity he adopted after the physical alteration occurred. In the context of the trial this defense made perfect sense, for the defendant needed to justify his marriage to Caño to avoid being condemned on the charges of sodomy, male impersonation, and scorn for matrimony. Hence, Céspedes described his marriage as a natural choice:

> [Since] he ran around with many women, he wanted to marry and not to have to make love to anyone but his wife, and for this reason he married and he did not think that in doing so he erred, in fact he thought that he was in God's service.[43]

Céspedes even named several sexual partners as witnesses to verify his sexual history. As further outside evidence that his masculinity was never in doubt, he explained that his wife "always took him for a man since he is and has been one." The defendant introduced more proof of his sexual prowess by recalling that his ex-lover, a widow named Isabel Ortiz, protested his marriage to Caño because Céspedes previously had promised to marry her.[44]

The most conclusive, official proof of Céspedes's claim to male identity came from the proclamation of his masculinity by medical authorities at the time of his marriage in May 1586, when he was found to be a man by the doctors who examined him on behalf of the church. Nine doctors testified that Céspedes had a male member, although the first two (Casas and Martínez) mentioned a small mark between the penis and the anus, saying they could "not determine whether or not it is a female sex."[45] Moreover, one of the doctors, Francisco Díaz, found that Céspedes had "a virile member in good and perfect shape with two testicles."[46] When one of these men, Dr. Mantilla, was reinterviewed in July 1587, however, Céspedes claimed he had suffered a physical setback. The bodily change complicated his case considerably and probably led to his conviction. While Mantilla found Céspedes to be a man by looking at and touching him, the physician later said that "he has seen her and that presently she has a female sex and is a woman." The only feasible explanation—and certainly the only one that would protect Mantilla and the other physicians from prosecution—was that an "illusion of the devil" and Céspedes's own witchcraft had misled the doctors.[47]

Céspedes insisted that an illness had changed his body in the months before the trial. Various depositions attest to the defendant's discomfort and shock at these changes. Melchor López, the warden of Eleno's jail, referred to Céspedes as a woman and testified that Céspedes believed she was dying and that she talked about her member falling off. López explained that

Father Rozas even came to hear Céspedes's confession, and "Céspedes said that she was sick in her frontal area and that her member was falling off and that the cure she was applying was meant to make the member re-form."[48] Several others, including local citizens and prisoners, discussed the various comments and requests Céspedes made about disease, suggesting that Céspedes talked to others about his problem and that he experienced a high degree of anxiety and pain.

Céspedes was no stranger to applying remedies to the genital area. In fact, the only confession he made regarding his dually sexed body was that he tried to seal the vaginal opening with "certain lavations of wine and balaustine and alcohol."[49] The Inquisition viewed this statement as a segue to similar admissions of either creating a substitute penis or conjuring the devil to create the illusion of such a member. Céspedes, who claimed to base his descriptions on personal bodily experience, saw no contradiction in this matter. While inquisitors inundated him with questions about bodily function and accused him of sexual misconduct and deception, Céspedes was equally vehement in his defense of his masculine body. It would be hard enough to explain why he had lived as a man for many years, but without physical evidence to justify this lifestyle change, Céspedes stood little chance of convincing the Holy Office.

The attention given to the penis during this trial cannot fail to impress anybody who reads the documents. Céspedes described in detail the initial appearance of his penis when he was a female adolescent. The scribe drew a line in the trial record to represent the length of the penis. Inquisitors, witnesses, and defendants alike discussed the form, function, and changeability of Céspedes's penis. Francisco Díaz, one of many doctors who testified, indicated on 15 September 1587 that he had found Céspedes to be a man who "had in size and form a male member proportionate to his body, neither large nor small, probably more large than small."[50] And even though María del Caño claimed that she never touched her husband's shameful parts (*partes vergonzosas*), the inquisitors found different ways to acquire information from her. They asked how the couple made love (Céspedes got on top and on Caño's side), if Caño ever found herself pregnant (once she suspected pregnancy, but then her period came), and if her husband ever "praised his male member" (he didn't).[51]

María del Caño's testimony contains highly personal information. Both she and Céspedes indicated during the questioning that she had never had sexual relations with anyone except her husband, who "took her virginity." Caño emphasized her limited sexual experience when she testified that she had "never been with another man to know what other men know."[52] Caño also said that she "begged and pleaded so much for Céspedes to show himself" that one day he gave her a brief opportunity to see his body. He walked around the bedroom with his shirt lifted up and instructed her to look at him. Then he quickly put his shirt down again, apparently before she got a good look.[53] As this example suggests, Caño presented herself as sexually inexperienced, but she also revealed that she and her husband had a relationship that allowed for requests about the other's body to be made and, to a certain degree, indulged.

Caño's deposition also gives us a sense of Céspedes's concern for his wife's well-being. When she visited him in jail in Ocaña, Céspedes told her "that his male member had been eaten by cancer and had gone into his body [and] that she should go to the church so that they would not arrest her."[54] Like her husband, Caño was under suspicion for illicit homosexual acts. By the end of the trial, inquisitors exonerated her: "The said woman could not understand that she was marrying anyone but a man, since the said Elena did the acts of a man."[55] In this case, doing the acts of a man refers to a very particular, heterosexual conceptualization of masculinity: Céspedes penetrated Caño with his penis, he ejaculated, and, though he never impregnated his wife, he had a physical protrusion (*bulto*) that she took for his male genitalia. Inquisitors took these details as evidence of Céspedes's performance of manliness. Either convinced by Caño's self-defense or lacking information to prosecute, they eventually let her go.

Inquisitors persisted in seeking to shatter what they perceived as Céspedes's charade of male impersonation. By focusing on the physical evidence of the body, they pinned their definition of masculinity on a normative conceptualization of biological male sex. The task at hand was to identify the minimal trappings of masculinity, and then to determine whether Céspedes possessed such trappings. Did he have a penis? Was it in proportion to his body? Did he look like a man? The Inquisition put the medical experts in a compromised position, since those who had found Céspedes to be a man in 1586 were now called upon to revise their initial assessments. This group of experts found the defendant devoid of male genitalia. They also insisted he showed no sign of ever having been a man *or* a hermaphrodite. Without testicles and a penis, Céspedes was defined as a woman and, therefore, a trickster.

Nonetheless, the defendant worked hard to defend his manliness. Specifically, he emphasized his private and public compliance with the standards of masculinity. His sexual partners confirmed that his body worked like a man's. True, he occasionally had a period, but his wife and Isabel Ortiz corroborated his claims on working genitalia. His transformations from hosemaker and weaver to tailor, soldier, and surgeon suggest that he was an opportunist whose unusual physical circumstances and ambitious character helped him move up the social ladder. He learned several crafts, became a soldier, and learned to perform surgery. He even mentioned that, after getting licensed as a surgeon, he lived in Yepes with María del Caño but then, "on account of there being no surgeon in Ocaña, he went to live there."[56]

The move to Ocaña, which also led to the denouncement of his hermaphroditism to the authorities, is described in such a way as to emphasize two different aspects of Céspedes's character. It made economic sense that a surgeon who supported his wife would move to a town in need of his services. By practicing a skilled trade, he offered an important service to society. We cannot know whether Céspedes was primarily opportunistic or whether he also had a sense of responsibility to a society into which he had inserted himself through a rather circuitous route. Such questions of motivation and character are, finally, untenable. His self-fashioning helped him become a productive and valuable citizen. As Céspedes argued to the tribunal, he had value to society and medical knowledge that justified his unusual physical characteristics.

The attention to genitalia and sexual function in the case reveals that the "truth" of Céspedes's sex mattered deeply to the inquisitors. His ethnic difference might also have contributed to the Inquisition's desire to strip him of his masculinity, as well as of his place in society. Céspedes defended his masculinity in terms of public and private performance. Yet the dominant culture was unaccommodating with regard to the public nature of his assimilation. Instead, inquisitors focused solely on the private, looking for physiological proof of his unorthodoxy. In this sense, Céspedes's body offered a legitimate vehicle for punishing the intangible offense of assimilation. In addition to ambiguous genitalia, he had brown skin, a slave brand, and pierced ears. Freed slaves were not uncommon in the Iberian Peninsula during the period. Their numbers were higher in Andalusia than elsewhere, suggesting that their integration might have been more easily tolerated in the South than in other areas of Spain.[57] With regard to the perceived threat of the Moriscos in the sixteenth century, Burshatin and others have pointed out that the Spanish state forced Moriscos to stop wearing their traditional dress and to speak as proper Christians in this period.[58]

The insistence on Céspedes's femininity reflected a belief in an inherently stable and unchanging identity. The inquisitors' reaction to Céspedes has much in common with the purity-of-blood statutes passed in the sixteenth century. These so-called *limpieza de sangre* laws made it more difficult for people who called themselves Christians to be functioning, integrated members of society. Granting more rights and protections to those who could trace their Christian lineage than to those who simply called themselves Christians, the statutes created a system by which private lives became a matter of public inquiry. As in cases in which law-abiding, church-going *conversos* were tried for Judaizing, inquisitors looked beyond Céspedes's public identity to his private life. They rejected the original doctors' reports that declared Céspedes a man and accused him of bribing medical officials. A new string of examinations reversed this judgment, with everyone stating quite plainly that Céspedes had never been a man, had only a female sex, and, as one surgeon noted, had the height, face, and speech of a woman, not of a man.[59] Everyone assumed that Céspedes must belong to one sex or the other, and it was his great misfortune that the Inquisition conceived of masculinity in perhaps the only way that excluded him. Without evidence of male genitalia, he did not stand a chance.

A BODY ON TRIAL

The Inquisition put Céspedes's body on trial by discussing, examining, and prodding it for two years. The case hinged on defining masculinity in such a way as to prevent outsiders—those who were biologically or ethnically different—from enjoying the benefits accorded to men whose physiology and Old Christian, Spanish identity allowed them to be fully integrated into society. Indeed, faced with the possibility of redefining masculinity, the options for the inquisitors were limited. If they let Céspedes into their club of men, then they would be allowing a nonnormative, branded ex-slave with brown skin and pierced ears into their midst. More urgently, perhaps, the inquisitors needed to consider the implications of such a decision: They would be sending the message that alternative configurations of masculinity were acceptable. Much concerned about setting examples for the public, inquisitors often elaborated on the meaning of their judgments when they announced sentences. In turn, these sentences were reiterated and dramatized in the public arena of the penitential and punitive ceremony known as the auto de fe. As with many other cases in which defendants were spared from the stake, the inquisitors proclaimed "equitable and merciful" treatment and emphasized that Céspedes could have been "gravely punished" (fol. III.83).

The declaration of the sentence—which included the abjuration of sins in an auto de fe, two hundred lashings, and ten years' unpaid service in reclusion at a hospital—emphasized that the punishment was meant as an example to others so that "similar deception and tricks are not committed again."[60] The officials concluded that Céspedes "had never been a hermaphrodite . . . and all of the acts that as a man she said she had done were [done] with certain artifice [*artificio*], and everything was a trick and not natural."[61] As a trickster (*burladora*), Céspedes had preyed on women, deceived medical authorities, and, by implication, tricked soldiers, neighbors, and patients into believing he was a man.[62]

The evidence cited throughout the case as a basis for calling Céspedes a *burladora* is purely sexual in nature. Elena pretended to be Eleno, used trickery to appear to have male genitalia, and had the audacity to marry a woman with the approval of the church. The stakes were much higher than mere sexual trickery. As Alice Domurat Dreger has observed about hermaphroditism today:

> Most of us are used to the idea of two sexes, and most of us are used to being only one. . . . The questioned body forces us to ask what exactly it is—if anything—that makes the rest of us unquestionable. It forces the not-so-easy question of what it means to be a "normal" male or a "normal" female.[63]

In spite of the persistence of the one-sex anatomical model that saw females as defective males through the early modern period, the idea of two separate genders reigned in the daily lives of the people.[64] Cultural authorities, such as inquisitors who judged heretics, church officials who granted marriage licenses, or doctors who assessed individual bodies, demonstrated their dedication to keeping the two sexes neatly defined and decidedly distinct. Through medical and legal investigations into the sexual and physical histories of one hermaphrodite, the Inquisition established what it meant to be a normal man. The implicit questions put to inquisitors by this case were numerous. How could an individual be both a man and a woman? How should inquisitors respond to the narrative of a mother-turned-soldier who claimed to be a man? The intersections of race and gender made manifest in the very person of Eleno/a de Céspedes complicated the dominant definitions of heterodoxy that the Inquisition was charged with enforcing.

Rather than criminalizing hermaphroditism, the inquisitorial judgment stigmatized the nonnormative body, issuing a threat to others who might try to refashion themselves. Up against the living example of the defendant, who successfully negotiated female and male identities for more than forty years, the Inquisition denied that identity was negotiable, particularly for individuals who appropriated the benefits of the dominant ethnicity, class, religion, or sex. So Céspedes, with a nonnormative body that had a vaginal opening but no penis or testicles, was categorized as a deviant woman.[65]

A well-heeled mechanism of social control, the Holy Office broadened its definition of heresy in the sixteenth century to purge society of suspect citizens and outsiders. Medical advice was needed to explain Céspedes's physical anomalies, however. Due to the changes in Céspedes's physical features, all the medical authorities in this case revised their initial assessments of Céspedes as a man and unanimously agreed that he was a woman who showed no signs whatsoever of having been a man or a hermaphrodite. The unanimity on this last matter makes the doctors' statements read more like collusion than professional opinion, since many of the same men had previously found Céspedes to be a man. Although the defendant tried to counter their assessment with several learned sources about hermaphroditism, his arguments fell on deaf ears. This dynamic—of pitting scientific argumentation based on direct observation against historical research—confirms that various explanations of hermaphroditism existed in Spain during the early modern period.[66] In combination with the suspiciously unanimous verdict about the absence of any signs of hermaphroditism, the dynamic also suggests that the Inquisition willfully chose to exclude the possibility of hermaphroditism. Instead, inquisitors accused the defendant of having a satanic pact that gave the illusion of male genitalia. From the inquisitors' standpoint, the rejection of the mere possibility of Céspedes's intersexuality was crucial, for it crushed any claims the defendant might have on masculinity. Working within a complex framework informed by concerns about ethnicity, class, religion, and gender, the Inquisition kept the branded mulatto hermaphrodite Eleno de Céspedes out of the ranks of men.

A MAN AND A WOMAN

Rife with anxieties about gender, class, and ethnicity, this case drew the boundaries of masculinity in a way that guaranteed the exclusion of Eleno de Céspedes. But what does the treatment of intersexed individuals tell us about the conceptualization of the category of woman in this period? Recall, for a moment, our nun-turned-man Magdalena Muñoz. Like other hermaphrodites in the period, Muñoz and Céspedes found that their bodies attracted public attention once their intersexuality became known or suspected. Muñoz was a curiosity among the other nuns, who believed that she had manly strength and characteristics. Nonetheless, Muñoz was confirmed to be a woman by nuns who, on many occasions, examined her while she was sleeping.[67] Only when Fray Torres and his colleague certified that Muñoz's swelling in the groin area had produced a phallus was Muñoz called a man and released from the convent. Joyfully, Muñoz's father received his "manly son," whom Torres described as a liberated prisoner.[68]

In the context of Eleno de Céspedes's Inquisition case, the narrative of joy and relief expressed by Fray Torres makes more sense. A man locked away in a woman's body, Muñoz was liberated by a natural transformation that rescued his manliness from a prison of femininity. Even though Muñoz acted like a man and had physical characteristics that seemed masculine, not until a penis appeared was he able to be a man, to leave the supposed prison of the convent and inherit his father's estate.

The Muñoz case illuminates one key aspect of the Inquisition's treatment of Céspedes. If we believe that Céspedes had a form of hermaphroditism, then we see that it did not matter that Eleno acted like a man. Without a visible phallus, he lacked the minimal requirements for manhood. It is a great irony of this case that Céspedes's punishment was gender reassignment, for this is a person who lived as both man and woman during one lifetime and who showed a capacity for self-transformation.

In stripping the defendant of his masculine identity, the Inquisition stripped him of his profession, his marriage, and his wife. Publicly whipped and humiliated, he lost all that he had worked toward for more than two decades. Like the gender-confused references to Magdalena Muñoz as both *hijo* and *ella*, the inquisitors played into the gender confusion they sought to avoid. They declared Céspedes a woman and sentenced him to ten years' unpaid labor in a hospital. A standard sentence for bigamists and other heretics, the unpaid hospital labor involved an ironic twist in the case of Céspedes, as it placed the convict in a setting in which he could deploy the knowledge and skills he had acquired as a man, but only as an unpaid woman.

Letters received from hospital authorities and included in the case file attest to the problems created by this solution. Apparently Céspedes was such a popular figure that people came from all over to see the woman-surgeon. The first letter, written by an official in the Hospital del Rey in Toledo on 23 February 1589, describes "the great commotion and embarrassment that the entrance of said Elena de Céspedes has caused because many people come to see and be cured by her."[69] Subsequent letters confirm the commotion: Francisco de Aguilar requested that inquisitors remove Céspedes from the hospital so that the institution could "serve with the peace and quiet that it used to enjoy." A final letter indicates that "because the word had spread that the said [Céspedes] is a surgeon and that she cures many illnesses, the numbers of people who come to see her are so high that it does not allow her to comply calmly with her seclusion."[70] With no other documentation, it is hard to know what to make of this situation. Perhaps Céspedes become known as a freak of nature, drawing voyeurs from far and wide. Perhaps his popularity signifies a triumph of sorts over inquisitorial attempts to contain individual difference and he managed, in spite of the Inquisition, to become a popular surgeon. Or perhaps he became, as Burshatin suggests, a butch woman in skirts whom we should celebrate today as a voice of "exemplary *mestizaje*."[71]

Once the trial documents end, the sources tell us nothing about Céspedes's own feelings about his new position as a woman living in the hospital. The sources do not answer our questions about whether Céspedes enjoyed this popularity, if he settled into his imposed identity as a woman, if he was a victim of voyeurism, or if he enjoyed his role as healer. Looking back on this case more than four hundred years after the fact, we might be tempted to take pleasure in the ironies of the inquisitors' making. It is tempting, for example, to imagine Céspedes reveling in his popularity, to imagine inquisitors anguishing about the notoriety they themselves created. Such acts of the imagination find no proof in the documentation. By looking to Céspedes as a "proud transgendered subject," for example, we are imputing a deeper psychological profile and broader conclusions than the evidence allows. It is comforting to see victims as triumphing over their oppressors, yet I find it difficult to imagine a person living a wholly contented life after suffering severe physical ailments, clipping away at his penis and testicles, losing both his livelihood and his wife, and being forced to change his identity. We should not overlook the great emotional, physical, and economic trauma to which the Inquisition subjected him. Indeed, it seems implausible to suggest that, after such an ordeal, anyone could appreciate the ironies of such a sentence.

If Inquisition survivors can claim any kind of victory, then Eleno de Céspedes's triumph was one that, perhaps, we would have been unable to appreciate until very recently. Born a woman, Céspedes negotiated the challenges of self-definition as he fashioned himself into a man and integrated himself into Spanish society. He experienced life as a female ex-slave in that culture. As a woman, Céspedes married a man, had a child, and worked in relatively low-paying jobs. Regardless of what really happened to his body, it seems clear that he later experienced the same culture as a man, gaining many benefits in terms of freedom of movement and professional opportunity. While the Inquisition tried to reverse this triumph of self-definition, the trial record affords a chance to retrace the steps of Céspedes's life and to understand his defense of his identity change.

A testament to the complex relationship between gender and authority in early modern Spain, Céspedes's case records one individual's struggle to establish and defend an identity that would allow him upward mobility in educational, professional, and personal terms. Regardless of which scientific, historical, or medical arguments the defendant used to argue for access to those privileges, the Inquisition excluded him on the basis of his suspect claim to masculinity. By giving voice to his unique life story and arguing cogently for the right to live as he chose, Eleno de Céspedes should go down in the annals of history as someone who articulated through rhetoric and through lived example that being different—a mulatto, a slave, a hermaph-rodite—should not exclude one from the professional and social benefits ac-corded only to a select few. Céspedes fought for acceptance as a man, and his attempt to define gender based on peculiar physiology highlights larger cultural anxieties about maintaining clear, fixed lines between the sexes. In-quisitors attempted to keep the sexes separate, and Céspedes could not con-vince them of his manliness if he could not produce a masculine body.

The very extremes of the Céspedes case give us access to specific cul-tural definitions of masculinity and femininity. In addition to revealing the period's anxiety about defining men and women, this unique trial exem-plifies the divergence between rigid definitions of gender and individuals' lived experiences. Cultural authorities articulated specific gender codes, but that Céspedes lived for years as a man suggests it was difficult to impose those codes on the Spanish citizenry. As an outline of the attempts of cul-tural authorities to contain individual difference, the Céspedes Inquisition trial presents a host of complex responses to the culture of control in early modern Spain.

2

Bernarda Manuel

Defending Femininity to the Holy Office

On a November day in 1650, a thirty-four-year-old woman was taken to an Inquisition chamber, where, to avoid torture, she declared her innocence and informed her jailers that she had "the curse of women"—her period.[1] When inquisitors were not put off by this invocation of a bodily taboo, Bernarda Manuel (c. 1616–?) avoided torture by confessing to having observed the Law of Moses. She then gave an explicit account of the sins she had committed against the church since first learning about Judaism from a nursemaid at age eight. She admitted to fasting occasionally and to keeping the Sabbath, and she named several other Judaizers. Finally, Manuel affirmed that Catholicism was the true religion and the only route to salvation.

Poignant as it is to read this woman's forced renunciation of her religious beliefs and practices, Manuel's confession is not unique among cases of *conversos*.[2] Like many suspected Crypto-Jews tried by the Inquisition, in the end she confessed to the heretical activities she had denied during her eleven-month trial. In keeping with strategies meant to deter further accusations, Manuel put the blame on a proselytizing servant who, if she existed at all, probably could not be located by the Inquisition. Although Manuel provided some details about her alleged Judaism, it is impossible to glean an accurate understanding of her religious beliefs from her confession. Acting under pressure and responding to specific accusations, Manuel gave the information necessary to appease her inquisitors.

Was Manuel a practicing Jew, or was she simply a Catholic descendant of Jews caught in the Inquisition's mission to purge the country of all signs of heterodoxy? The signs point toward a converso background, although it is impossible to know whether she ever practiced Judaism. Among scholars of Spanish Jewry, debate persists as to whether Jewish practices and culture continued after the first wave of inquisitorial furor in the fifteenth and six-teenth centuries.[3] I believe that Manuel's story is one of the hundreds that provide insight into what seems to have been a thriving, albeit clandestine, converso culture. Manuel's parents immigrated to Spain from the Algarve re-gion of southern Portugal around 1630. It is likely that they were conversos who left Portugal either to avoid prosecution by that country's increasingly vigilant Inquisition or to take advantage of the proconverso reforms of Philip IV and his favorite, the Count-Duke of Olivares, in the 1620s.[4] That her family immigrated to Seville might suggest that they sought a new home among the large converso population in that city. Her father's profession as a doctor and her husband's as a cloth merchant might be clues to family back-ground, as conversos comprised a large part of those trades.[5] It is worth not-ing that Manuel's husband tried to deflect blame onto her during his Judaiz-ing trial by testifying that Manuel, her three sisters, and her brother-in-law tried to convert him to Judaism. Whether the couple and their families did indeed observe Jewish practices cannot be known for certain, but the details surrounding them suggest that at the very least they came from a converso background. Like many descendants of the persecuted Jews, they may well have observed both Catholic and Judaic rituals.

Regardless of whether conversos' confessions reflected the truth of their religious beliefs or merely parroted what the Inquisition wanted to hear, we cannot help but notice the double meaning behind Manuel's affirmation that Catholicism was the only route to salvation. Indeed, had she refused to make such a confession, Manuel could have been banished, whipped, or even "re-laxed," a process by which the Inquisition, an arm of the church, avoided kill-ing, instead turning individuals over to the secular arm of the law for public execution. Her admission of guilt and her express desire for reconciliation with the church led to lesser punishments. The Inquisition confiscated all her worldly goods, obligated her to wear a penitential garment (*sanbenito*), and forced her to abjure heretical activities during the public spectacle of an auto de fe. Finally, they sentenced her to perpetual imprisonment (*cárcel perpetua*).

Bernarda Manuel's is a story about immigrants and Jews, but her Inqui-sition trial gives us a glimpse into more than just religious and ethnic intol-erance. In a compelling twelve-page autobiographical statement (*memorial*) written in her own hand, Manuel crafted a defense that rested on her im-peccable record as a virtuous Christian mother and wife. She also portrayed herself as a woman at the mercy of a mentally ill and abusive husband. Man-uel detailed the hardship that her husband's paranoia and hostility created for her and her family. At the end of the document, she appealed to in-quisitors to recognize her innocence, asking them, "How am I to blame?"—"*¿Q[ué] culpa tengo yo?*" (fol. 38, 1.17–20). As suggested by her declarations of victimization and innocence, the record of Bernarda Manuel's conviction by the Holy Office offers a stark example of a tale of domestic strife ignored by the authorities.

The connection to the history of domestic violence is but one of the fascinating aspects of Manuel's trial and her handwritten memorial.[6] The self-portrayal of a consummate wife and mother lays bare the dominant definitions of femininity in seventeenth-century Spain, showing in no uncertain terms the outline of the appropriate gender codes that Manuel perceived to be at work. Manuel defended herself by mobilizing rhetoric of motherhood and femininity; her question "How am I to blame?" points to larger questions about gender, religion, and personal responsibility. The trial record reveals individuals' relationships in a culture whose gender codes were intertwined with religion and citizenship. Seeking to make her voice heard by the tribunal, the merchant-class conversa immigrant sought authority in the roles of wife and mother—the roles that most reliably accorded women legitimacy. The failure of this strategy tells us as much about Bernarda Manuel's expectations as it does about the disenfranchisement of women and other minorities in inquisitional Spain.

A WOMAN'S STORY

The disadvantaged position occupied by Manuel related to her personal life and to the sociopolitical landscape of Spain during her lifetime. Like other Portuguese immigrants in the mid–seventeenth century, Manuel faced heightened risks.[7] Many Spanish Jews fled to Portugal in the early years of inquisitorial terror. Yet Spain's annexation of its neighbor in 1580—and the accompanying imposition of a strict Inquisition—led to Portuguese converso immigration beginning in the late 1500s. Those who immigrated decades later at the behest of the Count-Duke of Olivares were welcome: They filled an economic vacuum created by exile and violence. Yet by 1640 the nation of Portugal was in revolt. By 1643, Olivares had fallen from power. These changes left the immigrant conversos open to renewed prejudice and persecution.[8] By 1650, under the guidance of the harsh inquisitor general Diego de Arce y Reynoso, the Inquisition had stepped up its prosecution of conversos.[9]

In addition to belonging to a group that had fallen out of favor, Manuel was socially marginalized by the circumstances of her strained marriage. As the memorial describes in the opening paragraph, Antonio Borges proposed marriage when Manuel was twenty-two. Her male relatives cautioned against the alliance:

[They] did not think that I should marry this man because Antonio Borges had a bad disposition because the woman he had been married to had died on account of the trouble he caused her; and they thought I should consider that his two brothers had left their wives and they didn't want him to do the same to me, to which I responded that I would never marry such a man.[10]

Convinced by those who advocated the marriage that Borges "was a good man and that he would [never do anything] to her and would treat his wife like all honorable men do," she agreed to marry him.[11] Three weeks later, Manuel's initial fears were confirmed:

[M]y father received a letter from one of our uncles in which he said that if his niece was still not married that she should not marry Antonio Borges out of fear that he would kill his niece just as he killed his other wife because he came to treat her in such a way that he even kept an unsheathed dagger between him and his wife in bed.[12]

Manuel concludes this introductory section with a pointed description of her emotional strife as a newlywed: "[A]nd so, sir, the fear that I conceived was so great that neither by day nor by night did my heart have any rest and this fear lasted until I had children."[13] Whether her children provided her with protection or simply with a new focus is a question to address later. In spite of the decreased anxiety she experienced after childbirth, she never found sustained relief from Borges's crazy spells (*locuras*).

Aside from her children, siblings, and father, Manuel mentions few social contacts in Seville, where she lived as a married woman for a decade before traveling to Alicante and then settling in Madrid. Her husband's controlling behavior probably limited her social interaction. She testified that she went out only to go to church or to visit family, that Borges followed her and "did not allow her to communicate with anybody." Manuel elaborates on her isolation by describing the house where they lived in the Sevillian district of Triana for six months as located in a remote spot near the river. During that time, by her account, she talked with only one person outside her family.[14]

Manuel's narrative of a threatening marriage that isolated her and left her exposed to her husband's *locuras* was meant to discredit her accuser. Although that person's identity had been withheld from her, Manuel assumed correctly that her husband had told inquisitors she was a practicing Jew. Indeed, on 18 January 1650, Borges, himself imprisoned for Judaizing, told the inquisitors that his wife "declared to him that she was an observer and a believer of the Law of Moses, in whose observance he has seen her."[15] Although Borges subsequently withdrew the accusations, saying he was "crazy and without judgment" when he made them, the Inquisition nonetheless proceeded with its prosecution of Manuel.[16]

Working under the assumption that her husband had turned her in, Bernarda Manuel portrayed herself to the tribunal as a psychologically abused wife. Her defense appealed to the logic of the *tacha*, the system by which defendants could remove hostile prosecution witnesses. Renée Levine Melammed explains the tacha as a "trying" and "exasperating" system but also points out that it probably was "the only successful technique utilized by the defense." The exasperation stemmed from the need to provide a list of people who had reason to provide false testimony against the defendant, plus the names of two others who could verify each enmity. Melammed speculates on the use this mechanism:

> It is not surprising to discover long *tacha* lists, for the defendant, sitting for long periods of time in a cell, would reconstruct his or her life and think of numerous incidents and tensions during his or her lifetime that might have influenced someone to provide incriminating testimony.[17]

We do not know whether Manuel divined or was told the name of her accuser, but throughout her trial she focused her efforts on destabilizing her husband's reliability as a witness.[18]

In fact, Manuel's memorial, which she describes in the deposition as "sheets of paper written in my own hand," begins with an explanation of this thought process: "I say, sir, that I have run through my mind and I don't find anybody who could do me such great harm."[19] She then names her husband as the only possible exception to this otherwise clean record of family and acquaintances.

Even though the memorial contains intimately drawn depictions of her experiences, Manuel remains at a distance. While writing this document, she was a prisoner and a defendant, bound by legal considerations. This was her best chance to represent herself to the tribunal in a way that would convince the Inquisition of her innocence. Her lawyer might have advised her to write the document and to put Borges at the center, although Manuel never indicated that she wrote at someone else's behest. Whether she made the decision herself or her lawyer counseled her to write, the most likely scenario shows Manuel holding the power to shape the story, to offer a portrait of her family that might convince the tribunal of her innocence.

Working within these limitations and writing under the pressure of an ongoing trial, she still could have chosen from many different narratives.

Most obviously, she could have written about her church-going experiences, her children's Catholicism, or her knowledge of church doctrine. Witnesses testified about Manuel's attendance of mass and her knowledge of Catholic prayer, for example. Among all the stories she could have told in a document whose composition she likely controlled, she chose to tell the story of her life as a victim of a violent husband. Based on what she wrote in the document, we can surmise that Manuel sought to discredit Borges's mental stability and, as a result, to discredit his testimony to the Inquisition. By focusing on her husband's violent behavior, Manuel must have hoped that inquisitors would respond with sympathy to her role as a victimized wife.

While Manuel's trial structurally resembles other Inquisition cases— with depositions, accusations, and judgments written by scribes and signed by various witnesses and officials—the autobiographical document contains rich information about her experiences as an immigrant, daughter, sister, wife, neighbor, friend, and mother. Like any autobiography, Manuel's memorial weaves together select stories and information, allowing us to learn as much about her actual experiences as what her expectations were with regard to the tribunal's response. Her attempts to discredit Borges's testimony suggest that she expected the Inquisition to follow its own guidelines for thorough and fair investigation. The gap between her perceptions and the realities of Inquisition practices speaks to the disempowered position of many during the period—including women, Portuguese immigrants, and suspected Judaizers.

The defense based on spousal abuse and neglect had little effect, as inquisitors essentially ignored the information presented in Manuel's document. They did not locate most of the witnesses she named, and they disregarded the argument she made about her plight as a mistreated wife. In spite of testimony by defense witnesses who supported Manuel's claims, Borges's original accusation of his wife's Judaizing determined the outcome of the case. On 7 November 1650, Bernarda Manuel followed the course of many defendants before her: She confessed and repented rather than succumb to torture. Her memorial offers an unusual opportunity for us to analyze not the verifiably true life story of a thirty-four-year-old woman, but the strategies of self-representation an immigrant conversa used in an effort to have her case dismissed by the Inquisition. In conjunction with the trial record itself, this document's negotiation of marriage, religion, and violence offers a chance to piece together one woman's understanding of the codes of conduct governing gender in seventeenth-century Spain.

THE MARTYR DEFENSE

From the Inquisition's perspective, Manuel's trial did not hinge on gender roles in the least. At first, the accused was not informed about why she had been brought before the tribunal: Like the names of witnesses and accusers, charges were kept secret so as to obtain the broadest-reaching testimonies possible. We must remember that Inquisition trials took place in secrecy. As Richard Kagan has explained:

> Unlike a criminal trial conducted to establish innocence or guilt, the trial of faith was premised on the guilt of the accused. Once the inquisitors had voted to pursue the case (*votos*), the guilt of the accused was assumed and the purpose of the trial was to extract a confession.[20]

The Inquisition had jurisdiction over religious heresy, and it defined that category broadly to include fornication, blasphemy, bigamy, and sodomy along with Judaism, Protestantism, Islam, and witchcraft. Given that Manuel's husband was already in custody, the likelihood that he was her accuser and Judaizing the crime probably was evident.

The formal accusation against Manuel was wide reaching. She was accused of observing the Law of Moses, proselytizing, and committing offenses against the Catholic church; wearing clean clothes, resting, and fasting on Saturdays; refusing to eat various foods prohibited by Judaism; attempting to flee the country; and conjuring a spell using a statue of Christ. Based almost entirely on Borges's statements, the accusations found marginal support in only one witness. Manuel's eleven-year-old daughter, Inés, told the authorities that she had seen her father whip a small statue of Christ. This testimony implicated Manuel, her sister, and her brother-in-law, who were said to be present when the events occurred at the sister's home during Christmas in Seville.

Interestingly, Inés did not name her mother as a participant in these events. Instead, the girl described her mother as sitting in a separate room, feeling "afflicted," and crying until she fainted. Nor was Manuel named in the other testimonies given during this initial information-gathering phase. Two converso prisoners in Seville, Francisco Duarte and Francisco López, said nothing about Manuel, but did provide anecdotes about Borges's desire to go to Italy, presumably in search of religious freedom.

The descriptions of Judaizing given by witnesses and embellished upon by the inquisitors fell squarely within the boundaries of Jewish practices witnesses reported to the Inquisition. The circularity of this procedure should not be overlooked: Inquisition procedures were infused with witness baiting, as the Judaizing cases illustrate. Melammed explains that, when the tribunals were first established, Inquisition representatives held public information sessions at which they told people how to identify Judaizers and other heretics. Following these sessions, a grace period ensued during which people came forward to confess a broad range of sin and heresy.[21] The meticulous record keeping of this initial phase allowed the Inquisition to gather details about Jewish and other practices. Later this information was used to prosecute those absolved during the grace period, as well as to identify Crypto-Jews, bait witnesses, and elicit pro forma confessions.[22] The spectacle of public punishment, which included the renunciation of heresy and the reading of prisoners' sins in town squares and churches, also helped spread limited, often erroneous, information about Jewish practices.[23]

The patterned rhetoric of Inquisition cases poses many problems for interpretation. The similarities among accusations, testimonies, and confessions make it difficult to reconstruct events, let alone to understand the motivations of the people involved.[24] Unlike the thousands of witnesses and defendants whose words come down through the filter of Inquisition scribes, Bernarda Manuel stands out because her own words appear as part of her defense. Similar to standard defense testimonies in its attempt to deflect suspicion, her document lets us examine the psyche of a woman living on the cultural margins and, in the moment we meet her, fighting for her life.

While Inquisition cases almost always included an autobiographical deposition, defendants in Spain rarely wrote anything designated for inclusion in their cases. This was particularly true for nonaristocratic and nonclergy members of society, who comprised the illiterate majority. Scribes and officials wrote most material included in the trials, but the tribunals sometimes appropriated letters and notes as evidence. Other materials—such as religious biographies and autobiographies—also came under Inquisition scrutiny and are referred to in the records.[25] In their origins at least, such texts seem more predictable and less surprising than Manuel's autobiographical document, for their subjects generally belonged to the influential classes, fraternized with powerful individuals, or, at the very least, had high levels of education. Those with good connections often used their influence and education to shake off accusations of heresy. During the same year as Manuel's trial, for instance, the well-connected mystical author Sor María de Agreda (1602–65) was interrogated, but her case was never brought to trial.[26]

The immigrant conversa Bernarda Manuel was not as fortunate. Yet she did have the unusual benefit of literacy, which she used to present her own version of the story to the tribunal and, in doing so, to exploit gender expectations to her benefit. By the time Manuel submitted her document to the tribunal, she had heard and denied the charges against her and had been assigned a defense lawyer, Gabriel de Parejas. She had told the tribunal that, when she married Antonio, he had a reputation for being a prickly man with a "terrible nature."[27] In her deposition, Manuel portrayed herself as a woman trapped in a relationship of fear, thus trying to make the accusations of her own proselytizing seem incredible. Specifically, she denied that she was strong-willed enough to convert others:

> I was a weak woman with a weak nature, [so] I would have needed to be daring to persuade the said Antonio Borges or anybody else to observe the Law of Moses. I was so fearful in his presence that I did not even dare to speak or to communicate with anybody except the many servants we had.[28]

The representation of the victimized wife, of a woman so paralyzed with fear that she confined her interaction to speaking with household servants, makes us wonder to what extent we really can understand Bernarda Manuel.

Like other defendants, Manuel was constrained by the questions asked of her and the pressures exerted on her during the trial. We know that she claimed to be weak and fearful, but we also know that her written and spoken testimonies were motivated by the very real desire to escape the charges brought against her. The coherent arguments put forth in Manuel's depositions and her written statement suggest that she was clever enough to devise and implement a defense strategy that informed her self-representation throughout the trial.

Since Manuel probably controlled the shape, style, and content of her memorial, the document allows us to learn more about her than we can usually know about any defendant in these trials. First, the document shows that Manuel received a relatively solid education, probably in her native language of Portuguese. In a time of low literacy levels (especially for women), Manuel knew how to write. Her writing abilities offer further proof of a vibrant Iberian converso culture invested in educating women, yet we might not have known anything about her education without this document. Her text is written in Spanish, but Portuguese heavily influences its syntax, spelling, and grammar.[29]

Manuel's writing differs from the Inquisition scribe's rendition of her spoken words, as he did not distinguish between the defendant's speech and that of other witnesses or officials at any point in the record. In contrast, her first-person, handwritten memorial does not mask her immigrant status. Indeed, there is a marked difference between Manuel's language in the memorial and her language in the rest of the trial record. This disparity casts serious doubt on the belief of some scholars that Inquisition scribes faithfully recorded all speech particularities, mannerisms, and gestures.[30] The disparity between Manuel's writing and her recorded speech should serve as a cautionary note to scholars who take for granted that depositions from any tribunal—whether inquisitional or secular—represent an exact record of what was said during proceedings. Further, Manuel's trial record reveals the extent to which scribes controlled the representation of the ideas, words, and emotions of defendants and witnesses.

Yet Manuel's memorial opens another line of inquiry into the possibility for personal control in a legalistic environment driven by formulaic discourse and the inquisitors' goal of securing confessions. That is, her document responds to the various chapters contained in the formal accusation against her, but her own self-validation and Borges's deauthorization emerge as the driving forces behind the text. From the beginning, she presents her husband's history of aggression as his primary flaw, using the opening page to emphasize her initial reluctance to marry him. The emphasis on the anxiety-producing marriage sets the tone for the entire document, leading the modern reader to question the motivations behind this focus. Perhaps Manuel thought her best defense was an offense: Rather than deal head-on with accusations of her own heresy, she confronted the inquisitors with the flawed nature of the proceedings by proving that the man who initiated the trial was violent and unreliable.

After providing an evidentiary discussion of her husband's history of violence, Manuel directly responds to the accusation that she kept the Sabbath. She claims that she worked harder on Saturday than on any other day and that her maids could attest to the Christian behavior in the household on this day, which was often spent preparing the family's Sunday clothes (fol. 33–33v). Rooted in Catholicism, the defense of her fasting practices contains familiar rhetoric as well:

> [T]his is another false witness because I don't know any fasts except those mandated by the holy Catholic faith, and these I did very little because I was always raising a child [i.e., nursing] or pregnant.[31]

Having identified herself first as a daughter, sister, and niece who trusted her fiancé enough to marry him, Bernarda now capitalizes on her role as a Catholic mother. As the second mention of motherhood, this reference to the physical realities of childbearing and child rearing grounds Manuel's testimony firmly in the realm of motherhood.

Manuel's strategy for self-representation takes form in these passages about marriage and motherhood. She wants to portray herself as a devoted wife whose principal source of authority was her role as a mother. Manuel attempts to convince the Inquisition that her devotion to family contrasted with Borges's mistreatment of his wives. Unlike her husband, she put her family first: "No matter how many problems I had in my household, I always sat at the table to calm my husband and children."[32] The references to breastfeeding and maternalism clarify Manuel's assertion that her fear of her husband subsided upon the birth of her first child. These references also suggest that Manuel found power and protection in her reproductive role. Perhaps she cultivated this power over twelve years of marriage to an increasingly unstable man who acted with restraint when he witnessed his wife in a maternal role.

Other evidence for the control that Manuel might have exerted through maternalism can be found in her record of childbirth. At the time of the trial, Manuel had five children between the ages of eleven and a few months, and she mentioned no miscarriages or deaths. Based on the ages Manuel gave for the children at the time of the trial, we know that two and a half years separated each of them. The relatively programmatic spacing between births in the absence of any known miscarriages suggests that Manuel may have used breastfeeding and motherhood to gain control over her domestic life.

An important source of control for women, reproductive spacing can be achieved by nursing for a long time and enforcing a taboo on sex during lactation. In this regard, we should recall Manuel's depiction of her abusive marriage: She described a marriage that was threatening from the start, one that provoked a fear that lasted until she had children.[33] If Manuel's husband did indeed threaten violence when they were newlyweds and if the threats subsided with the birth of a child, as the document suggests, then Manuel's desire to prolong her role as a nursing mother would make perfect sense.[34] Childbirth and child rearing protected her from violence and, perhaps, from having sex with a man whom she feared. Manuel's later reference to breastfeeding suggests that she also used nursing to avoid Catholic dietary restrictions. Even if she did not do this, she at least perceived that the Inquisition would view pregnancy and nursing as legitimate excuses for avoiding such restrictions and thus included it in her memorial. Likewise, she mentioned making personal sacrifices such as sitting at the dinner table to keep the family peace.

All these issues capture the potency of Bernarda Manuel's role as a mother. A source of authority and legitimacy, motherhood seems to have afforded her legitimate means by which she could calm her husband's threatening behavior. If she was a practicing Jew, then the seemingly prolonged periods of nursing, in addition to her pregnancies, afforded her a justifiable reason for not obeying Catholic dietary guidelines. Manuel's attempts at cultivating control through maternalism is evidenced by the birth spacing as well as by her choice of strategy in the torture chamber—when she claimed to have her period—and, most obviously, in the memorial itself. Perhaps she invoked the taboo of menstruation to avoid torture because she had previous success with invoking breastfeeding, pregnancy, and menses to avoid sex with her husband. Moreover, if she was Jewish, then sex during menstruation would have been prohibited anyway. The details surrounding motherhood and the female body suggest that the identity that had given Bernarda Manuel the most control in her personal life was in fact her feminine identity. It follows, then, that Manuel would embrace an idealized depiction of herself as the perfectly loyal mother and wife in her memorial.

The defendant's reliance on her maternal identity for protection and power explains, too, why religious orthodoxy plays a lesser role throughout her memorial. Indeed, she provides only a smattering of evidence for her Christian beliefs. Notably, she claims that it would have been impossible to practice Judaism because of her husband's fervent devotion to Catholicism: Borges fasted, mortified himself, and kneeled before a portrait of the Virgin when he was too ill to attend mass. She concludes this section by challenging the logic of the accusations against her: "It is not possible to believe that I would have done different fasts than those mandated by the holy church in front of a man as Catholic as he said he was."[35] The important part of this phrase comes at the end: "as Catholic as he said he was." Manuel almost certainly knew that her husband had been imprisoned for Judaizing, but by writing about his devotional practices she indicates that theirs was a Catholic household and intimates that heterodoxy had no place in their home. As in the rest of the memorial, Manuel re-creates her domestic life and, in this particular instance, she finds an acceptable way to tell the inquisitors why she never informed on her husband.

Manuel elaborated on this self-defense in responding to the accusation that she participated in a Christmas ceremony in which Borges whipped a small Christ figure in Seville three years before the trial. Such an absurd accusation, which appears in other cases as well, reflects a stereotype of Jewish delight in the crucifixion.[36] Manuel fervently denies any knowledge of such a ceremony in her memorial, explaining that it rained so much that Christmas that she could not even visit her father and brothers because of the high water levels. Moreover, she describes herself as a woman who "only left her house to go to mass and to my father's house," and who always stayed in on Christmas: "Neither when I was single nor when married did I ever leave my house on this night."[37]

The portrait of an isolated, obedient, and virtuous wife takes on martyr-like qualities in the remaining pages of the memorial. In the first two folios, Manuel describes Borges's behavior and disposition without giving extensive details, but his threats and paranoia come to the fore beginning with the response to the fourth chapter of the accusation. This section rested on an alleged trip to Alicante, which several witnesses believed to be the point of departure for Borges's trip to Italy. It was thought that he wanted to flee Spain to be able to practice Judaism freely, so the accusation carried serious weight.[38] Manuel tries to distance herself from the trip by admitting that she traveled to Alicante, but only at Borges's insistence. In fact, her version claims that when Borges explained that they would go first to Alicante and then to Rome, Manuel flatly refused to go. Borges responded angrily.

> He told me that if I did not want to go with him wherever it may be that he swore to God that he was going to leave me with my children and go where I would never know anything more of him and if the reluctance I felt was because I was leaving my father, honorable women after getting married did not have to be with their fathers but rather had an obligation to be with their husband[s] even if they went to hell.[39]

Borges then threatened to leave Manuel and mentioned the precedent for this action in his own family, confirming that his brothers already had left their wives (fol. 34). With these considerations in mind, Manuel accompanied her husband to Alicante. With her cousins' help, she convinced Borges to go to Madrid rather than risk the voyage to Italy. But when the family arrived in Madrid, Manuel's troubles began again and, eventually, culminated with her arrest by the Inquisition.

As a preface to the account of Borges's strange behavior in Madrid, Manuel anticipates inquisitorial skepticism:

> I don't doubt that you will say to me how can we believe that an honorable man, the son of good parents, married for twelve years, and with five children was going to raise such a fuss without there being a reason. To this I respond, sir, that from the day he came to Madrid an idea so ugly has entered into his head that he says that I have made a grave offense against his honor.[40]

Her husband's furor was such, she claims, that "many times I saw death in front of my eyes." By her account, only God's intervention saved her.[41]

In Manuel's telling of the tale, Borges's increasingly irrational behavior included accusing his wife of infidelity and threatening to kill her. He found no proof and so could not take her life. He then turned to verbal abuse: "[H]e began to treat me so badly with words that there was not one vile name he did not call me to my face every hour."[42] These verbal assaults affected Manuel, who says she began to have fainting attacks. Manuel relates that, when Borges saw the effect that his behavior had on her, he scolded her,

> saying why did I have to take the things [he said] to heart since I knew that he was crazy and he affirmed with many oaths that he knew very well that there was no man who had a more honorable wife than he did.[43]

Manuel's descriptions capture the confusion created by the unpredictability of her husband's behavior.[44] His contented stages would not last even a whole day. In front of the children, he began to accuse her of adultery and sexual impurity. Then, hours later, he would use the excuse of his insanity when repenting for his irrational statements (fol. 35, ll. 18–22). According to Manuel, he declared himself crazy and out of his mind.[45] Manuel's reactions to Borges's volatility included crying, fainting, and begging her husband for rational explanations.

In conjunction with Borges's increasingly erratic behavior, Manuel's fear and desperation grow more apparent throughout the document. For instance, Borges initially accepted his illness—which may have resulted from complications with syphilis or any number of other disease processes—as divine punishment for having mistreated his wife. He later revised this account and blamed Manuel for making him sick in return for all the bad things he had said about her (fol. 35). Convinced that Manuel would kill him, Borges embarked on a new plan. He moved his bed so he could sleep in a different room, then locked Manuel and the children in another room at night. Unsatisfied that this sufficiently isolated his wife from others and suspicious that she had spoken to her brother-in-law at midnight about a new murder plot, Borges made Manuel sleep with him. At this point Borges began to keep a dagger in his bed so he could kill her if the urge struck.[46] Out of fear that Manuel would poison him, he made the children drink and eat before he would touch anything she prepared, and he even went so far as to lock up his medicine so she could not tamper with it.

Manuel's desperate attempts to understand Borges got her nowhere, and her memorial depicts his words and actions as falling squarely in the realm of paranoia. She begged him to identify the people he thought were trying to kill him, but he responded vaguely, indicating that he "wanted to go around the world so as not to die at the hands of traitors."[47] Once he called Manuel "the worst of all of them." On Christmas, she said he came running through the door and locked it behind him, complained that someone was trying to kill him, and said "he would not have any rest until he took his vengeance on me."[48] Like the descriptions that follow, this incident exemplifies Borges's shifting emotions and volatility.

The representation of a paranoid husband whose emotions change from moment to moment suggests a family life riddled with the threat of violence. Underscoring the portrait of turbulent domesticity, the cycle of violence and repentance repeats itself twice more in the memorial, with the time between outbursts growing shorter and with the intensity of each incident increasing. After the Christmastime paranoia and death threats, Manuel lived in fear of the next flare-up. On 7 January, the violent, tense phase wound down when Borges was overcome with guilt over his behavior and outwardly showed his contrition to the whole family. Eating the food Manuel served him and sharing it with his children, he begged his wife for forgiveness, and Manuel

> told him that I already forgave him thinking that he was asking for that pardon for the offenses he had done to me . . . and all day long he walked around very content with the pardon I had given him.[49]

Borges then went to confession, an action that seems to be in line with his desire for forgiveness. But that night, when he called Manuel to come to his bed, she felt fear once more: "I got out of my bed with tremendous fear saying to myself 'people never change.'"[50]

What follows is perhaps the most intimate scene detailed in Manuel's document. At Borges's request, she got into bed with him. He then told her if she really loved him, she would kill him: "Kill me with this dagger and I will pay for what I have done . . . I see that you do not deserve it and that you are innocent and it would be best that you kill me."[51] His contrition continued through Saturday, but on Sunday, 9 January, Borges got up, blessed his children, left for mass, and never returned. Since Borges's testimony against Manuel was taken on 18 January, we can assume that the Inquisition arrested him soon after he left for church that day.

Manuel does not conclude her discussion of Borges with his departure, however. Structured chronologically until this point, the document now backtracks to include select incidents that strengthen the portrayal of Borges as unstable and violent. Informing the inquisitors that Borges had threatened to leave for the Indies with two of their children and had urged her to go to her father's or brothers' houses, Manuel wrote: "I told him that I would rather die at his hands than leave my own house since I was innocent of having offended him."[52]

After naming several possible witnesses for her defense and explaining that she never kept the Jewish Sabbath, Manuel returns to the topic of her husband to talk about his "craziness so without foundation."[53] This included Borges's desire to kill his brother-in-law.[54] On a different occasion he walked in the door "like a tiger," convinced that everyone was dishonoring him and that somebody was trying to kill him.[55] This theme of being stalked by traitors continues: Once Borges interpreted a mishap with a Moorish man who passed by on the street as a sign that "somebody who did not like him wanted to set fire to the house."[56] In an incident confirmed by their eldest, Inés, in her testimony for the defense, Borges once ordered that two dead partridges, meant for eating, be thrown into the well. Inés testified that Borges also wanted to throw her and Manuel into the well. In Manuel's version, Borges later accused his wife of putting something in his mouth when he slept, and then insulted his daughter by saying that the "girl would end up just as bad as her mother."[57]

Throughout the memorial, Manuel makes a clear distinction between her husband's normal and violent states. In terms of rhetorical strategy, this acknowledgement of normal phases adds credibility to the descriptions of the abnormal behavior. Manuel explains Borges's misperceptions of reality as a result of his imagination, which, in her view, had the effect of making him see things as the opposite of what they really were. Her husband's skewed perceptions also translated into mistrusting, strange behavior. Even when she went to mass or on family visits, Borges followed her. Like many male characters in the literature of the period, Borges watched to see if his wife took a circuitous route or met someone on the way. Manuel even challenged Borges on the vacillation of his behavior: One day when she perceived him as "more humane," she asked if he believed that the things he saw were, in actuality, true. On this occasion, Borges attributed his behavior to Satan, calling his visions "a temptation of the devil that incited him to take revenge."[58]

In a final account of Borges's own awareness of his *locuras*, Manuel explains that her husband repeatedly asked her not to take the spells to heart, so that the children could grow up with both parents. Borges blamed his palsy (*perlesía*) for his actions. Manuel writes that because it was an illness that begins in the neck, "it takes away a good part of one's judgment."[59] Although a quick paragraph was added, the original ending of Manuel's document concludes with an emphasis on her husband's craziness (she says *loco* and *locuras* twice in the last twenty lines) and with a request for mercy from the inquisitors.[60]

A FAILED STRATEGY

Manuel's document begins with her ill-fated decision at the not-so-young age of twenty-two to marry a man with a history of domestic violence, and it ends with a plea for compassion. By highlighting her husband's unpredictability, aggression, and paranoia, Manuel builds a case against Antonio Gómez Borges as a physically and mentally ill man who, at one point, wanted to flee to Italy for unspecified reasons. The focus on Borges comes at a cost to Manuel, however. Although she mentions her own Catholicism, the emphasis on Borges obfuscates this aspect of her defense. Manuel's knowledge of standard prayers was not brought up by inquisitors until the time of Manuel's confession, when she recited prayers as evidence of her Catholic faith. This certainly could have been included in her memorial, but instead Manuel chose to deal with each accusation directly: She did not fast inappropriately; she wore dirty clothes on Saturdays; she was not party to the alleged Christ-whipping ceremony.

The concerns that emerge from this memorial deal with domestic, not religious, matters. Manuel says what she must in this arena: She asserts that she lived in a Catholic household because, if she didn't, she would be accused of failing to turn in her husband for Judaizing. She provides names of witnesses who can attest to her daily behavior and to the strength of her Catholicism, and she highlights her role as a good mother concerned about her children. As a continuation of this strategy, the defense asked the witnesses whether they knew that Borges had mistreated Manuel, that he wanted to kill her, and that she "lived in great fear of losing her life."[61] While other defense questions ask about Manuel's Catholicism and her participation in alleged Jewish activities in Seville, this particular question speaks to the heart of her defense, which depended on discrediting Borges.

In one way or another, all the witnesses for the defense supported the depiction of Borges as an unfit husband. Alfonso Rodríguez Borges and his wife, Catalina Pereira, both described their relative as insane.[62] Rodríguez Borges also asserted that "with his bad condition, craziness, and jealousy, the said Antonio Gómez Borges occasioned the death of his first wife, whose name he cannot remember."[63] Pereira discussed Borges in similar terms, saying that she never dared speak to him about his wife "because he was crazy and out of control, on account of which the said doña Bernarda always lived with great fear of her husband's taking her life."[64] Repeated throughout these testimonies is the assertion that Borges "gave Manuel a bad life" (*le daba mala vida*). This euphemism addresses the jealousy, mistreatment, and strange behavior exhibited by Borges in his marriage. Alfonso Rodríguez Borges, his wife, and his maid, as well as Manuel's daughter Inés, two acquaintances from the community, and a priest, Fray Padre de León, all testified that Borges "gave her a bad life." The witnesses' discussion of Borges's cruelty and instability ranges here from killing his first wife to making Manuel sleep on the floor, trying to inflict violence on her and others, and terrorizing her with threats. Even a priest testified that Borges, when ill, declared his desire to leave his wife if he could find a way (fol. 45).

Although these witnesses also attested to Manuel's own devotion to Catholicism, they focused almost exclusively on Borges's character and behavior. The factors that contributed to this focus originated with both the defense questions and the identities of the witnesses. The defense could put forth its own questions, which were designed to elicit exonerating testimony from the witnesses it chose. However, the Inquisition was charged with locating and bringing in witnesses, which meant that it was in the inquisitors' hands to find the people named by the defendant. In this case, all the witnesses knew Manuel or Borges, but none of them could address the alleged Christmastime heresy, since none was from Seville. Instead, the witnesses made general statements about Manuel's good Christian behavior and confirmed the portrait that she had given of herself as a woman who, in the words of many, "lived as a martyr."[65]

In some respects, the emphasis on the relationship between Manuel and Borges reiterates the emphasis on gender in Manuel's memorial: The handwritten document and the defense questions blame Borges for failing in his role as patriarch and subjecting his wife and family to undue stress. The martyr defense failed, however. Although the witnesses vouched for Manuel's Catholicism, nobody was able to confirm her story about the floods in Seville keeping her homebound during the alleged Christ-whipping ceremony. Inquisitors heard that Manuel attended church and lived as a Christian, but they were not persuaded of her innocence.

The summary of the case emphasizes Manuel's role as a proselytizer in Seville. It also accuses Manuel of whipping herself, fasting, keeping the Sabbath, having covert meetings in Seville, putting cloth above doorways, and engaging in other miscellaneous behaviors that inquisitors associated with Judaism. Given that the trial had shown insufficient evidence to condemn Manuel, the inquisitors summoned her to the torture chamber.

While conventional in its admissions and structure, Manuel's confession provides further insight into the domestic life described in the memorial.

When she confessed, she explained the origins of her Jewish beliefs and admitted to fasting and keeping the Sabbath. She also described her husband's conversion to Judaism: After she informed him of her beliefs, he told her he would observe her religion. Manuel also stated that, in an act of kindness, Borges fasted for her during a pregnancy so as not to endanger her health. This depiction of Borges's sensitivity contrasts with his aggressive behavior outlined in the memorial, a contrast that testifies to his vacillation between extreme emotional states. It also suggests that, in spite of the heartache Borges caused her, Manuel cared for him or, at a minimum, appreciated his capacity for tenderness, for why else would she have included such stories in her confession?

Manuel describes herself many times in the memorial as a woman living in isolation in her home. One touching story in her confession allows us to imagine her connections to other community members. En route to Alicante, Manuel and her traveling companion, doña Blanca, identified themselves to each other as practicing Jews. Having forged this bond, they fasted in Alicante without telling their husbands.[66] The confession thus gives a sense of two women's bond over their religious practices. It also serves as a testimony to the betrayal demanded by the Holy Office: After repenting for her errant religiosity, Manuel named several observers, including her brother-in-law Gaspar de Castro and his sister, and the servant she described as introducing her to the faith at age eight. The inquisitors apparently were satisfied with the confession and condemned Manuel to perpetual imprisonment.

Since the Inquisition claimed to initiate cases only when sufficient evidence had been collected, it had an extremely low rate of case dismissals. Most defendants could hope only to be judged lightly. If we think in terms of the pressures and realities of the time, then we might see Manuel as lucky. She gave the inquisitors what they wanted: a confession containing specific details about her Jewish practices and about other Judaizers. In exchange, she was not tortured and she was not killed.

In terms of what she said and wrote, Manuel's presentation of her story had no measurable or recorded impact on the inquisitors. No reference to Borges's abusive behavior appears anywhere but in the memorial and in the questions asked by the defense. The tribunal (*Consulta de fe*) that reviewed cases and made sentencing decisions did not mention Manuel's self-defense or Borges's suspect motives for accusing her. The obfuscation of her words and of supporting testimony suggests that, from the inquisitors' perspective, the portrait of an abused wife and mother was irrelevant to the case. This rejection of a defense grounded in gender codes raises questions about Manuel's expectations. Why might she and her lawyer have thought that a gendered argument could sway the Holy Office?

FAITH ON TRIAL

Bernarda Manuel wrote an eloquent defense of her position as a victimized wife. The puzzling aspect of her narrative is why she thought this strategy might work. In seventeenth-century Europe, domestic violence did not carry the overwhelmingly negative connotations it does in the twenty-first century. Many moralist writers condemned men's violence to a certain degree, but they also qualified their statements and, in given circumstances, upheld a man's right to beat his wife. As Mariló Vigil explains, Juan Luis Vives rejected wife beating as base behavior, but Vicente Mexía cautioned women to be obedient so as to avoid being beaten. Francisco de Osuna denigrated judges who punished men for beating their wives, and he indicated that men, particularly those of the middle and lower classes, licitly could beat their intractable wives. The opinions of these three influential writers suggest, at the very least, that violence against women in the home was not universally condemned and, in many cases, was recommended as a way to discipline wives and daughters.[67]

In addition to Manuel's own account, other Inquisition records contain information on domestic violence. María Helena Sánchez Ortega has mined sorcery trial records for the prayers of women tried as sorceresses and has found evidence to suggest that such chants were used by women as a potential weapon against violent men in their lives.[68] Inquisitors did not respond to evidence of victimization or fear, however. Alleged sorceresses were convicted, and as Manuel's example suggests, the presence of abuse in a woman's life did not necessarily affect trial outcomes.

The overarching issues of masculinity and patriarchal authority lie at the center of Manuel's reasoning. Although her attack on Borges had its legal basis in the *tacha*, the emphasis on her husband's unreliability in her document made an appeal to the inquisitors as male authority figures. It is well known that women in the period were considered male property in many ways: Fathers, brothers, and husbands had the responsibility of protecting women and keeping them in line. Likewise, the implementation of the purity-of-blood statutes in the sixteenth century translated into an intensification of the pressures on men to police women's chastity and fidelity. As mentioned in the discussion of Eleno/a de Céspedes, these statutes legitimized a fear of contamination. They also reinforced prescriptive gender roles in which fathers and husbands took on the responsibility of preserving the integrity of their family lineage by making sure that the women of the family did not have illicit sexual contact. The power over genealogical integrity and familial honor lay in the bodies of women, which in turn were under the control of men.[69]

Bernarda Manuel's depiction of herself as a weak, obedient, and caring woman replicates prescriptive norms for femininity in the period. All the activities and events she narrates took place in her home. She left her house only to go to church or to visit her family. She sat down to eat with her children and husband even when she felt sick with sadness or fear. She writes with surprise of Borges's "evil thoughts" of her purported adultery, as if the very idea of an affair were unthinkable. As Manuel explains of their life in Madrid, Borges kept trying "to find some smoke in support of his evil thoughts," but "where there is no fire there cannot be smoke."[70] In terms of maternalism, sexual purity, and religious and domestic obedience, Manuel portrayed herself as meeting the expectations of femininity put forth in such rigidly confining books as Fray Luis de León's *The Perfect Wife* (*La perfecta casada*, 1583). In other words, Manuel claims to have played by all the rules that dictated proper female behavior. The focus on her husband's instability and her own consummate femininity in the memorial suggests that Manuel expected the Inquisition tribunal—an authoritative body with the power to dictate and enforce cultural norms—to recognize her compliance.

This leads us to speculate about Manuel's own position as she put pen to paper to defend herself. From the Inquisition's perspective, the case of Bernarda Manuel was merely one of thousands of trials about ridding the country of heterodoxy and difference, about defending Catholicism as the one true faith. For Manuel, it seems that this was a trial about faith of a different kind: faith in a cultural system that dictated private and public behavior and, in return, rewarded compliance; faith that the patriarchy would live up to the promises it made to women who complied with its mandates. Manuel articulated her plea for a just hearing from the inquisitors throughout the memorial. Toward the end of the document she addressed the inquisitors directly with the question that tugs at our hearts centuries later:

> Now I say to you, sir, that if his heart told him that the dirty clothes I wore on Saturdays were clean and . . . the real fasts were false and all that was good his imagination told him was bad, *how am I to blame?* [¿*qué culpa tengo yo?*][71]

With this rhetorical flourish—¿*qué culpa tengo yo?*—Manuel asked the inquisitors to sympathize with her powerlessness. As a wife who had borne the brunt of her husband's volatility for twelve years and now stood accused by him, Manuel presented herself as a victim.

The representation of Manuel's innocence and victimization dominated her discourse throughout the trial. Importantly, her claims found confirmation in the witnesses' testimonies. The pervasiveness of this rhetoric—of virtuous wife and mother, of fearful victim—suggests the possibility that another element of faith was on trial: the faith in the Inquisition to comply with its procedures, to strike testimonies of one's enemies, and to carry out justice. In the end, the Inquisition disregarded Manuel's testimony and, as in nearly every other case against Judaizers, condemned her for heresy.

Even if the inquisitors ignored Manuel's memorial, her handwritten words provide a rare glimpse into the domestic life of a seventeenth-century woman. Her immigrant status and, perhaps, religious beliefs made her a suspicious outsider in a closed society. As a Portuguese woman accused of Judaizing, Manuel was a victim of the violence of her times. As the wife of an abusive, mentally ill man, she was a victim of domestic violence. Bernarda Manuel's intimately drawn story of fear and victimization forms an important chapter in the long history of religious intolerance and domestic violence, more often than not characterized by silence and captured in official documents that fail to give voice to the victims. Manuel dared to ask what many other victims may not have been able to ask: *¿Qué culpa tengo yo?* Today, this question rings with ambiguity. Was she asking what guilt an abused wife shares with her abuser? What a mother of five is to do when her husband becomes mentally unstable? Or did she want the inquisitors to tell her what blame there was in practicing a faith that, like their own religion, also promised salvation?

What Manuel really meant by her question we will never know. The layers of her narrative and the context in which we come across it make it impossible to know what responses she thought she might hear. In a way it did not matter, since the inquisitors did not respond. Centuries later, we can see that Bernarda Manuel's plea for mercy and understanding forms part of a long history of the silencing of victims of abuse. The difference with Bernarda Manuel was that she spoke out, and we have her words to show for it.

Bernarda Manuel's carefully crafted narrative reveals the powerful impact of gender codes in seventeenth-century culture. As the examples of Céspedes and Manuel both show, codes informing gender influenced people's presentation of themselves to the Inquisition. These defendants relied on strategies aimed at proving their compliance with normal gender expectations. This argument seems remarkable in the case of Céspedes, as he had to argue that his bodily change legitimized him to act as a man. Bernarda Manuel's attempt to prove her compliance with Christian femininity seems less unusual, and certainly was less sensational. Yet the connection Manuel drew between her femininity and her plea for protection makes explicit that, like Céspedes, she understood the dominant definitions of male and female. Both individuals appealed to those definitions in an attempt to free themselves from persecution. The Inquisition cases of Céspedes and Manuel illustrate the complex convergences of gender, ethnicity, and religion in the intolerant era of inquisitional Spain and reveal a deep understanding of those convergences among individuals of the nondominant classes.

PART II

Imagining Gender
Women and Their Readers

3

Women in Fiction

María de Zayas and Mariana de Carvajal

The trial records of Eleno/a de Céspedes and Bernarda Manuel lay bare the definitions of man and woman that operated in Spanish culture in the seventeenth century. The otherwise disparate cases overlapped in another key area: Both defendants could read and write. In a period of extremely low literacy rates, such education usually was limited to the upper classes and to those affiliated with the church. In this sense, Céspedes and Manuel were exceptional. At the higher levels of society, women's formal education most commonly remained in the realm of basic training in reading, writing, and the domestic arts. This is not to say that women did not write. To the contrary, they often corresponded for business and personal reasons. Moreover, convents, salons, and court culture provided the elite with opportunities to circulate manuscripts, take part in poetry competitions, and cultivate literary arts.

Yet if we look to the emerging book market of the seventeenth century, we find a dearth of Spanish women who wrote for the population at large. Unlike other parts of Europe, Spain saw only a handful of women writers published before 1700. Indeed, the best-known writers from the period were nuns who wrote within convent walls: Teresa of Avila and the Mexican nun Juana Inés de la Cruz (1648–95). Hundreds of other nuns also wrote prose, poetry, plays, and letters that document the creative and historical lives of women religious. Outside the convent, the book market remained in the control of men, and only a few women successfully penetrated that market. Published writers included the poet/playwright Ana Caro Mallén de Soto (c. 1600–?), who is known to have received payment for her works, and a trio of authors of prose fiction: Mariana de Carvajal (c. 1610–?), Leonor de Meneses (c. 1620–64), and María de Zayas y Sotomayor (c. 1590–?). A

half-dozen, including Caro and Zayas, also wrote dramatic texts intended
for public performance. Together, these women formed Spain's first cohort
of women who wrote for the public.

This cohort encompassed women of upper-class backgrounds who
were privy to an excellent education. The women's life paths varied considerably once they were adults. Carvajal was a mother of nine when she was
widowed and left to work through her family's economic problems, perhaps
taking up the pen as a means of making extra income. Meneses, too, was a
wife and mother, who reportedly died as a result of giving birth. Zayas is
not known ever to have married or borne children. Intellectually, the women
were powerful, as evidenced by the control over baroque literary style they
demonstrated in their texts.[1]

These were some of the first women to step onto the literary scene in
a public manner, and so it is no coincidence that the literature they produced for the book market gives us an extraordinary amount of information
about the topics that women deemed appropriate for public consumption.
The texts they produced allow us to gauge the means by which women who
wrote for the male-dominated book market brought their issues and concerns to the public. In spite of their historical importance, very few of these
writers have been incorporated into broader discussions about the literature
and culture of early modern Europe. Even in the realm of Hispanic literary
studies, women writers continue to receive short shrift in the classroom and
in scholarship.[2] Yet, as the following discussion illustrates, the integration of
women's texts into the literary and cultural histories of the period promises
to enhance our understanding of the development of the book market and
of a readership unaccustomed to reading books written by women.

The focus on women's issues in the texts of two of Spain's seventeenth-
century female authors presents us with an excellent point of entry into
women's literature. María de Zayas and Mariana de Carvajal are intimately
related in a literary sense, as Carvajal may well have chosen the genre of the
novella based in part on her predecessor's great success. Zayas figures among
only two or three women writers read by scholars and students in the twenty-
first century and, in conjunction with Saint Teresa and Sor Juana, intrigues
modern audiences with fiction that as recently as 2001 has been called "racy."[3]
On the other hand, Carvajal seems to lack the luster and intrigue that draws
us again and again to her predecessor. Reading these writers' texts together
can help open up the larger question of what it means to recuperate women's
writing, as well as shed light on what it meant to be a woman writing for a
public that may have been hostile to female intellectuals.

Writing for that public clearly presented challenges, to which María de
Zayas and Mariana de Carvajal left numerous clues in the prefaces to their

novella collections. Zayas adopts a self-denigrating pose when she introduces her stylistically complex volume of ten novellas as her "scribbles." She then defends women's intellectual capacities and criticizes men for denying women the education they deserve. In recognition of the challenge she faces, Zayas retreats at the end of the preface, claiming that since she was born a woman, she has no obligation to write well.[4]

Carvajal uses different techniques to place gender at the center of her own brief preface. Initially, she refers to her willingness to field criticism about her novellas. She then uses a jolting turn of phrase when she calls her book "a useless abortion of my short wit." Invoked again in the second paragraph, motherhood does more than provide the basis for metaphor; Carvajal uses it to oblige readers to judge her kindly. She pleads for a sympathetic reading of the tales, which center on a widow and an orphan, informing us that "it is the pressing obligation of a noble heart to alleviate such disconsolate pain."[5] Given that Carvajal herself was a widow with household and child-rearing responsibilities, her appeal is personal and dramatic.

Both Zayas and Carvajal thus use femininity in the dual tropes of humility and noblesse oblige. Both mobilize their female identities as a justification for humble attitudes vis-à-vis literary production. Both remind nobles of their obligation to respect women. Conveying self-consciousness about the role of women in the public sphere, the authors' prefaces reveal a need to justify women's place in the book market, to convince consumers to read women's writing.[6]

The discussions of gender and sexuality in the Céspedes and Manuel cases find a complement in the treatment of these issues in the fiction of María de Zayas and Mariana de Carvajal.[7] As we have seen, the defendants and witnesses in the Céspedes and Manuel trials provided information about definitions of acceptable gender behavior, including details on daily activities, marital expectations, and mothering experiences. Likewise, the fiction of Zayas and her less popular successor, Carvajal, provides us with information about the topics women writers deemed appropriate for public consumption. If Céspedes and Manuel allow us to access the lived experience of gender in early modern Spain, many women wrote creative texts that engaged the meanings of gender in the period. The texts of Zayas and Carvajal, for example, pay extensive attention to female friendship and sexuality, allowing us to glean an understanding of the fluid boundaries of female friendship and desire as expressed in the fiction of highly educated, aristocratic women. These fictional representations provide a counterpoint, and thus a challenge, to the real-life restrictions on gender and sexuality that affected the lives of people from such diverse backgrounds as those of Zayas, Carvajal, Manuel, and Céspedes.

Zayas and Carvajal represent a fascinating case of comparison in terms of how they have been read and who reads them now. Both authors are available in modern editions, yet Zayas clearly is the more popular of the two with today's readers. Even though Carvajal has received some critical attention, much commentary has viewed her as a second-rate, conventional writer who pales in comparison to her more recognizably feminist predecessor.[8] As Noël Valis has indicated in one of the best articles to date on Carvajal, literary histories have portrayed the two as opposites:

> Zayas was the aberration; Carvajal confirmed the rule. Yet this lesser talent is of no less interest to us today, for surely the quiet voice of womanly submission inscribed paradoxically upon the assertive act of writing itself also speaks a language worth learning, tells us something about ourselves and the cultural past out of which we still operate.[9]

The issues of ideological conformity and literary quality raised by Valis help explain why Carvajal has not figured more prominently in early modern women's studies. Valis correctly dismisses concerns over Carvajal's "lesser talent" and advocates instead that we read Carvajal because her "quiet voice of womanly submission" has the potential to teach us something about women's position vis-à-vis patriarchy, to illuminate the tensions and contradictions that surfaced when women wrote for publication in the seventeenth century.

The analyses of Zayas's "Love for the Sake of Conquest" ("Amar sólo por vencer") and Carvajal's "Love Conquers All" ("Celos vengan desprecios") that follow focus on the representations of women's desire and relationships. Reading women authors in conjunction with each other and in the context of other archival sources helps us better understand how elite, educated early modern women viewed the role of gender in their culture, as well as how they viewed the act of literary creation. In the realm of the imaginary, we can see that women writers sought to validate women's experiences and legitimize female authority, friendship, and sexuality. Zayas and Carvajal vetted anxiety in their prefaces, but they also took the liberty of creating female-centered fictional worlds in which sexuality and friendship played important roles in the development of character and plot. The apparent contradiction between the authors' prefatory material and their fiction suggests that both writers had faith in their ability to pique the public's curiosity with regard to women's issues. When considered together, the novella collections of Zayas and Carvajal offer a richly layered portrayal of women's social interaction and eroticism. My analysis delineates the connections between the authors' representations of women's issues, thus providing a methodology for integrating more female authors into the literary canon.[10]

WOMEN AND DESIRE

Cervantes's *Exemplary Novels* (*Novelas ejemplares*, 1613) popularized the novella genre, which enjoyed a large readership in Spain during the first half of the seventeenth century. Codified in its plots, themes, and characterizations, the Golden Age novella heavily relied on reader expectations; indeed, critics believe that readers knew the structure of the novella before they even opened the books.[11] Zayas and Carvajal thwart, or at least challenge, reader expectations from the very start by announcing their gender and infusing their prefaces with woman-centered language. The references to their own identities as women writers explicitly confront readers with the anomaly of the authors' gender and implicitly hint that the narrative will be different from male-authored texts.

The defense of women's intellectual capacities in Zayas's *Enchantments of Love* (*Novelas amorosas*, 1637) sets the stage for the pro-woman rhetoric of this volume and for its straightforwardly feminist second part, *The Disenchantments of Love* (*Desengaños amorosos*, 1647). The absence of a politically charged tone emerges as a major difference between Zayas's collection and Carvajal's shorter, one-volume *Christmas in Madrid* (*Navidades de Madrid*, 1663). Despite an abundance of differences—including Zayas's criticism of men, her focus on violence, and her direct calls for social change—these framed novella collections share a concern for foregrounding women at all levels of the narrative. By shifting our attention to this important aspect of the texts, we can encourage a more serious consideration of the commonalities among women writers of the time. While this model, which focuses on similar thematics in women's writing, might be applied to many other texts with different results, in the case of Zayas and Carvajal it allows us to see how both writers explore the landscape of women's friendship and desire.

The novella collections, whose primary stories are situated in women's homes and centered on the daily life of female protagonists, unquestionably focus on women. Zayas depicts her protagonist, Lisis, as a single woman trying to overcome her disillusionment with love. Carvajal portrays a widow, Lucrecia, as the protagonist of her frame tale. Storytelling has a curative function for both characters. Directed by Lisis, the soirees in Zayas's two-part collection help the protagonist overcome illness (in *The Enchantments*) and celebrate her upcoming wedding (in *The Disenchantments*). Carvajal's Lucrecia, whose husband dies in October, spends the Christmas holidays with friends, telling stories during a five-day party similar to the soirees held in Lisis's home. Lavishly detailed descriptions of domestic settings permeate the collections, creating a feminized space in which the stories will be told.

Perhaps more important than their similar styles and settings, both frame tales trace characters' interactions with each other. This interaction centers on male-female relations, but it extends to mothers and daughters and female friends. Lisis, for example, acts as an obedient daughter to her mother, Laura, and forms a strong friendship with her slave and companion, Zelima/Isabel. All three women join the convent at the end of *The Disenchantments*. Widows, mothers, and their children populate Carvajal's frame tale as well. Both collections pair men with women from the beginning, describing courtship in terms of matched clothing of men and women (in Zayas) or in the descriptions of gift exchange and characters' amorous intentions (in Carvajal).

The depiction of women as decision makers in control of storytelling, entertaining, and parenting locates them at the center of the frame tales and encourages readers to follow this focus through to the novellas proper. Moreover, erotic desire structures the plots of the frame tales, and, in true Italian tradition, the tales themselves flesh out variations on this theme. In placing women front and center, the collections are similar to other female-authored texts, such as the plays featured in Teresa Soufas's *Women's Acts*, in that they give readers a glimpse into women writers' perceptions of women's issues. If the prefaces reorient the genre toward women, at least two novellas—Zayas's "Love for the Sake of Conquest" and Carvajal's "Love Conquers All"—introduce various possibilities for female desire. These tales about young single women emphasize the importance of women's social interaction with each other and explore the meanings of female homoeroticism. In spite of significant stylistic and ideological differences between Zayas and Carvajal, their publications offer complementary conceptualizations of women's desire.

In its structure and themes, Zayas's *Disenchantments* demands a woman-focused reading. Changing the storytelling rules from the less ideologically charged *Enchantments of Love*, Lisis says that only women may participate in the narration of stories at her soiree and that they must tell true stories of men's deception.[12] These extremely violent, pessimistic tales about women's relationships with men give Lisis justification for leaving her fiancé and withdrawing to a convent at the end of the volume. The sixth of the ten tales confirms the despairing mood. Like the female protagonists of the majority of *The Disenchantments*, Laurela is killed by her family members in "Love for the Sake of Conquest." What we now refer to as heterosexual (male-female) relations result in the woman's deception, disillusionment, and death.[13] By contrast, the interaction the young protagonist has with other women is depicted as safe and rewarding.

As readers of Zayas know, the first part of this novella seems strangely disconnected from the violent ending. Before Laurela is betrayed and victimized, the tale focuses on the infiltration of this fourteen-year-old's home by a cross-dressed male suitor. Disguised as Estefanía, Esteban enters the house with the excuse that s/he needs employment. Impressed with Esteban/Estefanía's appearance and musical abilities, Laurela welcomes her as a sister and a friend, with kisses and hugs that prompt Esteban/Estefanía to announce "her" displeasure at not having been born a man (*Desengaños*, p. 306). Laurela's interest is piqued, and will remain so throughout the charade. Portrayed as a sheltered girl whose education has consisted of dancing, singing, and sewing with other women, Laurela lacks worldly experience, which seems to justify her heightened curiosity and naïveté. At one point, for instance, she asks what Esteban/Estefanía would do if she were a man. Esteban/Estefanía's response is as straightforward as the subsequent discussions of female-female love: "I would love you and serve you until I won you, just as I shall so long as I live, for the power of love can also include a woman's love for another woman just as it does a suitor's love for his lady."[14]

Working first as a servant and then as a handmaid, Esteban/Estefanía spends more than a year in the house as Laurela's confidante and companion. Dodging the advances of Laurela's father, Esteban/Estefanía frequently expresses love for Laurela. The interaction among the characters during this period constitutes an unprecedented defense of women's love for each other. Some readers have been critical of what they see as the incoherent characterization and narrative of the tale. Yet I agree with Mary Gossy, who responds by relating the cross-dressing episode to a larger message: "What I would argue here is that Zayas's first concern is not to tell a good Aristotelian story, but rather simply to represent a possibility."[15] The possibility, of course, is that of women's desire for each other.

Esteban/Estefanía's defenses of female-female love reach the level of all-out debate. Playing the role of cultural interpreter, Esteban/Estefanía speaks knowledgeably about the validity of female-female love and men's ignoble behavior in courtship and sex:

[S]ince the soul is the same in male and female, it matters not whether I'm a man or a woman. Souls aren't male or female and true love dwells in the soul, not in the body. One who loves the body with only the body cannot say that is love; it's lust. (*DL*, p. 224)[16]

Following this defense of spiritual/emotional love, Esteban/Estefanía denounces men for disparaging and deceiving women. As in other moments in the text, Esteban/Estefanía's declarations of same-sex love provoke mocking and laughter. Suspicious of the outsider's true gender, the other maids want to know if Esteban/Estefanía really is a woman and, if so, what "she" expects to gain from this undying love.

The negotiation of ambiguous gender identity—questioned or mocked by almost everyone except Laurela—raises the issue of reader and critical response. Many modern readers are quick to identify the lesbian undertones of this story. On the other hand, we cannot know with any precision the extent to which homoeroticism, particularly female homoeroticism, was intelligible to early modern readers. Nor can we know for sure whether our own readings of early modern sexuality (of any sort) accurately decipher the erotic codes in the texts. As Mario DiGangi has pointed out in *The Homoerotics of Early Modern Drama*, we cannot expect to decipher the codes of sexuality with exactitude. We cannot know, for example, which acts were considered more sexual than others, or which expressions of sexuality were acceptable within the language of friendship.[17] However, the chiding and doubt of Zayas's other characters provide a gauge of possible reactions to expressions of female-female desire. As Gossy indicates of the scene when the characters try to find out whether Esteban/Estefanía is a man or a woman: "They cannot fully accept that a woman could love another woman, and so keep looking for a male body to resolve their doubt."[18]

Insofar as Zayas inscribes a range of responses to the homoeroticism of the tale, she goes much further than merely exploring the possibility of female-female desire. Ranging from skepticism and playfulness to serious discursive exploration, these reactions give us measures of the various ways female homoeroticism registered and signified in the early modern imagination. The absence of any visceral reaction to female homoeroticism in "Love for the Sake of Conquest" suggests that the characters do not perceive the phenomenon as a significant threat. Even if the father, Bernardo, is discomfited by his inability to convince Estefanía to have sex with him, the characters do not (and perhaps cannot) see the homoeroticism expressed by Esteban/Estefanía as anything more than a nonthreatening extension of female friendship. In contrast to the violently negative portrayal of male homoerotic acts in "Marriage Abroad, Portent of Doom" ("Mal presagio casar lejos") in *The Disenchantments*, no character in "Love for the Sake of Conquest" rejects outright the possibility of women's love for each other. Indeed, Zayas's portrayal of men's sexual relations with each other in the grim "Marriage Abroad"—in which the protagonist discovers her husband having an affair with his male page and subsequently burns her marriage bed—suggests that male homoeroticism registered negatively in the imagination of seventeenth-century Spaniards. This abject depiction of male homosexual acts corresponds to what we know about legal and inquisitorial prosecution of sodomites, a category that could (but usually did not) include women.[19]

In "Love for the Sake of Conquest," the reaction of the father, Bernardo, upon discovering Esteban/Estefanía's true sex provides yet another suggestion of the negative role of male homoeroticism. While Bernardo had allowed the handmaid to show extreme fondness for Laurela, he later becomes so enraged at his daughter's sexual impurity that he kills her. The text gives no indication as to whether this vengeful attitude has more to do with the father's confusion over his own attraction to a woman who ends up being a man, or with the loss of honor caused by his daughter's illicit affair. Perhaps both factors play a part in Laurela's tragic murder.

In contrast to the unease with male homoeroticism, female homoeroticism avoids vilification in this tale. The young Laurela emerges as the most willing of all the characters to entertain ideas about women's love for each other. Laurela's intense curiosity about female-female love contrasts with the others' dubious comments. She stands out because, unlike her father and the others, she does not mock Esteban/Estefanía's declarations of woman-woman love. Her innocence entails a lack of prejudicial apparatus that might inspire her to react with criticism or scorn. She and Esteban/Estefanía emerge as the only characters genuinely interested in the articulation and defense of female homoeroticism. Laurela's presexual, narcissistic innocence seems to allow for this curiosity: The depiction of this character as an adolescent girl exclusively interested in a small, private world of women blunts her purportedly naive interest in female-female desire. Ignorant of all matters sexual because she "didn't know what it meant to love or to be loved," she remains in a purely homosocial stage, and therefore represents the perfect foil to Esteban/Estefanía's homoerotic courtship (*DL*, p. 206).[20] Laurela wants to spend time only with other girls or women; she has no interest in male suitors until her father arranges a marriage contract on her behalf. Above all, she has no knowledge of sexuality. The threat of male sexuality (what Esteban/Estefanía calls "appetite") and the potential threat of homoeroticism (the love promoted by Esteban/Estefanía) are practically nonexistent because of the protected environment in which Laurela, in spite of her fourteen years, lives as an indulged child with her family and attendants.

The fiction of innocence comes to a halt with the awakening of desire. Indeed, Esteban's entry into the household disrupts the unsustainable isolation of Laurela's world. Unlike many plots in which a father's arrangement of a marriage contract wreaks havoc on the emotions of his daughter, Laurela reacts happily to the marriage suggested by her father. The welcoming stance suggests that she will make the "natural" transition to a heteroerotic union. The subsequent interaction with Esteban/Estefanía complicates this transition significantly. In several senses, Esteban/Estefanía destroys the possibility of Laurela's easy entry into adult sexuality. Rather than follow the expected course of contractual marriage, the young Laurela is wooed by a young "handmaid," then hears that same handmaid's confession that s/he is a man. Finally, the same suitor lies about his nobility to gain Laurela's trust and favor. At this point he also undermines the previous arguments he had made about homoeroticism, confronting Laurela with the impossibility of female homoerotic love: "Who has ever seen a woman fall in love with another woman?" (*DL*, p. 227).[21]

For Laurela, the knowledge of Esteban's male identity brings a new consciousness about her mixed sexual feelings. Angry and disturbed, she decides that she has so compromised herself that suicide is the only option. Esteban/Estefanía prevents Laurela from killing herself and, in a moment critical to Laurela's sexual confusion, takes pity on the girl. S/he tells her that the gender confession was a joke, that s/he really is a woman and not a man. Confronted with these contradictory statements and her own awareness of sexual desire for this woman/man, Laurela spends a feverish night of indecision. The outcome of the story follows the pattern of the other novellas in *The Disenchantments of Love*. After a month of illness, Laurela flees with Esteban and has sex with him. Following his abandonment of her, Laurela's relatives impose their own punishment, pushing a wall over onto her and her handmaid and killing them both.

Before deteriorating into a tale of betrayal and violence, "Love for the Sake of Conquest" constructs an intimate domestic world that allows for a relatively open exploration of female-female desire. Esteban's cross-dressing functions as one of the major factors that allow for dialogues and declarations about women's love for each other: Since readers know Estaban is really a man, they probably read his discussions of same-sex love as veiled declarations of his own feelings for Laurela. The open nature of Zayas's exploration of female homoeroticism suggests that such eroticism was not perceived as threatening to the social order. Zayas gives us more clues about the intelligibility of this desire through comments about Laurela's and the others' reactions to Esteban/Estefanía's declarations:

> [S]he and the other women thought it was simply folly, but it amused them and made them laugh whenever they saw her play the exaggerated and courtly role of lover, lamenting Laurela's disdain and weeping from jealousy. They were surprised that a woman could be so much in love with another woman, but it never crossed their minds that things might be other than they seemed. (*DL*, p. 217, modified translation)[22]

According to this description, the characters do not wholly reject the notion of female-female love. Instead, in their amusement over the situation, the women are astonished by what they see as folly.

Beyond the tacit acceptance of homoeroticism expressed by the other characters throughout the tale, Esteban/Estefanía's defenses of female-female desire forthrightly reject the primacy of heteroeroticism. Esteban/Estefanía repeatedly proclaims to love Laurela, and persists in the face of mockery. This love provides much fodder for jokes, but never is repudiated outright. Even Laurela's father participates in the jests, stating his preference for the handmaid's female sex: "I prefer you as a woman and not a man" (*DL*, p. 216).[23] Esteban/Estefanía responds with another declaration of the right to choose one's object of desire: "Each person seeks and desires what he needs" (ibid., modified translation).[24] These examples clearly indicate that Laurela comes of age in an environment in which situations charged with homoeroticism constitute her first introduction to sexuality.

The pressures of Laurela's impending arranged marriage bring Esteban to confess his male identity. Subsequently, Laurela struggles to come to terms with the complexities of sexuality. As she considers the implications of Esteban/Estefanía's male identity, Laurela begins to think of her handmaid as a man and, by morning, believes that she loves him. By dawn, Laurela is so invested in the heteroerotic nature of this love that she experiences a moment of panic about Esteban's identity: "She began to worry that the maid might really be Estefanía and not don Esteban" (*DL*, p. 229).[25] As readers, we see that Laurela's admission of love for Esteban acknowledges the homoerotic nature of their courtship. Laurela's worries about Esteban's true identity confirm that she has made what Zayas portrays as the transition to male-female desire.

The introduction of the dangerous, seductive power of desire propels Laurela into the adult world of male-female relationships. Filled with sex, lies, and violence, this world proves dangerous to Laurela, whose life is ended by her honor-obsessed father, uncle, and aunt. The gruesome nature of the murder suggests an attempt to bury the sexual dishonor. Yet, as Amy Katz Kaminsky points out, Zayas "does not politely avert her glance from the death of the woman. Laurela's head is split open by the falling wall, and she suffocates in the rubble."[26] The dangers of the patriarchal sexual economy sharply contrast with the depiction of female homoeroticism and homosociality as nonthreatening and even nurturing. Indeed, whereas homoerotic desire did not endanger Laurela, heteroeroticism leads to her death.

Zayas's unprecedented endorsement of female-female desire in "Love for the Sake of Conquest" destabilizes the status of male-female desire as the only natural erotic arrangement. In a more veiled manner, Mariana de

Carvajal's "Love Conquers All" engages similar issues of female friendship
and eroticism through the portrayal of an older, wiser protagonist. As Shifra Armon has noted, social interaction is a main theme in *Christmas in
Madrid*.[27] Specifically, *homosocial* interaction provides the focal point for
this, the sixth of eight tales in the collection. In fact, we might see Carvajal's
Narcisa, an adult who constructs a homosocial life for herself, as a savvy
version of the younger Laurela.

The tale begins with Narcisa tiring of her two suitors, Duke Arnaldo
and Count Leonido. The men's sword fighting and public denunciations of
Narcisa's cruelty lead her to petition the viceroy for help. Unsuccessful in
this venture, "she was so disgusted that, to vent her anger, she treated them
with even harsher contempt."[28] In contrast to her disdain for men, Narcisa
is "beloved by all her women friends," and "pride[s] herself on being as courteous and affable with the women as she was cruel with the men" ("Carvajal,"
p. 273).[29]

Narcisa's close relationships with women, particularly with her cousin
Clori, develop primarily in the bucolic environment of her country house,
a liminal space where Narcisa solidifies her friendships and seeks refuge
from suitors. Furthermore, the relationships motivate much of Narcisa's
travel in the tale. Her friends urge her to visit the countryside, where they
spend time making garlands and praising Narcisa's beauty. Unlike many
texts that depict women as envious of each other, Narcisa is said to inspire no jealousy precisely because she she treats her friends with "loving
kindness" (*amoroso cariño* [*Navidades*, p. 121]). In these and other ways,
Carvajal emphasizes the positive aspects of female friendships. The female-
focused world of the protagonist also reinforces DiGangi's suggestion that
we need to "acknowledge the homoerotic possibilities within the language
of friendship."[30]

Among those who have highlighted the importance of female friendship in Carvajal's fiction, Valis has suggested that "Narcisa's initial dislike of
men is counterbalanced by her loving relationship with women, though it
would be risky to interpret an implied lesbianism in this case."[31] Narcisa's
homosociality does contain a current of homoeroticism insofar as her allegiances lie entirely with women and she reacts positively to women's desire
but negatively to men's. Specifically, when women make demands, Narcisa
accommodates them, yet she rejects all but one man's expressions of desire.
The narrative emphasizes this pattern of female-oriented affection: Narcisa
takes Rosana's suggestion that they go to the country, she enjoys the company of her female friends, and when they find themselves lonely without
her, she promises to return to them in Milan.

As in Laurela's story, male desire endangers women in "Love Conquers

All." Laurela found her honor compromised by Esteban's revelation and courtship, which in turn led to more violence. Likewise, the men who fight for Narcisa's hand in marriage also assault her. Leonido trespasses on her property in the country, threatening to take revenge for her disdainful behavior. Arnaldo's offenses progress from minor inconvenience (he steals her glove in church) to physical threats (he attempts to kidnap and rape her). Only the interventions of the mysterious Spanish suitor, Duarte, save Narcisa from real violence. Finally, Narcisa and Clori, whose friendship forms the emotional backbone of the tale, marry Duarte and Leonido, respectively. In the end, Narcisa's wedding is said to please her friends, and Clori and Leonido live peacefully and harmoniously for many years (*Navidades*, p. 131). As in many other short stories in Carvajal's *Christmas in Madrid* and in Zayas's *The Enchantments of Love*, the marriage ending reestablishes the patriarchal order, putting the active female characters in their properly subordinate roles.[32]

Armon has observed that "[e]ach of Carvajal's *novelas* delineates a set of obstacles to marriage and a corresponding set of strategies for overcoming them."[33] In Narcisa's case, in addition to the suitors' bad behavior, female friendship and the emotional investment in a female-centered lifestyle constitute further obstacles to marriage. While the narrative focuses on Duarte's efforts to stifle the other men's inappropriate, violent competition for Narcisa's hand, her own willingness to entertain Duarte's advances and to give up her homosociality also form part of the transition toward the marriage ending. Described as living free from love, Narcisa shocks her cousin when she expresses interest in the man who saves her from Leonido in the garden. Like the *mujer esquiva*—the stock character who refuses to marry—Narcisa shuns men until the disguised Duarte comes onto the scene. In response to Clori's astonishment at this newfound love, Narcisa responds: "Well, don't be astonished, . . . for if I was born free of love, I am not free of having been born a woman" ("Carvajal," pp. 274–75).[34] Recognizing that others view her as disdainful of men, Narcisa also asserts as indisputable the fact of women's attraction to men. In a word, Narcisa's self-conscious declaration—"I am not free of having been born a woman"—confirms heteroeroticism as the natural state of desire.

While Zayas depicts the nonthreatening arrangement of female-female desire in stark contrast to a dangerous patriarchal sexual economy, Carvajal represents male-female desire as a naturalized erotic arrangement; that is, Carvajal's Narcisa experiences the transition to heteroeroticism as natural. Similarly, Laurela accepts the idea of a marriage contract, but we should keep in mind the absence of real desire in this arrangement. In contrast to the acceptance of the contractual marriage, Laurela experiences doubt and shock when Esteban/Estefanía confronts her with defining her own desire—with deciding whether she truly loves him/her. In this moment, Laurela's apparently easy transition toward male-female relations loses its stability. At the heart of Laurela's vacillation over whether she truly loves Esteban are questions far more difficult than mere contractual acquiescence: The situation forces Laurela to decipher her feelings about friendship and desire, about homosociality and homoeroticism.

Like Zayas's "Love for the Sake of Conquest," Carvajal's "Love Conquers All" fleshes out various aspects of women's homosocial interaction. In both tales, the female protagonists' desire centers for an extended period on the urge to please, entertain, and satisfy other women. With the exceptions of Esteban's performance of a feminine role and Duarte's exemplary courtship, the tales present masculinity as needlessly violent and egoistic. The counterpoint to men's competitive, honor-driven actions can be found in positive representations of women's affective alliances and, to varying degrees, homoeroticism.

To decipher further the implications of these characters' female-centered affections, we must recognize that, in both novellas, women's devotion to each other is presented as a homosocial stage that precedes the normative sexual awakening. In this sense, Zayas and Carvajal depict female homosociality and even homoeroticism as passing phenomena. As DiGangi notes, other authors similarly depict such desire: "In the Renaissance, . . . same-sex desire cemented normative bonds between men (e.g. through court patronage) and between women (e.g. through premarital friendship)." The nonthreatening aspect of premarital female eroticism and homosociality relies on the representation of this phenomenon "as a harmless, temporary dalliance preceding or subsumed under [the woman's] orderly desire for and subordination to a man."[35] The notion of female homosociality or even homoeroticism as "a harmless, temporary dalliance" applies to Laurela's and Narcisa's experiences only in part. Identified primarily with women during the premarital stage, both characters occupy what we might call today a lesbian subject position and what we can call a woman-identified subject position for the early modern period. Neither character pines away in anticipation of a man's attentions; in fact, their attentions are focused on other women, and the introduction of heteroerotic desire produces shock (in Laurela's case) and, for the older Narcisa—who was despairing of men's incompetence—a pleasant surprise.

These female allegiances amount to more than dalliance. The authors depict Laurela's and Narcisa's lives as organized primarily around relationships with other women and, importantly, around female desire. Zayas represents various reactions to homoeroticism, thus making "Love for the Sake of Conquest" transcend standard depictions of female friendship. Like Zayas, Carvajal was interested in giving readers access to the networks of friendship and forces of desire at work in women's lives.

WOMEN AND SEXUALITY

We cannot know what Zayas and Carvajal experienced when they presented their work to the public for consumption and criticism. It is intriguing to note that both wrote woman-centered fiction in which friendship and sexuality occupied center stage. The exploration of women's friendships and the suggestion of homoerotic bonds heighten the connections between these texts and those of other women in the same century. The open-ended nature of Laurela's and Narcisa's desire makes Zayas's and Carvajal's tales read as complementary explorations of the mutability and variety of women's affective and erotic relationships. In turn, this analysis of emotional bonds provides a potentially powerful framework for reconstructing the affective elements of the lives of early modern women.[36]

The comparison of the two writers' works suggests that—rather than focus on the marriage endings in Carvajal or on the violent resolutions in Zayas's *Disenchantments*—we can turn to the broad range of relationships female characters have with each other to learn more about female authors' representations of femininity and friendship. Carvajal's positive representation of women's friendships has most commonly drawn critics' attention. Conversely, Zayas has been seen as negatively portraying relationships among women.[37] Yet, as some critics have noted, both authors emphasize the feminine in their prefaces and in their frame tales, and both emphasize the interconnectedness of women's lives.[38] Notably, Kaminsky argues that Zayas foregrounded "what her contemporaries take for granted: men's cruelty to women, and what they ignore: women's need for each other."[39] With this emphasis on the creation of a legitimate intellectual space for women in mind, we can see that the frame tales in *The Disenchantments* and *Christmas in Madrid* encourage us to focus on women's bonds with each other. Such arguments also highlight our claim that Zayas rejects the idea that female-female bonding represents only a temporary dalliance in women's movement toward sexual relationships with men.

At the end of *The Disenchantments*, Lisis announces that the suffering of the female characters in the novellas has convinced her to withdraw from her upcoming marriage and enter a convent. This rejection of the current state of male-female relationships is explicit and unequivocal. By taking the hands of two female friends and leaving the soiree, Lisis highlights the gravity of her announcement. Not only does she refuse to marry, she also refuses to be in the company of men. Instead she chooses the safety and comfort of a woman-only environment. In a less dramatic style, Carvajal also endorses the importance of women's relationships with each other and portrays women as decision makers in the frame tale. Two widowed friends, Lucrecia and Juana, occupy central positions in *Christmas in Madrid*, even though much of the action centers on courtship among the younger generation. Although the text begins with Lucrecia's family's move to Madrid, the husband barely figures as a character. His death serves as the catalyst for the storytelling, and his confidence in his wife's prudence characterizes Lucrecia from the beginning as a responsible head of household. Women's ability to assume traditionally male duties also surfaces in the widow Juana's story. As a strict mother worried about her daughter's future, Juana does not allow the seventeen-year-old Leonor to leave the house, except to go to mass. The sound judgment of the mothers pays off, as they are able to arrange good marriages for the next generation. The volume concludes with characters anticipating more festivities, expressing good wishes for friendship, and departing with warm embraces.

The emphasis on friendship at the end of *Christmas in Madrid* and of *The Disenchantments of Love* provides an additional point of entry into the interconnectedness of women's lives. Zayas explores the fluidity of women's desire in "Love for the Sake of Conquest," where the trope of a cross-dressed male provides an excuse for defending women's love for each other. In tracing the bonds between Narcisa and her female friends, Carvajal also speaks to the intensity of women's friendship, which in "Love Conquers All" includes a female protagonist who responds repeatedly and obediently to women's desires. Outsiders' laughter, men's frustration, and general curiosity are only some of the reactions we see to these characters' homosocial lives and, in Zayas, to a defense of female-female love. By ascribing such responses to women who live surrounded by women, who reject men, or who discuss homoeroticism, the authors give us clues about how we might decipher women's desire in early modern texts. Without the more direct engagement of such issues presented in Zayas's texts, however, we might not be inclined to see similar patterns in Carvajal.

These authors' fictionalized depictions of sexuality and friendship bring us back to a reconsideration of the issues of sexuality and authority in Eleno/a de Céspedes and Bernarda Manuel. Details of Céspedes's sexual relationships provoked a strong negative reaction from inquisitors, who feared that a lesbian was in their midst. This real-life example of a perceived homosexual alliance cautions readers of early modern fiction not to conflate fictional representation with historical reality. While Zayas depicted a world in which female homoeroticism led merely to derision and mockery, Eleno/a de Céspedes aroused inquisitorial suspicion precisely because of a body and sexual practices that seemed outside the norm. The reference Manuel made to her friendship with another *conversa* similarly finds its counterpoint in the fiction of Zayas and Carvajal, both of whom portray female friendship and community as the backbone of their tales.

Carvajal's and Zayas's novellas provide a glimpse into the complexities of women's interpersonal relationships. Both authors' frame tales firmly emphasize women's friendship and strength of character. Zayas's complex representation of homoeroticism is complemented by Carvajal's more contained depiction of a female character's woman-centered identity. Similarly, their presentation of such topics to the book market reveals the issues the authors deemed of interest to the public. The insecurity—whether feigned or real—exhibited in the prefaces to both collections suggests that these women were anxious about the reception of their fiction by the reading public. Rather than capitulate to this insecurity, María de Zayas and Mariana de Carvajal forged new ground by writing fiction centered on women's emotions and desire.

We might postulate, then, that Zayas and Carvajal introduced the Spanish reading public to alternative definitions of gender and desire. Rather than represent female characters as secondary in plots based on honor or adventure, as was common, these authors portrayed complex worlds in which female characters occupied central roles. Women writers such as Zayas and Carvajal thus confronted the public with evidence of women's intellectual capabilities, as well as positive fictional representations of women's concerns and competency in a whole range of areas. We do not know the extent to which these and other authors influenced expectations and beliefs about women. Yet we can assert that their representations of women's interactions with each other introduced more expansive, positive images of women to readers and buyers of books. In a world in which femininity was defined within strict boundaries, Zayas and Carvajal broke new ground and legitimized the female experience as a valid—even interesting—topic for public discussion and consumption.

4

Women Onstage

Angela de Azevedo, María de Zayas, and Ana Caro

I n an age in which probably less than one-quarter of the population could read, reactions to writers like María de Zayas and Mariana de Carvajal would have come primarily from people who heard texts read aloud to them. Nonetheless, the authors' principal buyers likely belonged to the upper echelons of Spanish society.[1] Theater, however, accessed a broader public. In Spain, as in England, the late sixteenth century brought theater to the masses. Shakespeare's Spanish counterpart, Lope de Vega, produced hundreds of plays (*comedias*) and enjoyed unsurpassed popularity as the de facto national playwright. Until recently, it was supposed that women's participation in this burgeoning industry was limited to acting and directing. Yet the rediscovery of female-authored dramas and the publication of those texts by Teresa S. Soufas and others has opened up new lines of inquiry into theater history.[2]

At least a handful of women dramatists in Spain wrote texts apparently destined for the public stage. These plays challenge many fundamental assumptions that scholars have made for years about Spanish culture and literature. Women's plays do not take up questions of historical change, feudalism, or the caste structure of Spanish society, as do many of the canonical dramas studied by Anthony J. Cascardi and others in terms of their engagement with what Cascardi eloquently terms "ideologies of history."[3] Rather than evoke the seemingly irrational violence of the honor code or articulate male characters' preoccupations with love and honor, the women's texts often deal with gender and social restrictions.

Very little is known about the female dramatists, and no evidence has emerged that any of the dozen or so known plays was performed in a public theater.[4] The lack of information on performance has not dissuaded critics from speculating on likely performance venues, ranging from literary salons to the public theater (in the venues known as *corrales*). Soufas suggests that manuscripts were likely circulated in literary circles; that Azevedo, as court attendant to Philip IV's wife Isabel de Borbón, perhaps had palace audiences; and that Caro, the first female writer known to have professional status, perhaps saw her plays performed in a public theater.

Regardless of whether the plays were performed in their day, it is significant that women wrote for the theater masses. Furthermore, these dramatic texts are rich in detail about gender relations. To date, most of the related scholarship has focused on questions of gender difference. Critics' readings of friendship and love in these texts have shown that the plays contrast with the male perspectives of Spanish theater. Classical comedies by Shakespeare, Lope, and others depict topsy-turvy worlds in which order is restored through marriage at the end. The shrew is tamed, Portia sheds her lawyerly attire, and Rosalind makes her match. Unlike many celebrated female characters penned by men, the protagonists of women-authored texts often have a choice about their erotic pursuits. In making these choices, they remain focused on articulating and attaining their desire rather than on pleasing or appeasing the men around them. Thus the female dramatists' plays offer tremendous material for the consideration of women's interactions with each other.

While we do not know whether any early modern Spanish woman's work was produced for the public theaters, the plot lines, characterizations, and stage directions suggest that a few female dramatists aspired to see their work onstage. The issues these playwrights deemed appropriate for public consumption overlap with the questions of friendship and sexuality in the fiction of Zayas and Carvajal. The main point of difference between men's and women's plays relates to the gender focus. Since theater presents endless possibilities for interpretation in performance, these questions are treated with more ambiguity than we might see in prose fiction. Even male-authored plays that center on women's desire tend to turn to the concerns of men by the end. In plays by women writers, women remain the focus.

Playwrights of the period followed the outline of the genre quite closely. Spanish plays had three acts and approximately three thousand lines and followed familiar plots either to tragic or comedic effect. Yet in spite of their adherence to generic restrictions, the women's comedies' focus on female eroticism and desire breaks with convention. The five dramatists known to us today are Angela de Azevedo (c. 1600–?), Ana Caro Mallén de Soto (c. 1600–?), Leonor de la Cueva y Silva (b. 1600s), Feliciana Enríquez de Guzmán (b. 1500s), and María de Zayas y Sotomayor (c. 1590–?). Of these, only Caro is on record as having received payments for her plays, in this case for public performances in Seville. As the only woman known to have been a professional playwright in the first decades of the seventeenth century, the Andalusian stands out from her peers. It is, therefore, perhaps not a coincidence that she and Zayas, the other known successful woman writer of the period, are said to have been friends in Madrid. Aside from this passing reference, we know only that the women shared an upper-class, privileged background and a devotion to writing.[5]

There are many similarities among the oeuvres of these dramatists. In contrast to most male-authored texts, the plays cling to a woman-centered discourse that undermines dominant codes of gender and eroticism. Three texts from the period 1620–40 communicate the dramatists' interest in portraying gender not as a fixed, unchanging category, but as something performed by women and men to achieve their desires.[6] As we will see, these plays by Angela de Azevedo, María de Zayas, and Ana Caro turn this interest in women's gender performance into an exploration of female eroticism, displacing male characters and violating sexual norms. Through an analysis of the boundaries of female desire in these dramatic texts, this chapter suggests a framework for reading other women's creative writing in the period, for it points to the ways in which three women present and sometimes sustain alternative expressions of femininity and female desire.[7]

Before delving into the women dramatists' depictions of desire, it is important to highlight the role of sexuality and gender in most comic texts produced for the early modern stage. The genre of comedy follows the predictable path from disorder to apparent order, from the messiness of single life to the purported stability of marriage. Dawn Smith has noted the reassuring quality of this formula, in which audiences know that the plays "will end in marriages [and] the laws of society will be re-imposed."[8] Whether or not audiences or readers take the final marital pairings as a definitive restoration of order is certainly up for debate. Does the audience (and do we as readers) really believe, at the end of canonical plays such as Lope de Vega's *The Foolish Lady* (*La dama boba*), that the clever women have learned submission and will never speak out again? Does Angela's marriage in Calderón's *The Phantom Lady* (*La dama duende*) convince us that this heretofore active woman will step easily into the role of passive wife? Smith addresses underlying tensions of the genre: "Today, we appreciate the rich ironies of these plots and suspect that at least some members of the seventeenth-century audience looked beyond the diverting entertainment and conventional happy endings to a more sobering truth."[9] The restoration of patriarchal order is most evident in the marriage endings and in men's return to power, yet the sobering truth about cultural restrictions on gender can be discovered in the many subversions and inversions of this hierarchy before the predictable final scenes.[10]

The overriding structures of comedia are tied inexorably to sexual and social conventions. In this fundamental sense, the plots and themes of early modern comedy comply with traditional Western narrative structures. No matter what the first acts (or chapters or stanzas) bring in terms of sexuality and gender transgression, standard plots culminate with male-female pairings or, at the very least, they present these pairings as normative and desirable. In a study of these patterns, *Come as You Are*, Judith Roof theorizes the relationship between narrative and sexuality. In her analysis of reading practices, Roof notes that we tend to read "toward the satisfaction of the end."[11] Rather than solely anticipate the male-female pairing at the end, she advocates that we examine the ways in which moments of deviance challenge the standard organizing structures of plots and, of interest for our purposes, gender and eroticism.

Like those who have reveled in the middle acts of a Shakespeare play, Roof looks to the middle of the action for traces of subversion. She observes that the imposition of patriarchal principles of social organization in narrative endings "both forces *and* enables multiple sexual possibilities in the middle."[12] Elaborating on a strategy that looks to the unfolding of desire as a way to understand the meaning behind these principles of social organization, critic Sally O'Driscoll advocates that we "question the closed narrative system of heterosexual desire and read the text for what it can reveal about the construction of normative sexuality."[13] These theoretical perspectives provide a guide for reading women-authored comedia. The focus on women and desire in Azevedo, Zayas, and Caro challenges the meaning of the marriages by shifting our eye to the sacrifices demanded of women in a culture that treats them as objects to be controlled and exchanged.

PINNING DOWN SEXUALITY: ANGELA DE AZEVEDO'S *FEIGNED DEATH*

Azevedo, Zayas, and Caro pointedly lay bare the structures of competition and the restrictions women faced in a culture of contractual marriage and limited female independence. While Azevedo's *Feigned Death* (*El muerto disimulado*) does not deal with female homoeroticism, it does challenge the limitations placed on women in questions of desire.

Azevedo was born in Lisbon near the beginning of the seventeenth century and later moved with her husband to Madrid, where she served as a lady-in-waiting to Queen Isabel de Borbón in the court of Philip IV. Upon widowhood, Azevedo entered a Benedictine convent with her only daughter.[14] The excellent education Azevedo received as a result of her privilege is reflected in her extant plays, two of which deal with religious themes.[15] The

third, *The Feigned Death*, is written in the secular tradition and here is read as
a social critique that crosses gender boundaries and criticizes patriarchy. This
reading establishes a baseline of social criticism that can be found in women's
comedia and sets the stage for an analysis of the more daring sexual border
crossings in Zayas's and Caro's plays. Like many male-authored dramas, the
women's texts show characters self-consciously playing out their gender roles.
Here, though, the sustained attention to women's concerns allows for a more
incisive, and sometimes subversive, exploration of gender performance.

The Feigned Death is based on various coincidences that result in the
cross-dressed female protagonist's falling in love with her brother's putative
murderer. The play exploits the themes of competition and violence, pitting daughter against father, brother against sister, and women against each
other. Jacinta faces violence at the beginning of the play when her father
threatens to kill her because she refuses to marry the man of his choice. The
cross-dressed protagonist, Lisarda, who seeks revenge for the deaths of her
father and brother, also must deal with men's violent ways. Soon after appearing onstage dressed as a man, Lisarda/Lisardo has found her brother's
killer and, much to her surprise, fallen in love with him. This complication
proves even more complex than it appears, as the lover and presumed murderer, Alvaro, is in love with another woman. Lisarda, speaking as the male
Lisardo, agrees to say that s/he killed her brother so that Alvaro can go
through with his marriage to Jacinta. The third primary conflict of the play
also stems from the violent nature of sexuality under patriarchy: The ever-
rash Alvaro spends much time discussing his wish to kill his sister, Beatriz,
and her purported lover.

The first act pairs force and competition with sexuality on several levels.
Jacinta almost has marriage imposed upon her by her father; love has
Lisarda in its hold; and Beatriz claims that sexual desire takes precedence
over all other concerns.[16] All three women put their lives on the line for desire. They encounter serious, even violent, resistance to their valuation of
sexual love over familial obligation. Act 1 thus highlights the consequences
faced by women who dare to challenge the lack of freedom afforded them
by existing social structures. Several dicta can be surmised from the initial
scenes: Women must marry, even if it is against their will; men rely on violence in matters of honor; and competition governs all relationships. By
showing women's interventions into these familiar patterns of behavior—all
of which appear in countless other Golden Age plays—Azevedo exposes
the workings of a social structure that denies women a voice and leaves little
room for nonviolent reconciliation.

The rest of *The Feigned Death* works through the basic themes of competition, violence, and desire presented in the first act. All these issues put

into relief the constraints placed on women. Lisarda's brother Clarindo returns home alive and well. Dressed as a woman, he has the twofold mission of avenging his attempted murder and testing Jacinta's love for him. Cross-dressed characters and resistant women progressively disrupt the social order in the play. Moreover, the authority figures (Jacinta's father and Alvaro) continually misjudge and underestimate the women around them. Alvaro's anger over Beatriz's relationship with Alberto reveals the extent to which men control, but fail to understand, women's sexuality. While the father, Rodrigo, advocates the marriage between Beatriz and Alberto because "many marry for love," Alvaro opposes the match because of supposed improprieties and because of Alberto's lesser fortune.[17]

The conflicts between women and their male protectors in *The Feigned Death* point to men's desire to control women. Nonetheless, this is a female-focused play. As in *The Foolish Lady*, *The Phantom Lady*, and other comedies still popular today, women's loyalty and ingenuity allow them to achieve their desired matches at the end. Successfully ending the cycle of violence, Lisarda reveals her identity and her love, begging her brother not to kill Alvaro. Facing death if he refuses to comply, Alvaro accepts the match. Clarindo offers his hand to Jacinta. The father, Rodrigo, finally steps in to make the match that he has advocated all along: He asks Alvaro to approve of Alberto's marriage to Beatriz. The men previously showed a complete misunderstanding of women's capacity for desire, as both Alvaro and Rodrigo misinterpreted their charges' emotions.[18] By the end, however, the women are paired with the men they love, and the men assert their authority by approving the marriages.

Azevedo's representation of the male protectors' failures to understand women articulates a strong critique of the limitations placed on women under patriarchy and of the failings of patriarchy to accommodate women's concerns. The success with which the strong-willed female characters resist male control and influence the outcome of the play validates women's intellectual, physical, and emotional strength. Finally, the forceful nature of marriage matches and the violence associated with gender relations call attention to the male orientation of the structures and values that informed sexuality in the early modern period.

GENDER AND EROTICISM:
MARÍA DE ZAYAS'S *FRIENDSHIP BETRAYED*
AND ANA CARO'S *VALOR, OFFENSE, WOMAN*

Revealing the structural underpinnings of gender and sexuality, *The Feigned Death* shows female subjects struggling independently against the sexual economy to achieve their desired matches. This pattern of isolated women contrasts with the intermingling of women's lives in Zayas's *Friendship Betrayed* (*La traición en la amistad*) and Caro's *Valor, Offense, Woman* (*Valor, agravio y mujer*). Just as competition informs nearly every relationship in Azevedo's text, Zayas's and Caro's characters often work against each other to gain the objects of their desire. Zayas and Caro wrote responses to the Don Juan myth, so it comes as no surprise that the texts center on desire and that the heroes obtain their erotic objects. These patterns might go unremarked save for one difference: The heroes are women, and their erotic objects are men. Azevedo reveals the ways in which the sexual economy subordinates and manipulates women; Zayas and Caro flesh out this theme by portraying women characters whose resistance to men's machinations causes them to interact with other women. This glance at women's interaction allows for female homoeroticism in both plays. While *The Feigned Death* offers a decisive critique of gender and desire under patriarchy, *Friendship Betrayed* and *Valor, Offense, Woman* beg a reading that pays attention to the ways in which women undermine cultural paradigms of sex and gender.

Zayas's only known play constructs a world of friendship and betrayal. In *Friendship Betrayed*, collaboration among women is validated, while competition among them seems to be discouraged openly. *Friendship Betrayed* deals with the gendered codes of love and desire by focusing on a woman who has an insatiable appetite for love and sex. Fenisa's unchecked desire leads her to seduce or attempt to seduce almost every male character in the play. She is every woman's rival, and it is her betrayal of her female friends that gives the play its title. In the first scene, when the protagonist, Marcia, tells Fenisa of her newfound love for Liseo, she puts Fenisa's friendship to the test, insisting that a real friend would not urge her to stop loving this man.[19] Fenisa's defense of friendship is entirely superficial, as her interaction with Marcia reveals. Rather than support Marcia in her "war of love," Fenisa attempts to dissuade her because, as she reveals to the audience, she has fallen in love with Liseo after looking at his portrait.[20]

Furious with her friend's betrayal, Marcia leaves. Fenisa stays on to contemplate her choice of love over friendship and decides that, in the battle of affection, "friendship has fallen to the ground and love is victorious."[21] The dichotomy between friendship and desire is established in this first scene, in which Fenisa initiates a series of betrayals. As the play unfolds, Fenisa devises schemes to court Liseo and other men, while other women—Marcia, Belisa, and Laura—try to maintain a hold on the men of their choice.

It is unusual for an early modern play to focus so sharply on women's desire. As Catherine Larson has stated about Zayas's women characters, they "are proactive and dynamic, challenging the traditional view of women in the *comedia*."[22] Add to these gripping characterizations the cooperation seen among all the women except Fenisa and we have an exception in the classical Spanish canon: This is a truly feminized play in which structures of competition and desire are presented from the female perspective, and in which the audience glimpses the workings of women's friendships. Here the women work together to achieve their desired matches. The world is topsy-turvy, and the chaos is due, in large part, to the various gender-role switches that occur: Women act, men often only react, and even Don Juan himself is manipulated, while the sexually insatiable Fenisa and the other women manipulate. Explaining the many ways critics have dealt with this complexity, Larson summarizes: "It may well be that the most important element of [*Friendship Betrayed*] is that it asks us to ask questions about the nature of relationships between men and women."[23]

In addition to the questions it raises about male-female relations, *Friendship Betrayed* provides richly suggestive detail about female-female interaction. If we look away from the relationships between men and women to women's relationships with each other, the play clearly "asks us to ask questions" about the nature of female homosocialism which, in act 2, expands to include homoeroticism. As mentioned, the opening scene of *Friendship Betrayed* pits female friendship against sexual desire as Fenisa consciously casts Marcia aside so as to pursue Liseo, her chosen man of the moment. The first scene in act 2 contrasts sharply with this exposition, for here we see Marcia ruminating over the intangibility and instability of desire immediately before she is confronted with what seems to be—and could easily be performed as—a highly charged attraction to another woman.

As the second act opens, Marcia delivers a soliloquy about the intense contradictions of love (*Traición*, ll. 863–76). Based on the tension created by opposing terms, Marcia's language is typically baroque in its awareness of the unreliability of emotion and language. By fleshing out the unpredictable, elusive nature of desire, the speech anticipates the highly charged homoerotic scene that follows when Marcia and Belisa receive an unidentified female visitor.

Although the subsequent scene revolves around the visitor's intention to repair her relationship with a man, the interaction among the three women is marked by eroticized language. Belisa escorts the trembling Laura, whose head and face are covered, into her cousin's quarters. Marcia and Laura are each impressed by the other's appearance. Indeed, they take time to size each other up before speaking directly to one another. Marcia, for example, speaks to Belisa about the woman: "Does dawn not arrive, dear cousin, with such great presumption?"[24] Equally courteous and perhaps even taken with her hostess, Laura responds that Marcia's beauty is so extreme that she can barely speak: "Your figure is so striking; it has unsettled me, and in just seeing you I myself am almost in love with you."[25] Laura's unease is explained by her revelation that Marcia is her rival in love. As Laura explains, Liseo had promised to marry her. She has come to make the weighty request that Marcia stop returning his favors so that he will comply with his marriage obligation.

Laura's reaction to Marcia can be explained in terms of rivalry and competition, yet Marcia and her cousin's charged rhetoric cannot be untangled quite so easily. The fact that Marcia speaks *of* Laura twice before speaking *to* her directly establishes a curious dynamic that continues when the women deliver more asides after addressing each other directly. While Laura continues to muse aloud about her own cowardice, Marcia comments to her cousin on Laura's confused appearance. Further exchanges about the women's beauty resonate with the descriptions in act 1, scene 1 of Fenisa and Marcia's experiences of falling in love with a man at first sight.

If Marcia and Laura merely compliment each other, Belisa raises the stakes considerably by emphasizing homoeroticism through the introduction of the rhetoric of courtship: "There is nothing better than sight when I am taking in such loveliness. May Heaven give you good fortune that matches your beauty!"[26] Laura responds courteously, kissing Belisa's hand in gratitude. However, Marcia interrupts this interaction between the others by abruptly changing the subject back to Laura's visit and demanding that Laura tell her why she has come.

In spite of Marcia's attempt to draw Laura's attention to herself or her need to intervene in the overt homoeroticism, Belisa continues praise Laura extensively and even goes so far as to cast her admiration in chivalric terms: "I am your servant, and I swear that from this hour on, my will is captive to yours."[27] This is the second time in the scene that Belisa puts herself in the position of a man; she has already said that if she were a man, she would give all her affection to Laura.[28] Belisa's evident interest in (and even attraction to) Laura highlights the constraints placed on sexuality. By declaring herself Laura's servant and, in terms of courtly love, her deliverer, Belisa simultaneously points to the boundaries both of acceptable desire and of gender roles: It is impossible for her to publicly act on Laura's behalf, as this is an active role reserved for men. Hence the women must develop a covert scheme by which Liseo will make good on his marriage promise to Laura.

The eroticized interaction among the women has provoked a variety of comment from critics. Soufas notes "the suggestion of a brief erotic attraction" among the women, for example.[29] Susan Paun de García validates the strong feelings among the women as love, but only as "love in the sense of friendship."[30] However, the homosocial and homoerotic interaction can be seen as having a cumulative effect in which the boundaries of women's desire expand to include the possibility of female-female eroticism. Coming on the heels of Marcia's sonnet about the unpredictability of love, and following a first act that revolves around male-female matches, this scene stands out for its feminized eroticism, for its possible homoerotic competition between two women for another woman, and for the almost hyperbolic cooperation among women who plan to remedy the wrongs of a male-female relationship. This scene breaks down the dichotomy between homosocial friendship and heterosexual love by adding the element of homoeroticism to the erotic choices already present in the play. Indeed, Belisa's declaration—"from this hour on, my will is captive to yours"—can be read as sealing the homoeroticism with a pact, suggesting that it will survive beyond an initial scene among the women.

It is clear, however, that the homoeroticism does not figure among the permanent erotic choices. The heterosexual impulse inevitably moves the plot and provides its resolution. The subsequent scene between Juan and Belisa restores the primacy of heteroeroticism as Belisa renews her love for Juan. Yet if we consider the homoerotic element as we look at Fenisa, the character who has refused allegiance to women in favor of alliances with as many men as possible, we see that the first scene of act 2 adds an important dimension to Fenisa's exclusion at the end of the play.

Demonized for her sexual choices as well as for her refusal to make sacrifices that other women have been shown making for each other, Fenisa stands alone at the end. The comic figure León goes so far as to offer Fenisa up to the public: "Dear Sirs, Fenisa remains without lovers as you can see. If anybody wants her, ask her address of me."[31] Fenisa's solitude has been interpreted as a punishment (since she is not paired with a man and has no female friends), as well as an affirmation of her challenge to the dominant order.[32]

If we consider the homoerotic interaction, we can see that Fenisa is being punished in three fundamental ways: She is excluded from a match with a man, from friendship with women, *and* from the homoerotic possibilities that the scene with Marcia, Belisa, and Laura allows us to imagine. Inasmuch as Fenisa rejects female friendship and opts for heterosexual courtship and sex, she finds herself excluded from the many possibilities of women's friendship and desire. Through its validation of female homosocialism, *Friendship Betrayed* expands the boundaries of desire by including female homoeroticism as a legitimate facet of women's relationships with each other. Ultimately, the fleeting homoeroticism in Zayas's play is betrayed by the drive toward the marriages at the end.

Of Ana Caro's two known secular plays, *Valor, Offense, Woman* has a plot that allows for a sustained homoerotic reading. Based on cross-dressing, this plot comes undone only when the cross-dressed character reveals her true identity. The familiar story lends itself to an exploration of female homoeroticism: Seeking to force Don Juan to comply with his promise to marry her, Leonor has cross-dressed and traveled to Brussels. There she finds Juan in love with another woman. The remainder of the play revolves around Leonor/Leonardo's courtship of this woman, Estela, a courtship aimed at releasing Juan from the clutches of another woman's love. The end brings several marriages, including the expected match between Leonor and Juan.

The representation of gender in this play upsets prescriptive codes of conduct, particularly those related to masculinity and heterosexuality. From the beginning, Caro exposes the reliance of masculinity on violence and aggression. The opening scene, in which Estela and her cousin Lisarda are lost in the wilderness during a terrific storm, anticipates the violent actions of the men who will soon appear. Mother Nature's violence pales in comparison to that of the three bandits, who tie up the women, rob them, and prepare to do worse damage. Only Juan's well-timed entrance saves the women from further aggression, and his valiant fighting drives the men away and inspires Estela's love.

By presenting women in distress and men as rescuers, the opening scene evokes several gender stereotypes. It is worth noting, however, that the forest scene undermines these stereotypes at the same time it sets them up. Estela makes the mistake of assuming that all men are reliable, for when she sees the three bandits coming near, she thanks God for her good fortune. Indeed, the very presence of the women (who are dressed as hunters) in the forest during such a storm suggests that the women are more adventurous than one might expect. However, the bandits prove to be unreliable and the women, particularly Estela, wind up needing men to rescue them. The play establishes, then upsets, expectations, and this gender instability directly relates to Leonor's cross-dressed performance throughout the play.

Following up on the violence exhibited by several men in the first scene, Leonor explicitly equates masculinity with violence when explaining the existential change effected by Juan's abandonment of her. Clinging to her masculine identity, Leonor denies that only her appearance has changed: "I am who I am. You were fooling yourself if you imagine me to be a woman, Ribete; the offense changed my very being."[33] Leonor demands that her servant Ribete think of her as a man because she has undergone a violent transformation. With this new identity she will stop at nothing—including violence and the deception of another woman—to right the wrongs done to her. Indeed, she intends to kill Juan and avenge her honor. In several ways, then, Leonor expresses her awareness of the reliance of masculinity on violence and trickery, and sees herself as having been forced into performing an active, possibly violent, masculine role in order to exact revenge.

The fervor with which Leonor proceeds to woo Juan's newfound love, Estela, can be read as an equally intense performance of gender. Like the rest of Leonor's performance of masculinity, the courtship of Estela leaves aside aggression and emphasizes intellect. Aware of Juan's love for Estela, Leonor determines that her only salvation lies in an expert performance of courtship. Estela, who refuses all wooers, falls almost immediately for the intriguing new arrival, Leonor/Leonardo. Although three other men unsuccessfully woo Estela, Leonor/Leonardo is the only character able to secure and maintain this woman's affection. Immediately following Estela's rejection of Juan and Ludovico, Leonor/Leonardo delivers a long, flowery speech that will accomplish what the men have failed to do: secure Estela's love. After showing some initial resistance to Leonor/Leonardo's rhetoric, Estela is moved to praise her new suitor's powers of persuasion, upon which the cross-dressed woman becomes the first "man" invited into Estela's life.[34]

This interaction between the women brims with multiple possibilities and problems. To begin with, Leonor's conscious manipulation of another woman occurs in the service of heterosexuality, for Leonor's primary goal is to find a way to force Juan to marry her. In this way, Caro uses Leonor's machinations to expose the sacrifices made by women in the sexual economy. Another problem is that Estela is portrayed as fickle in love. In a short time, she falls in love with Juan, purports to reject him along with the prince, and then falls for a woman whom she takes for a man.

But Estela's fervent and continued interest in Leonor/Leonardo should give us pause. In terms of the dynamics between women in this particular scene, two interpretations present themselves. As Soufas has noted, the scene can be read as women's "mutual recognition of what is truly appealing to them with regard to love and devotion."[35] That is, it can be read as a scene in which two women are given an opportunity to model their notion of ideal heterosexual courtship. Or, if we continue to read for homoeroticism, this scene, and Estela's expressions of love that follow, can be read as women's expansion of the boundaries of desire, as women's expression of what they want from each other in love. The emphasis on the unpredictability of gender in the initial scenes sets up this expansive representation of women's desire. The final scene rests uneasily on the same theme: the instability of desire.

Soufas concludes: "Caro does not build into her plot any overt homoerotic substructure for Estela and Leonor."[36] The pairings of Juan and Leonor, Fernando and Estela, and Prince Ludovico and Lisarda at the end of the play certainly support this conclusion. However, if we keep our eye on the homoerotic dimension, it is possible to locate a sustained homoeroticism that culminates in an awkward interaction between Estela and Leonor/ Leonardo in the final moments of the play. While Estela remains a devoted lover until the very end, Leonor devotes herself to getting Juan to marry her and to helping Prince Ludovico court Estela. This uneven dynamic—by which Estela's desire increases and Leonor's is increasingly displaced—creates the final tension of the play. With Juan's marriage promise secured through trickery and with broken promises now mended, Leonor abandons her crusade to find a violent remedy to her solution. Marriage stands in for murder, in a sense, and Leonor chooses femininity once again. To the surprise of the others, she exits the stage as a man and reenters dressed as a beautiful woman. Leonor pardons the men for their precipitous and unfounded claims about her fickleness in love. Then she explains her situation and verbally reclaims her female self: "I was Leonardo, but now I return to being Leonor."[37]

This proclamation of identity sets up a key moment. While Juan and the men are able to recognize the change (an obvious one, given Leonor's garments and the explanation of her actions), Estela remains unconvinced. In the first and final overtly homoerotic interaction—the first time that both women know the biological sex of the other—Estela asks poignantly, "Leonardo, you were deceiving me?" Leonor responds, "It was necessary, Estela."[38] The choice of words in Spanish captures the gravity of the situation: Leonor says, "Fue fuerza," thus justifying the betrayal in terms of the violence ("fuerza") that, by her own account, changed her very being ("mudó mi ser"). This exchange makes room for Estela's own match with another man. Interestingly, this male-female pairing is couched in terms of the relationship between the two women. Estela answers Leonor with a decision to marry Leonor's brother Fernando. Rather than direct her declaration to Fernando himself, Estela continues to speak to Leonor: "Let us remain sisters, lovely Leonor."[39] With this, she asks Fernando for his hand.

Fraught with tension, the final scene thus leaves much room for interpretation. The sacrifice of the homoerotic bond can be said to coincide with the rapid heterosexual pairings that often occur at the end of comedia. Equally important is the success with which Leonor's machinations obscure the homoerotic tension: Pleased with Leonor's tight control of her own fate, the audience or the reader responds by applauding her ingenuity. But what are we to make of Estela's choice of Fernando, a man in whom she has expressed no interest whatsoever, as a marriage partner? Like Estela's refusal to recognize Leonor/Leonardo's feminine identity, the choice of Fernando as a husband is a sign of resistance, an attempt to convert the temporary bond between the two women into a permanent one. The imminent disappearance of the female-female desire suggests that, like Leonor's own abrupt gender transformations, eroticism itself is changeable.[40]

Female homoeroticism is the least stable element in the play, for it must disappear for the text to come to a close. This absorption of unconventional desire can be explained, as Roof's study demonstrates, by the drive toward heterosexual endings.[41] The erotic bond between Leonor/Leonardo and Estela is forfeited to the heterosexual relationship between Leonor and Juan. By lingering on the very moment of forfeiture, the text prolongs the eroticism and highlights the act of betrayal. *Valor, Offense, Woman* thus sustains female homoeroticism until the final moments of the play, when women call each other sisters and create a permanent substitute for their fleeting erotic bond.

WOMEN ONSTAGE

In these plays, Angela de Azevedo, María de Zayas, and Ana Caro push the boundaries of social commentary usually found in Spanish classical theater by reorienting our attention toward women. Azevedo's *Feigned Death* exposes the ways in which women are pinned down by patriarchal structures informing sexuality. Her play also shows that men fail to understand women's compromised position within these social structures. Zayas and Caro focus on the variations of women's desire: *Friendship Betrayed* and *Valor, Offense, Woman* explore various possibilities of women's relationships with each other. All three plays show women's understanding of the behavior and sacrifices the marriage market demands of them. If Azevedo exposes men's failings and women's limited options in desire, Zayas gives us a glimpse into the cooperative and occasionally erotic aspects of women's homosocialism. Caro offers the most expansive vision of female sexuality by exploiting homoeroticism until the final moment and by lingering on the forfeiture of the female-female bond. We can speculate on the potential for performative subversion in these plays, each of which offers up moments that ostensibly or in point of fact explore same-sex eroticism: Lisarda/Lisardo gazes lovingly at Alvaro; Marcia, Belisa, and Laura praise each other extensively; and Estela pledges her love to Leonor/Leonardo. While we cannot precisely know the intelligibility of such desire from the seventeenth-century perspective, it is clear that, like other disorderly conduct in comedia, homoeroticism is meant to be contained by the marriage ending.[42]

Read as a group, these texts delineate women's role in a script that is both a literary tradition and a cultural reality. The pressures exerted on women are made patent through the interworkings of competition, violence, and desire. Through strong female characters and a focus on female perspectives, the authors critique the tenuous position women occupy in the sexual economy. If we read toward the expected marriage ending, we gloss over the multiple manifestations of women's desire and the various expressions of women's sexuality. We also miss the shifts that occur in the structures of competition and substitution, as women seeking to fulfill their own desire assist, deceive, and even court each other. In combination with the prose fiction published for the reading public, these dramatic texts provide perspectives on women's friendship and sexuality different from those in texts by men.

Free from the filter of the male author's pen, the small number of fictional texts written by women for the general public use the performative venue of theater and the imaginary realm of prose fiction to explore alternatives to limitations placed on women in early modern Spain. In writing for the public, a handful of elite women broke new boundaries. They entered the male-dominated literary culture and refused to replicate the exact plot lines and tropes found in men's writing. Through their texts, the authors introduced audiences to imaginary worlds in which women's concerns were treated as valid and women's desires received as much attention as men's. They offered up nuanced, expansive representations of female friendship and desire. The similarities among the tantalizing, even daring, depictions of gender and sexuality point to numerous possibilities—of the existence of intelligible female homoerotic codes and of a collective protest against misogyny and social control—that have yet to be studied fully.

We do not know, for instance, how individual readers or audience members responded to the texts. Were people reluctant to buy *The Enchantments of Love* when it first appeared on the market? Did the playwrights see their plays performed? If so, how did actors and audiences interpret the potentially homoerotic moments between women? The answers to these and other questions represent the key to understanding the impact of women intellectuals' entry into the public sphere of the time. Furthermore, the variety of representations of friendship and desire in these and other female-authored texts makes us question the extent to which they reflect women's real interactions with each other in early modern Spain. Women's texts tend to reject the reliance on violence that seems to have been both a cultural reality and a literary trope. Likewise, the fluidity of female friendship and the acceptance of female homoeroticism may well reflect the realities of women's lives in the period.

In examining the texts only, we can conclude that women's cultural production exposed the public to expansive, even egalitarian, definitions of gender and desire. While the authors adopt varying themes, plots, and styles, the validation of women's experiences and desires is central to all their texts.

By exposing the public to fiction focused on women's concerns, women writers of Spain's early modern period provided a framework for imagining gender differently. As a group, women who wrote for the public sphere produced literature that registered a protest against the restrictive gender codes and misogynist ideologies that pervaded Spanish culture of the seventeenth century.

PART III

Women's Worlds
Convent Culture

5

Nuns as Writers

The Cloister and Beyond

The sixteenth and seventeenth centuries saw significant change in women's literary activity on the Iberian Peninsula. We have seen that the public book market provided a space for a few privileged, talented women, such as Ana Caro, María de Zayas, and Mariana de Carvajal, to nurture careers as writers. Recent scholarship by an outstanding cohort has shown that convents represented one of the few spaces for nurturing women's intellects on a broader scale than was possible in the outside world.[1] Out of these all-female communities emerged a textual history that records a rich and variable convent culture.

To a large extent, that textual history conflicts with traditional assertions about women's place in early modern European society. It is a well-worn cliché that women in early modern Europe had few options and little control over their life choices. For most women, these choices were made by families more concerned with economics than with their daughters' wishes. Those of the lower classes generally could not afford the dowry necessary to enter convents, so their life paths were even further limited. Merchant- and upper-class families either married off their daughters or sent them to convents, the latter providing an honorable, sometimes cheaper, alternative to a marriage contract. Such social engineering extended beyond the household, as male authorities (including justice officials, as well as lovers, husbands, fathers, and brothers) forcibly placed women in what were known as conversion houses. Also called Magdalene houses, these institutions directed their efforts toward reforming prostitutes and other women of "ill-repute." In practice, they functioned as substitutes for jail. Whether men wanted to remove women from polite society or to punish them for illicit behavior, conversion houses offered a legitimate space for controlling women.

There was another side to this bleak picture of social control. New orders and foundations in post-Tridentine Catholic Europe helped present religious life as a viable alternative to marriage, spinsterhood, or even jail, so it is not surprising that the number of women living in the cloister grew exponentially during the period.[2] Those who willingly entered convents did so for different reasons. Many followed a religious calling. Others sought to avoid secular marriages, cultivate their intellects, or find solace upon becoming widows. Convent hierarchies reflected those of the outside world, with women of means having access to higher status and those of lesser wealth working as servants or enjoying lower rank. In Latin America, race also played a role, with all but those of European descent relegated to lower standing. Throughout the Hispanic world, many orders that accepted women of lesser means did so with the expectation that those individuals would help maintain the convent economy through their labor.[3]

Convents thus drew their populations from a large spectrum of class and educational backgrounds. While some women were placed at an early age, others came to the cloister as adolescents or as widows later in life. The social hierarchy of the outside world took hold *intramuros,* where wealthy women in the less strict orders were attended by servants and regularly visited by outsiders.[4] As Stacey Schlau has put it: "Religious life enabled some (mostly elite) early modern women, including those of Spain and Spanish America, to achieve a certain amount of freedom, within significant limits."[5] Each monastic order had its own regulations and each convent its own culture. Not all women were obligated to take vows. For many, living in a convent did not preclude them from receiving visitors. Regulations increased as a result of the post-Tridentine insistence on the cloistering of nuns. Nonetheless, only the reformed orders wanted their nuns to live wholly cut off from their previous, secular lives, declaring such women "dead to the world" (*muertas al siglo*). With the surge in third, uncloistered orders in the seventeenth century, the lack of strict division between religious and secular life became more apparent as women founded and operated communal houses, schools, and social programs.[6] At the same time, the risks of unconventional, non-Catholic religiosity increased. The persecution of Illuminists and the suspicion surrounding *beatas* (religious laywomen) attest to the diminishing tolerance for anything that approximated direct, unmediated contact with God.

Given the wide variation in the rules among orders and in the women's motivations and backgrounds, we should not be surprised at the equally rich variation among the thousands of texts produced in early modern convents. Those texts include convent records, business and personal letters, devotional literature, auto/biographies (*vidas*), spiritual guides, poems, plays, and novels.[7] Regardless of genre, many of these texts center on female spirituality, convent politics, and women's relationships with each other.

With the exceptions of texts by Sor Juana Inés de la Cruz and Saint Teresa, Hispanic religious women's writing often has been ignored. This lack of attention can be attributed to the problem of access to texts and to the tendency among those of us trained as secular humanists to shy away from religious topics. Faced with a limited number of texts produced by secular women and with the fact that convents housed the highest concentrations of educated women in pre-nineteenth-century Spain, scholars have begun to incorporate the convent into their gestalt of early modern women's lives. Piety, sanctity, religious practice, and spirituality lie at the center of many religious women's texts. Hagiography and other genres cultivated by religious men and women rely on formulae that give the texts the appearance of homogeneity and predictability. Hagiographic texts, which sought to legitimize spirituality by invoking saints' lives and biblical models, provide an excellent example of the realities of the period: Religious experience required careful explanation to avoid raising the specter of inquisitorial censure.

Female religious frequently wrote autobiographies and biographies to defend and explain unique spiritual experiences. They also wrote plays, poems, and prose fiction that explored the concerns of the outside world, as well as the challenges of convent life. The variability of convent literature confirms that we cannot think only in terms of a secular versus religious division for the early modern world. As evidenced by the treatment of themes such as motherhood and marriage in myriad texts by women, no strict divisions between secular and religious writers existed in the period.

Sor Juana's *Trials of a Household* (*Los empeños de una casa*, 1683) stands out as one of the most widely read (and performed) examples of a nun's secular-themed literature. Similarly, Sor Francisca de Santa Teresa's (1654–1709) "One Act Play about the Student and the Deaf Woman" ("Entremés del estudiante y la sorda") seems better suited for public theaters than for convent audiences.[8] Uncloistered women, by contrast, often turned to religious themes in their work. While María de Zayas downplayed the religious aspect of convent life and emphasized its potential for cultivating all-female communities, other women who lived outside the convent wrote literature focused on religious ideas and doctrine.[9] Dramas by Angela de Azevedo (*The Daisy from the Tajo River* [*La margarita del Tajo*]) and the Portuguese nun Joana Theodora de Souza (b. late 1600s; *The Great Wonder of Spain* [*El gran prodigio de España*]) dealt with hagiographic themes, which continued to gain popularity well into the eighteenth century.[10]

Such literature highlights the prominence of religion in early modern Hispanic culture. It also exemplifies the interplay between convents and the outside world. The variety of literature produced in convents reflects the high levels of education among many women religious, who were well versed in secular and religious writing traditions. They engaged both traditions in their own writing and brought an impressive breadth of knowledge to texts intended for secular and religious audiences. Sor Juana Inés de la Cruz's writings, for example, reflect a background in scientific, classical, and religious traditions. Her readership, too, was extensive: *The Answer* (*La Respuesta*) was published in Spain before it became known in her homeland of New Spain. Some works, such as the plays by Sor Marcela de San Félix (1605–88) or those of another Discalced Carmelite, Sor María de San Alberto (1568–1640), seem intended unquestionably for an audience of the author's peers. Other examples suggest that manuscripts circulated beyond convent walls more than we might imagine. This was the case with the *Vigil and Octavary of Saint John the Baptist* (*Vigilia y octavario de San Juan Baptista*) by the Cistercian nun Ana Francisca Abarca de Bolea (c. 1602–late 1680s). The *Vigil and Octavary*—part pastoral novel, part poetry collection—found its way from Abarca's niece and nephew to a series of censors before being published in 1679. Given that the author's other works also were published in Zaragoza, we can presume that she wrote for an *extramuros* community of readers, as well as for her family members and religious sisters.

Characterized by multiple genres, styles, and themes, convent literature constitutes a distinct subset of early modern cultural production, insofar as the authors shared the common circumstances of living in all-female religious communities. The convent wall functioned as both a barrier and a link between those communities and the outside world. Electa Arenal and Stacey Schlau and others have noted that convents functioned as permeable spaces from which women exerted political, ideological, and religious influence.[11] As Arenal and Schlau's wonderful book *Untold Sisters: Hispanic Nuns in Their Own Works* demonstrates for both Spain and Latin America, convent writing contains clues about the perceptions women religious had of themselves and of the world. Regardless of genre, topic, or style, convent writing often validates interpersonal relationships among women and emphasizes the powers of religious devotion. While women who wrote in convents often highlighted topics similar to those of nonconvent writers, the pressures that faced female religious differed in many significant ways from those faced by women outside convents. Where Zayas, Carvajal, Caro, and Azevedo focused on sexuality and marriage matches and put women's struggle for independence and agency at the center of their work, struggles in religious women's writing took on a different tenor, as many texts described a quest for spiritual perfection and personal and communal peace.

One of the principal differences among the writings of women religious lies in the diversity of their audience. Some texts circulated among nuns and confessors only, while others were published by book printers. Depending on the author and the intended audience, the texts produced by women religious variously idealize women's relationships, criticize a male power structure, and reinforce restrictions on female piety. Fictional convent literature affirms the rich variety of religious women's experience and the various configurations of relationships that cloistered women had with the outside world, as it provides a window into the unique situation of educated women living both apart from and as a part of early modern culture. This chapter focuses on representations of gender in fictional texts written by three nuns who lived on the Iberian Peninsula in the seventeenth century. Sor Violante do Ceo (1601–93), Sor Marcela de San Félix, and Abarca de Bolea wrote poetry and fiction that provide an excellent point of entry into the interplay between convent culture and the culture at large. Their richly varied texts give us access to early modern religious women's conceptualizations of gender and religion.

BEHIND AND BEYOND THE CONVENT WALL

The standard interpretation of religious writing used to hold that women wrote only to comply with their confessors' commands, but now we know that attitudes toward writing and the circumstances under which it took place varied from case to case. The circulation of manuscripts both intra- and extramuros provides one of many confirmations of the porosity of convent walls in the early modern period.[12] Writing for confessors, sisters, and, in some cases, for readers beyond the order, women religious often exhibited an acute awareness of their potential audience. Living in environments that validated their intellectual and spiritual capacities, female religious often infused their texts with a sense of confidence and investment in women's endeavors.

Women religious often wrote with assurance and humor about religious and nonreligious life. Nonetheless, cultural anxieties about heterodoxy infused all writing in the period. Pressures to marry and reproduce obviously did not operate within convent culture, but the positive aspects of that culture were offset by the limitations that still exist today with regard to women's role in the Catholic church. The urge to write about spiritual matters, for example, potentially conflicted with the prohibition against women's participation in theology. To navigate this difficult position, religious women called on rhetorical strategies to express complex ideas without challenging church orthodoxy. Like Zayas and Carvajal, who incorporated apologies into their prefaces, Saint Teresa and her cohort often called upon a rhetoric of humility and a colloquial style to avoid posing a threat to the church.

Saint Teresa, who managed to write complex theological treatises while also founding a new order, provides an excellent example of the connections between convents and the outside world. As her tireless search for financial backing suggests, religious women were connected to the outside world through economic necessity, educational background, personal experience, political savoir faire, and family ties. The reins of patronage also connected them to the outside world and, in the case of textual production, linked religious women with those entrusted to read, circulate, defend, and occasionally publish their writing. The reliance on patrons for economic assistance became more important in the seventeenth century, when the country experienced severe economic downturns. The dedications in many nuns' texts provide a glimpse into the importance of the links they and their communities had to the outside world. The range of writing produced in convents speaks to these connections, giving us insight into the relationships, values, and challenges that formed part of religious women's lives.

A surprising level of porosity characterized the relationship between those living within and outside of convent walls, so nuns often wrote with their sisters, male religious, and extramuros readers in mind. The intended audience depended on the type of text and the circumstances under which it was produced. As one of the most prominent genres, auto/biographical vidas aimed to memorialize unique religious experiences for the benefit of confessors, the larger religious community, and other Catholics. Vidas often aimed to publicize such experiences in the hopes of eventually achieving the beatification or even sanctification of the subject. Poetry, drama, and prose fiction functioned as artistic forms of religious devotion. They also served to strengthen authors' ties to their religious communities, as well as to patrons, relatives, and other readers.

In contrast to the narrowly defined goals of hagiography, nuns wrote other texts for a variety of reasons. Some produced works solely for the cloister, others circulated manuscripts among church officials, and others published for the general public. This spectrum of readership informed the production of each text, particularly since nuns faced pressures related to their intended audience when they made choices about how to represent convent life through fiction. Poetry, drama, and prose by Sor Violante do Ceo, Sor Marcela de San Félix, and Ana Abarca de Bolea exemplify this variety of purpose and readership. For each, writing aimed at other nuns, personal friends, or publication produced texts that varied in purpose, tone, and style. In spite of their different intended audiences, all three women wrote about female friendship and spirituality in ways that spoke to convent audiences *and* to the outside world. The bridges between intra- and extramuros life manifest themselves differently in each author's work. Gender and spirituality emerge as important themes in this literature, which demonstrates the writers' awareness of living both apart from and as part of the world beyond the convent wall.

A sonnet by Sor Violante do Ceo provides a framework for thinking about the influence of convent life on women's ideas about themselves. Sor Violante also draws attention to the permeability of the convent wall and the interaction between nuns and the outside world.[13] While we might suppose that the all-female populations of convents created an environment wholly divorced from secular life, Sor Violante's poem for her friend doña Bernarda Ferreira speaks in terms of commodities that belong to a world left behind:

> Belisa, friendship is a treasure
>> so deserving of eternal esteem
>> that it is insufficient to measure its worth
>> against the silver and gold of Arabia and Potosí.
> Friendship is a precious honor
>> that one treasures in presence and in absence;
>> and through which one shares the sadness, sorrow,
>> smiles, and tears of another.
> A bond of violence is not a friendship,
>> for friendship is based on sympathy,
>> from which loyalty reigns until death:
> This is the friendship that I would like to find,
>> this is what lives on between friends,
>> and this, Belisa, in the end, is my friendship.[14]

The language associated with friendship in this sonnet grips our attention precisely because of its connection to the material world. Sor Violante's reference to the spoils of overseas exploration links her poem to trade and imperialism. Contrasting hard currency with the immeasurable worth of an emotional bond, she argues that friendship has more value than the most exotic riches of the world. Undeniably material in its grounding, the sonnet localizes and interiorizes the question of worth. It also rejects what we now think of as a market economy for an emotional economy grounded in a relational world.

Sor Violante's poem moves easily between emotional and material references and, in so doing, forces us to think about the connections between the conceptions of gender in and out of the convent. The economic language of the poem devalues men's public activity while privileging female intimacy. Moreover, the poem assesses, then rejects, the material economy associated with men. The interconnectivity of the secular and the religious realms suggested by Sor Violante's sonnet captures important characteristics of religious women's lives. First, the references to Arabia and Potosí remind us that living in a cloister did not cut women off from the events of the outside world. Nor did convents present women with utopian conditions free from everyday financial, emotional, or political concerns. That Sor Violante relies on economic metaphors to convey love for her friend reminds us that convents had their own economies dependent on budgets, funding, and labor. The value attached to friendship defines an economy in which women's emotional lives offer far greater richness than anything pertaining to the masculine, materialist world. In a manuscript that may have circulated publicly, Sor Violante reaches to the outside world, ultimately placing a premium on the intimate, private realm of female friendship.

LOOKING IN: SOR MARCELA DE SAN FÉLIX'S COLOQUIOS AND LOAS

If Sor Violante speaks beyond the convent by appropriating the language of the secular world, Trinitarian nun and abbess Sor Marcela de San Félix draws us into the complexity of cloistered women's lives. Sor Marcela's extant works consist of six one-act allegorical plays (coloquios), seven prefatory poems (loas) for those plays, a corpus of poetry, and a brief biography of another nun. In addition to these texts, she wrote four manuscripts that she later destroyed, probably at the behest of her confessor. Her plays and *loas* were written explicitly for the all-female community of the Discalced Trinitarian Convent of San Ildefonso in Madrid. In the tradition of Saint Teresa and other nuns before her, Sor Marcela wrote to instruct her sisters in the nuances and challenges of the route to spiritual perfection.[15] Unlike Saint Teresa, however, she wrote with a heavy emphasis on entertainment, and the body of her work represents a fascinating manifestation of the early modern impulse to entertain while instructing.

Sor Marcela's allegorical plays trace the journey of a novice as she takes vows and seeks spiritual perfection. The earlier works depict various challenges to overcoming vice, while the later plays deal with more abstract matters, such as the holy sacrament and the parameters of proper religious devotion. In both theme and content, Sor Marcela's oeuvre presents the struggles faced by Trinitarian nuns seeking to overcome the pettiness of worldly affairs. Female characters bond to conquer vice and sin. Cooperation and mutuality lie at the heart of all the plays. Comical and instructive, Sor Marcela's works range in tone from reverential to incisively critical. Pleasure in the author's work emanates from her artistic dexterity as well as from the information she offers about convent life. Jokes about friars' gluttony, complaints about perennial food shortages, and references to the author's parents and her aged physical appearance account for many of the lighter moments.[16]

Beneath the humor lies a powerful articulation of the pressures and pleasures of female piety. As Arenal and Schlau have observed: "Playful but pointed interchanges in the *coloquios* and *loas* . . . show that daily existence in the convent often bore little resemblance to the idealized portrayals created for consumption *extramuros*.[17] Given the homogeneity of Sor Marcela's audience, such spontaneity and intense frankness make sense. Unlike the women who wrote for their confessors or others outside the convent community, Sor Marcela directed herself to an audience of insiders and thereby faced a reduced risk of running afoul of misinterpretation. The straightforward nature of this arrangement—by which she wrote plays to be performed by and for the convent community—provided a stable base from which Sor Marcela exploited her audience's shared experiences by making these central to her dramatic output.

In her six allegorical plays and their introductory loas, Sor Marcela advocates collaboration among women and pokes fun at the rigors of self-mortification. On the more serious side, through allegorical characters with abstract names, such as Soul, Appetite, Zeal, and Mortification, the plays depict the struggles of complying with proper female spirituality. In these coloquios, which were performed by Sor Marcela and her sisters, the author depicts a wide range of pressures that stem from female piety. The focus on piety puts forth a model of femininity that had both a purgative and a policing function for the Trinitarian nuns who watched and participated in the production of these plays.

Sor Marcela's six coloquios focus on the general themes of spiritual perfection and devotion. Soul figures as the protagonist in all the plays, and it is through her that we learn the difficulties and rewards of Catholic and, more specifically, Trinitarian religiosity. Confronted with the temptation of worldly appetites and sinful behavior, Soul must learn to listen to the advice of the female characters as she moves forward toward a more stable, rewarding relationship with God. The longest of these one-act plays would have taken up to two and a half hours to perform, and the preparation and performance of the pieces would have provided ample opportunity for instruction and entertainment during the all-important *recreos* (rest periods) that formed part of Trinitarian life.[18]

The purgative function of Sor Marcela's plays captures the modern reader's attention immediately. As Arenal and Schlau note, she used humor to air her criticism of various "personality types, lukewarm faith, and the weaknesses and vices of members of the Trinitarian community."[19] In general, Sor Marcela used humor to deal with difficult issues that affected her and her sisters. The struggle to transcend bodily and worldly desires lies at the heart of many of the coloquios, and humor mitigates the rigors of this struggle throughout Sor Marcela's work. For example, the best-known colo-quio, "The Death of Desire" ("Muerte del apetito"), features Desire, a ridicu-lous glutton who embodies every imaginable manifestation of desire. Soul tries to purge Desire from her life, yet is attracted to him and to his easy life-style. Torn between Mortification and Desire, Soul alternately defends and disparages her female support system before finally agreeing to embrace the virtuous life that Mortification and her sisters, Simplicity and Prayer, repre-sent. The serious theme—moving toward God and spiritual perfection—is offset by the excesses of Desire. Portrayed as a disgusting man, Desire spends much of the play elaborating on his insatiable physical needs. Alternating be-tween deep slumber and a state of needy consciousness, Desire tries to win the battle for Soul's heart. Finally, once Soul has embraced the teachings of her female friends, Purity kills Desire. When Desire comes back to life, the women tie him up and stab him to death. This scene depicts female solidarity as the cornerstone of the continuous struggle to achieve virtue.

The character Desire represents one of the best examples of Sor Mar-cela's sharp wit. While he operates at the level of excess in all bodily and earthly matters, Desire also provides a vehicle to parody the excesses of male monastic life. Upon his resuscitation, Desire requests food, drink, and all forms of entertainment, then says that he wants to become a friar, because at least then his needs will be met.[20] The scene of a recently resuscitated character trying to act on every imaginable impulse could not be more ri-diculous. Associations between the impulse for gratification and male mo-nastics must have provided wonderful laugh lines for the nuns, particularly given that Sor Marcela's plays often mention austerity and the lack of food as part of convent life.[21]

Reliant on humor to lighten the tone, "The Death of Desire" nonetheless contains a serious subtext, as it depicts the toll taken on the individual as she learns to leave behind worldly desire. The language of expurgation ap-pears regularly throughout Sor Marcela's work, reminding the nuns of the ongoing nature of this struggle. Just as Desire must be killed yet might reap-pear at any time, the character Negligence in the coloquio "The Holy Sacra-ment" ("El santísimo sacramento") must be tied up at the end so she will not wreak further havoc. At the end of "Indiscreet Zeal" ("El celo indiscreto"), the female characters try to devise a plan to purge their community of Zeal. So dangerous is this character that placing him in an insane asylum can-not work because he would only increase the other patients' misery.[22] Desire, Negligence, and Zeal must be purged from the community, tasks possible only through collective efforts.

Purgation emerges both as a theme and as an intended purpose of the plays. Through playful criticism of male ecclesiastics and of nuns who guard the pantry under lock and key, Sor Marcela provides an opportunity for the community to laugh together at the jokes they probably otherwise shared only in private. Plots that center on the need to overcome negative tendencies similarly allow the nuns' concerns to be aired in front of the entire group. The opportunity for collective laughter makes it easy to imagine that Sor Marcela provided a healthy outlet for tension. In this sense, the centrality of purgation to her texts acknowledges that a closed community can benefit from having humorous or other outlets for letting off collective frustration.

In addition to the purgative elements of the allegories, Sor Marcela's coloquios defined and reinforced the parameters of spirituality within her order. "The Death of Desire" models this spirituality for the audience, as Soul rejects Desire by learning from Simplicity, Prayer, and Mortification. Soul's struggle with Desire in this play and with Tepidity and Zeal in others conveys a key message of Sor Marcela's texts: The pressures of piety take their toll on individual nuns, but learning to rely on one's sisters for guidance can ease the burdens of religious life.

The emphasis on communal struggle ties in to the strict vision of female piety that occupies center stage in the coloquios. The plays exhibit a consciousness of the intense pressures—related to bodily mortification and extreme discipline—associated with piety, but they also endorse the righteousness of the expectations placed on Trinitarian nuns. While Sor Marcela's texts seem slightly irreverent and critical at times, they include a heavy dose of moral instruction. The modeling of a female support network provides one of the keys to understanding the moralism of these plays. Much of this network consists of female characters, but in "Indiscreet Zeal" two mute male characters play supporting roles when they arrive on the scene to take the annoying Zeal away.[23]

In the female family model inscribed into Sor Marcela's coloquios, every member has shared responsibilities, which include aiding others to fulfill the expectations of Trinitarian piety. Recognizing that the goal of spiritual perfection required support from the monastic community, the plays repeatedly articulate the importance of teaching and learning from one another. In "The Death of Desire," for example, Alma relies on her support system extensively by asking advice of Mortification and Simplicity. Moreover, Soul explicitly acknowledges her debt to Mortification: "I believe I have gained instruction from all that you have said" (p. 258).[24] Solidarity among the women is couched in familial terms, with references to genealogies and sisterly bonds making their way into many of the dialogues. The sisters who work together in "The Death of Desire" are so close, in fact, that Simplicity notes that the three are completely unified and never leave each other's company (p. 261; *Literatura*, p. 143, ll. 847–50). This unification provides a powerful front of resistance, as demonstrated by Desire's reaction to the virtuous sisters: While he feels threatened by the presence of Mortification, he becomes fearful when he realizes that Simplicity, whom he fears "more than hellfire," will soon arrive (p. 260).[25]

While some of the lessons in the texts are direct and unambiguous, Sor Marcela infuses her work with elements that undercut the apparent simplicity of the allegorical form. This complexity adds to the instructive purposes of the texts, as it contains many reminders of the ambiguities of spirituality. The refusal to define women as good and men as bad represents one obvious example of this complexity. Most of the negative characters are indeed male, but this scheme does not hold entirely. Indeed, much of this gender distinction might stem more from grammar than from the ascription of negative characteristics to men. The masculine character Love plays the role of the spouse in "The Virtues" ("Las virtudes"), for example. The appearance of negative female characters, such as Lies, who is called a "vile woman" and "the devil's daughter," reminds the audience that femininity should not be equated with goodness.[26] In Sor Marcela's world, it is not sufficient to call oneself a nun; one must strive constantly to do good work.

Sor Marcela's treatment of affective issues represents one of the most complex of the themes that run through her oeuvre. Love, for example, alternately figures as a site of conflict and as a means of reaching God. In "The Nativity," love represents the path to God, as laid out in a poetic speech by Contemplation:

> I would like to love God
> in such a simple way,
> that only his divine self
> would be the target of my love,
> and neither my growth,
> nor my rigorous redemption,
> nor my own preservation
> would increase my affection,
> but only his very existence
> as himself, without airs.[27]

As Contemplation's speech suggests, the characters in "The Nativity" find their way to God through love. Indeed, when Piety sees Christ with his family, she describes "the saintly and divine husband burning in the flames of love."[28]

While "The Nativity" and other plays portray love as the route to God, the depiction of love in "The Virtues" takes on a different valence. Elements of profane theater, which pepper many of Sor Marcela's plays, become particularly evident in the tug between desire and obligation in "The Virtues."[29] In this play, jealousy among female characters must be overcome for Soul to prepare herself to take Love as her spouse. Interestingly, the rivalry for Soul is cast in terms of love between friends and between lovers. Rejected by Soul in the first scene, Tepidity employs the language of love, referring to herself as a deceived woman (*burlada*). She tells Soul: "[S]ince I care about you so much I am voicing my loving complaints."[30] Soul later turns this into a maternal relationship when she notes that she cannot dismiss Tepidity so easily because, after all, the woman raised her.[31] Prayer competes for Soul's love as the play progresses and Tepidity's cajoling starts to take effect.

The language of love infuses the interaction between Soul and Prayer, who inquires about the rewards and happiness that Alma has received as a result of their association. When Prayer invites the future spouse, Love, onto the scene, she warns Soul to receive him with open arms. The exchange turns on courtship practices involving the two women and the man:

Prayer: I want to call Love in now.
          Soul, for God's sake, do not hide,
          and make sure you respond to him
          with more kindness than you did to me.
Soul: Just as sure as I will see him here,
          you can be sure that I belong to you.
Prayer: I want you to be his,
          as I am the go-between and nothing more.[32]

This language is clearly a product of the homosocial environment of the convent, as Soul's apparent confusion about her future partner points to the expansive view of love present in Sor Marcela's work and, one would suspect, in the environment of the convent itself. Soul mistakenly declares that she belongs to Prayer, an error that requires clarification.

The gender fluidity of this play portrays love as necessary for the community and its individuals. Love forms part of the healthy homosocial environment, in other words, just as it is a requirement for each nun's spiritual journey. In this play as in others, love can be complicated. Soul must learn to distinguish between healthy and detrimental love. Such a lesson appears in "In Praise of Religion" as well, when references to gossip and envy remind audience members that their individual choices affect those around them. The characterization of Soul as someone who desperately wants to please others reinforces the difficulties of learning to make distinctions. In "The Death of Desire" and "In Praise of Religion," Soul wants to please the female virtues, yet she cannot stop trying to placate Desire or Lies in either play. The mistakes made along the way have the potential to disrupt her spiritual journey and communal tranquility.[33]

The marriage between Love and Soul at the end of "The Virtues" emphasizes the importance of communal respect and love. Love insists that Soul try to placate the entire entourage of virtues (i.e., Abstinence, Modesty, Silence, Simplicity, and Poverty) in order to please him. Even the final lines of the coloquio play on the fluid meanings of love, as the character Love (presumably played by the author herself) asks forgiveness of the audience: "And pardon our errors since Love, who made us commit them, also can excuse them."[34] While the play conveys a general message of empathy and understanding, it also acknowledges the challenges that face women in the convent. Love, and all its good intentions, can cause one to make mistakes, but under the proper guidance, it can lead a believer to God. This duality, in which love functions as a source of both strength and weakness, serves as a further reminder of the need for women to instruct each other in making good choices.

Sor Marcela's dramatic texts fulfilled various roles for the nuns in her community. Most important, they provided an outlet for the airing of tension and criticism, as well as for the celebration of the positive aspects of Trinitarian life. They combined instruction with quick wit to preach a lighthearted yet serious approach to spirituality. Forgiveness and patience have a place in this schema: As Soul muddles her way through the many challenges of religious life, the other characters gently guide her toward the right decisions and behaviors. Sor Marcela's allegories take us on a journey that is doubly inward looking, as she examines the dynamics of convent life as well as the personal struggles of women religious with compliance with monastic piety. In a fundamental sense, then, the vision of Trinitarian spirituality portrayed by Sor Marcela addresses the pressures and rewards of being a woman in a closed religious community.

LOOKING OUT: ANA FRANCISCA ABARCA DE BOLEA'S *VIGIL AND OCTAVARY*

The Cistercian nun Ana Francisca Abarca de Bolea presents us with an entirely different model of exploring gender from that in Sor Marcela's work. In 1679, Abarca's only known fictional text was published in Zaragoza. *Vigil and Octavary of Saint John the Baptist*, a loosely configured pastoral novel, contrasts sharply with Sor Marcela de San Félix's direct engagement with female religiosity and Trinitarian life. While Sor Marcela sought to instruct and entertain her sisters through her plays, Abarca wrote at least one fictional work destined for an audience beyond convent walls. Sor Marcela wrote about convent culture, but, as we will see, Abarca engaged in the long-raging philosophical debate on the "woman question," also known as the *querelle des femmes*.[35]

Abarca had experience with the world of publishing before *Vigil and Octavary*. Other works of hers, including *Fourteen Cistercian Saints' Lives* (*Catorce vidas de santas de la orden del Cister*, 1655) and *Life of the Glorious Saint Susan, Virgin and Martyr* (*Vida de la gloriosa santa Susana, virgen y mártir*, 1671), were published in Zaragoza. Born about 1602 and placed in the convent at age three, Abarca rose to the position of abbess by 1672. She also enjoyed connections to Aragon's literary and social elite as a member of the same literary scene as the well-known writer Gracián and other prominent male intellectuals. The solidity of these bonds is evidenced by her correspondence and friendship with poets, professors, historians, and priests.[36]

The extensive prefatory material to *Vigil and Octavary* reflects these connections, as Abarca tells the story of the book's evolution and hints at the extent to which others, particularly men on the outside, played a role in getting it published. Her nephew, Tomás Abarca de Vilanova, lobbied to publish *Vigil and Octavary*, as did other Aragonese men such as Vicente de Alhambra and his son, Baltasar Sebastián de Alhambra. While it has been suggested that Abarca's niece, who also was a Cistercian nun, helped move the book toward publication, these men were instrumental in the text's publication.[37]

Laudatory writing in the first few pages of the book gives the impression that the men took pride in participating in the recuperative, collective endeavor of sponsoring and praising the nun's literary efforts. Sebastián de Alhambra captured this pride in a poem in which he mused: "This buried book / has been held for many years / in the grave of oblivion."[38] The poem refers to the long period of gestation of this pastoral novel. Indeed, parts of the book can be traced to as many as twenty-five years before its publication, suggesting that Abarca conceived of the loosely configured frame tale of shepherds celebrating the feast of Saint John as a way to incorporate poetry and prose composed over a long period of time.[39]

This presentation of *Vigil and Octavary* by male relatives, aristocrats, and censors draws attention to questions of gender and literary production as they relate to religious women's writing. Abarca's hybrid text, built around the nine-day festival of Saint John the Baptist, comprises satiric and religious poems, lists based on biblical references, and two novellas. At first glance, such heterogeneity of topic and form makes it difficult to locate and decipher any cogent message related to the women's issues we have seen in other female-authored texts. Views on female friendship, love, and spirituality simply do not occupy a place of privilege in Abarca's fiction. Yet her two novellas allow us to examine the interface between convent writing and the emerging book market. Abarca makes very specific use of the popular genre of the pastoral novel: Her text contains elements that parody negative representations of gender and gender relations in the dominant literature of the period. As we will see, she also weighed in on the debate on the worth of women (the querelle des femmes) by parodying misogynist literature in her novellas.

In contrast to Sor Marcela's cloistered dramatic production or even Sor Violante's poem addressed to a female friend, Abarca's fictional text engages very specifically with secular literary tradition. As a pastoral novel with two novellas built into it, *Vigil and Octavary* is structured around religious themes, but no specific treatment of women religious appears. The duality of the secular and religious reflects Abarca's life outside the convent, the fruit of literary labors whose audience lay beyond the convent wall.

To the modern reader, the treatment of women seems profoundly ambivalent in *Vigil and Octavary*. The text shows little interest in three-dimensional characters or sustained plot lines, making it especially difficult to generalize about the ideologies presented throughout. On the other hand, Abarca's pastoral characters comment on gender issues that, in a more sustained fashion, also appear in the two novellas included in the book. The principal narrative traces the travels of a group of shepherds who journey to a hermitage for the 24 June celebration of Saint John. The characters celebrate by singing, telling stories, attending mass, and having sumptuous banquets. In typical pastoral fashion, several characters fall in love and arrange their weddings during the course of the novel. Most of *Vigil and Octavary* focuses on religious celebration, which includes the recitation of poetry and songs by the various shepherds.

The loose configuration of *Vigil and Octavary* allows for the incorporation of diverse poems, stories, and humorous narrative sequences. Abarca embeds a series of contrasting attitudes and representations of women in the shepherds' lighthearted banter and in the two novellas told by these characters. The question of women's worth arises early in the novel, when the character Mileno recites poetry written by Abarca herself. In their praise, the shepherds indicate that the author deserved more than the second prize she received for the poem.[40] Moreover, the group speaks well "of many women who for their writings and good use of their lives were celebrated by historians and famous men."[41]

This interchange between male and female characters introduces the topic of women's worth. While the shepherds agree on women's intellectual and creative capacity in this instance, a subsequent episode reveals a rift between the male and female shepherds. Typical of the rhetoric associated with popular debates about the worth of women, the shepherds and shepherdesses disagree in their reactions to a poem about Orpheus's descent into hell in his search for Eurydice. The poem implies that women are fickle. The male characters praise the poem because, in the words of the omniscient narrator, "there is hardly any man who does not like to hear people speak badly of women."[42] The female characters, on the other hand, have no kind words for the message of the poem; the narrator comments that well-bred women "should ignore that which causes them sorrow."[43]

European debates on the woman question dated back to Christine de Pizan's claims to women's intellectual capacities in *The Book of the City of Ladies* (1405). The flurry of literary and philosophical texts that followed Pizan's intervention in a misogynist writing culture became known as the *querelle des femmes*. Involving hundreds, if not thousands, of texts that alternately defended and attacked women's intellectual capacities, the debates persisted up through the time that Abarca de Bolea wrote her late-seventeenth-century pastoral novel. Valorized by that tradition and presumably desirous of inserting her own text into the arguments, Abarca inscribed the debate into her text. Indeed, diverging opinions about women's worth are expressed throughout *Vigil and Octavary*. On the seventh day, for example, the characters perform acts of penance. For his part, the shepherd Feniso kneels at the women's feet and recites a misogynist poem ("Soneto contra las mujeres"). After listing examples of nature's harshest phenomena—such as the turbulent waves of the ocean and the unforgiving dryness of the desert—the sonnet concludes that the "fury that packs the greatest punch is the ire of a shifty woman."[44] This overtly misogynist language is in keeping with the arguments made by antiwoman rhetoricians who participated in the debate on the worth of women. Since many other comments in the text support women's intellectual endeavors and capabilities, Feniso's misogyny is out of step with the general endorsement of women by the narrator and others.

The various defenses of women in other moments of interaction among the shepherds outweigh Feniso's slanderous comments. On balance, the defense of women wins out in the primary narrative. The narrator comments that the admiration expressed for the shepherdess Anfrisa's poem to Saint Anne was well deserved, "even though incredulity and emulation often obscure the accomplishments of women."[45] Similarly, in the final pages, a prior comes on the scene and recites poetry composed by a woman, presumably a reference to Abarca herself. The narrator indicates that the group enjoys the recital and that they would have regretted missing the opportunity to hear "such well-written verse, especially since it was written by a woman."[46] The novel thus highlights the question of women's worth, particularly as it relates to intellectualism and artistry. While interaction among the pastoral characters reveals a tension between the sexes, the men and women generally endorse women's intellectual capabilities.

The secondary narratives in *Vigil and Octavary*—two novellas told by the shepherds themselves—engage gender issues through negative representations of women. The treatment of gender in the novellas seems so odd that, in one of the few modern studies on Abarca, Judith Whitenack has described reading the novellas as "strangely disturbing" because of the emphasis on the "vindication of wronged *males*, along with a concomitant pattern of female sin, repentance, and punishment."[47] As suggested by Whitenack's reaction, the depiction of women in the novellas seems problematic from the standpoint of the contemporary reader. Whitenack's analysis highlights the problem of gender in Abarca but does not resolve the contradictions between the pro-woman rhetoric of the pastoral novel and the misogyny of the novellas.

Yet by contextualizing Abarca within the tradition of the querelle des femmes, we can see that her novellas parody the views toward women found in dominant, male-authored literature. By building her novellas around standard plot lines and exaggerating the negative treatment of the female characters, Abarca's interpolated tales respond to those who would support Feniso in his antiwoman rhetoric. Whitenack's careful study of the close ties between literary tradition—of folktales primarily—and of Abarca's plot lines sets the stage for resolving ambiguous and often disturbing representations of gender that we as modern readers cannot help but find discomfiting. Indeed, Abarca's close engagement with plot lines familiar to readers allows us to trace the author's use of those plots to parody negative representations of women in men's texts.

Abarca's novellas are modeled closely on common tales of men's quests and adventures. Moreover, like countless other stories of their ilk, they depict the female characters as hopelessly useless or evil. Rather than take Abarca's replication of misogyny at face value, I suggest that, like the shepherd Feniso's misogynist sonnet, the novellas have the effect of challenging literary and rhetorical traditions that negatively portray women. Evidence for this challenge can be found by examining *Vigil and Octavary* as a cogent text rather than as a compilation of independent, unrelated shorter works. By placing standard tales within a larger text that challenges misogyny, Abarca questions an entire literary tradition that focuses on men and denigrates women.

Told by two male pastoral characters, the interpolated tales constitute the only sustained narratives of the entire novel. The first, "An Apology for Luck in Unhappy Circumstances" ("Apólogo de la ventura en la desdicha"), narrates a folk/fairy tale about a widower who gives his three sons magic talismans that eventually cause problems for one of the men. In presenting the treasures to his sons, the father reveals that he had met the boys' mother after a shipwreck on an uninhabited island. He rescued the foreign woman and lived with her for a year in the desert. The man taught her to speak his language, upon which he learned of her royal parentage and of her escape from an unwanted arranged marriage. To escape, the princess had stolen the magic objects and fled. Eventually she converted to Catholicism, married the boys' father, and, years later, left the talismans to her husband when she died.

The sons receive the objects under the condition that they each use part of the wealth the gifts will generate to build institutions devoted to good works and, in keeping with the theme of the text itself, dedicate the hospitals or schools to Saint John the Baptist. Complications begin when the youngest son, Lisardo, shows a complete lack of judgment and falls in love with Florisbella, to whom he reveals that his magic purse can generate precious metals. Florisbella, aided by her relative Casandra, lulls Lisardo into a state of happiness, which makes him leave the bag at her house. Florisbella publicly accuses Lisardo of witchcraft so that she can keep the treasure.

Lisardo spends the rest of the tale using his brothers' talismans as bait to help him retrieve his magic purse. Of course, the poor sap loses these as well. Only after eating magic fruit in the mountains can he recover his belongings by selling the apples and figs to the women, who subsequently grow horns and asses' ears. Lisandro relies on the good woman, Casandra, to help him recover the stolen goods. Dressed as a doctor who promises to remove the women's growths, Lisandro forces Casandra to undress and ties her hands and feet. Then he gives her "very cruel whippings using wide straps."[48] When Casandra betrays Florisbella and reveals the location of the magic objects, Lisardo dutifully unties her and, "pleased by the look on her face and her good treatment and knowing now about her good lineage and poverty, he told her that if she would help him recover his jewels he would marry her, taking her away to his country."[49] As Whitenack has noted, "Luck in Unhappy Circumstances" follows the formula for folktales about three magic objects, in which a woman tricks a man in order to secure the magic objects, he punishes her for the deception, and then he promises to marry her in exchange for return of the objects.[50] However, the details here transcend the requisite punishment and relate a scene of extended torture, in which the woman lets out a "cry that reached the heavens and penetrate[d] all of the rooms of the house."[51]

The subsequent torture of Florisbella follows the same pattern. Lisardo forces her to undress and ties her feet and hands to a post. Then he reveals his true identity, which surprises Florisbella so much that she faints, coming to her senses only after Lisardo whips her more. The "bad" woman confesses, packs her jewels and the treasures for Lisardo, and writes this story down "for the general warning of women who, with their trickery, diminish other people's estates."[52]

Throughout the tale, women shoulder the blame, even though the male protagonist shows pathologically bad judgment and makes repeated mistakes. Lisardo's carelessness leads to his troubles, and he fails on three different occasions to protect his family's magic treasures. Yet the misfortune of the title refers to the bad treatment he receives from Florisbella. The narrative thus turns on the depiction of an evil woman who eventually turns good, rather than on the bad judgment of the male protagonist. The details of the women's whippings complicate the otherwise perfunctory representation of Lisardo's successful attempt to recover his objects. Indeed, Casandra cries out so loudly that the others in the household conclude that the pain must be a result of the doctor's cure. A comment made by the frame-tale narrator, Mileno, reminds us of the overall negative depiction of women in the story. Mileno assures listeners that, in spite of being a woman, Casandra kept the secret of the true source of Lisardo's wealth (*Vigilia*, p. 107). To modern sensibilities, the whipping scenes remain the most jarring plot element. Reminiscent of torture experienced by real people in Inquisition chambers, Lisardo's torture of the women has the effect of saving them from themselves. By torturing the women, he is able to put Florisbella on the path that leads to her redemption and to lift Casandra out of her misery.

The second novella, "A Good Ending from a Bad Start" ("El fin bueno en mal principio"), repeats many of the same dominant ideologies about women and the same attitudes about men, although the stabilizing power of a woman's love counterbalances some of the negative depictions here. Written in the picaresque tradition, "A Good Ending" traces the adventures of two bumbling men, Fulgencio and Lisardo, in search of love. Interested in two cousins, Clara and Francisca, the men nonetheless mishandle the situation by receiving other female guests. This indiscreet behavior causes Clara to back out of the courtship and, even though her heart breaks, to enter a convent. Fulgencio spends the rest of the tale trying to win back Clara's love, but this requires that he earn his fortune. The tale becomes more convoluted when Lisardo hears that a duke has kidnapped his sister, and Isbella, a woman pretending to be the sister, tricks Lisardo into staying at her house to force him to marry her. Fulgencio falls prey to a woman named Flora, who convinces him to stuff himself into a trunk so that her husband will not discover him in her room. She then tells a servant to throw the trunk's key into the river and informs her husband that when she dies he should bury her belongings with her in the already packed trunk. He complies with her wish, which provides the impetus for many in town to laugh at the betrayed husband's blind obedience to an ill-intentioned wife. Meanwhile, buried in the basement of a monastery, Fulgencio must wait for Lisardo's improbable rescue.

Both men fall victim to women's manipulation in this tale, and the topic of female deception provides continuity to a series of mishaps experienced by the protagonists. Fulgencio explains that "a crazy woman's cruelty" landed him in the trunk, for example.[53] Moreover, when the townspeople laugh at Flora's funeral (knowing that she has manipulated her husband by requesting that he bury her jewels and dresses with her), their scoffing seems out of step with the fact that a woman has just died. When Lisardo seeks out the woman who tried to trick him into marriage, the neighbors warn him off because Isbella "made a living out of tricking and deceiving foreigners."[54] Once Lisardo rescues Fulgencio from his claustrophobic burial, the two men get so angry over Isbella's machinations that they threaten to kill her if she does not return the money she stole from Lisardo. Described as both "vile" and a "harpy" by the narrator, Isbella buckles under the death threats and confesses to having manipulated and stolen from Lisardo. She then repents, makes Lisardo the beneficiary of her new will, and dies. The money from her estate goes to a convent and, likewise, Clara makes large donations to a convent. Clara's modeling of virtue and Isbella's modeling of bad but repentant behavior are evocative of the female characters in "Luck in Unhappy Circumstances." Typical of the novella genre, the story ends with the marriages of the main characters.

Abarca's novellas relentlessly criticize unfeminine women and demonstrate almost complete leniency toward the stupidity of the male characters. Female virtue is praised, certainly; but two of the negative female characters—Floribella and Isbella—receive much criticism before they experience crises of conscience that move them to change their ways. Both women eventually repent, confess, and donate their money to religious causes. Yet the three male protagonists, all of whom make bad decisions that lead to life-threatening situations, receive very little criticism.

The absence of overtly critical remarks about the male characters directly conflicts with the emphasis on women's wrongdoing in the novellas. The text thus exposes the misogynist double standard to which women were subjected in literature and in the culture. The frame narrative provides a context for the misogynist dynamic in the novellas. In the frame, only the female shepherds fully endorse women's integrity, while the men endorse an antiwoman perspective. The depiction of women as cruel and deserving of punishment in the novellas thus appears to validate the male shepherds' claims of women's untrustworthy, evil natures. This is why it makes sense that Whitenack assessed her reading experience as "strangely disturbing."

Yet Abarca inscribes a clear pro-woman message into the texts. By basing her two novellas on familiar folktales, the author provides us with a key to deciphering the apparent contradictions in *Vigil and Octavary*. In the novellas, the female characters clearly are mistreated and held to higher standards than the male characters. Tortured, ridiculed, and criticized, the female characterizations are excessively denigrating. The bumbling male protagonists, on the other hand, remain the center of attention, receive little criticism, and attain their desire at the end of each novella. By embedding excessively denigrating representations of women into recognizably traditional novellas, Abarca draws attention to the negative treatment of women in dominant literary tradition. The antiwoman message of the folktales thus connects to the male shepherds' bad opinions of women. Since male shepherds tell the novellas and since they stick to the traditional narratives upon which these are based, the negativity toward women in the tales suggests that these shepherds think ill of women in part because of the literature with which they are familiar. Abarca uses the intercalated novellas, in other words, to show the relationship between representations of women—that is, what cultural production says about women—and individual attitudes toward women. This subtle but powerful move connects representation to reality, drawing attention to the consequences of misogynist literary traditions.

Through the representation of pro- and antiwoman ideologies in the frame tale, Abarca de Bolea acknowledges the possibility for legitimate debate about women's worth. The author then uses the novellas to demonstrate the unfair treatment of women in traditional literature. The connection between the two layers of the narrative—between the male shepherds and the stories they tell—delivers a persuasive message. Abarca de Bolea's *Vigil and Octavary* demonstrates through complex narrative strategies that the perpetration of negative representations of women is at least partly to blame for misogynist attitudes in the culture at large. Given Abarca's direct engagement with the querelle des femmes and her critique of denigrating representations of women, perhaps it is possible that she also wanted to call into question the legitimacy of the ongoing debates on women's worth. That is, from the perspective of a nun writing in the late seventeenth century, the querelle des femmes may have represented a tired argument that merely undermined women's intellectual work.

Vigil and Octavary reflects Abarca's dual life as an active literary figure and a cloistered nun, the sometimes contradictory forces likely encountered by someone whose work had an audience beyond convent walls. In contrast to her other work, *Vigil and Octavary* has its roots in the pastoral and framed novella traditions of secular literature. It is a book written for the book market, in other words, and so avoids the pressures of representing convent life to an extramuros readership.[55] Instead, it mixes religious and secular themes and traditions, hanging the poetry and novellas on a pastoral narrative of religious celebration.

Rather than draw the reading public into the culture of the convent, Abarca engaged the longstanding literary tradition of misogynist writing. The repeated defense of women's intellect in *Vigil and Octavary* contradicts the unforgiving portrayals of ill-intentioned female characters in the novellas. This contrast challenges readers to resolve the seemingly irresolvable conflict between cultural ideologies of women's inferiority and the fact that they were reading an erudite book written by a woman. This contradiction faced many readers of female-authored texts of the period. If individuals believed dominant rhetoric about women's inferiority, then intelligent texts written by women presented a conundrum. By inscribing into her texts a seemingly contradictory message about women, Abarca chose a sophisticated approach to the problem of whether readers would take her—a woman and a nun—seriously as a writer. At the very least, the inscription of these themes into the text would have forced readers to think about gender and the implications of reading women's literature.

We cannot know how the reading public reacted to Abarca's sophisticated protest of restrictive, denigrating gender codes. It is likely that readers recognized the adventure stories in *Vigil and Octavary* as tales they had heard numerous times before. The pro-woman rhetoric of the pastoral characters probably also resonated with readers, who would have been exposed to many versions of the debate on the worth of women. By building on familiar themes and language, Ana Abarca de Bolea probably managed to appease readers of all ideological persuasions with her entertaining text. Hundreds of years later we can delight in a work that appeared to embrace dominant gender ideologies but in fact parodied and rejected the double standard to which women were subjected in the culture.

CONVENT CULTURE AND CONVENT WRITING

Like many other examples of convent literature, the writing of the three nuns examined here reminds us of the permeability of the convent wall and makes it impossible to think that religious women lived disconnected from the world outside. These women wrote texts that engage the politics, culture, and economics of the secular world, thus giving us clues about their knowledge of and opinions about the world they left behind. For instance, Sor Violante's surprising metaphor of friendship flies in the face of the culture of conquest that permeated western European life throughout the seventeenth century. Her friendship sonnet reconceptualizes worth and creates an alternative market economy that parodies the economy of conquest.

Sor Marcela's is the only work examined here that was written exclusively for an audience of the author's peers. Yet even these texts directly engage with the outside world. From references to her famous father's talent to her own tainted lineage, the nun in her allegories shapes the raw material of Trinitarian life to fit the mold of popular secular theater. In the end, Sor Marcela's work captures the freedom afforded those nuns who wrote strictly for their cloistered sisters. In contrast to the genre of hagiography, in which authors defend religious experience by employing tropes of glorified suffering and martyrdom, Sor Marcela's drama discusses negative and positive elements of nuns' lives. Humor, self-parody, and criticism come together in messages of encouragement for the audience of Trinitarian sisters.

Sor Marcela's intimate, humorous depictions of convents contrast with the near absence of any topic related to female spirituality in Ana Abarca de Bolea's one fictional work. The differences between the two women's target audiences, chosen genres, and principal themes suggest that understanding representations of religious life becomes particularly complex when we take into account intended readership. The burden of representing oneself and one's religious community became more acute when texts were read beyond the convent walls. In the case of Sor Marcela's coloquios, the relative homogeneity of the audience allowed for a profound sense of self-awareness and self-parody that does not appear in most works produced in convent settings.

As suggested by the absence of such self-consciousness about convent life in Abarca de Bolea's *Vigil and Octavary*, the complexities of presenting one's religious community were perhaps better avoided when writing for an extramuros community. Abarca's fictional text circumvents these complexities. Even if the nun and her sisters originally used the poems in the *Vigil and Octavary* for their own festivities, the pieces then became part of a text that had more in common with other pastoral novels of its period than with most convent literature. Rooted in secular literary tradition, *Vigil and Octavary* provides a glimpse into one religious woman's adaptation and exploitation of familiar secular narratives.

In the frame narrative and in the two intercalated novellas, Abarca's representation of gender reflects many of the prevailing views about women in the early modern era. By basing her novellas so closely on stock characters and plot lines from folk stories and fairy tales, Abarca draws attention to a contrast between her own pastoral characters' support of women and the attacks on women in dominant literature and in the querelle des femmes. Whether her readers were aware of this contrast, we cannot know. From our perspective several centuries later, we can see that Abarca used the recognizable form of the folktale to reflect negative portrayals of women *back* at her reading public. The novellas aimed to make readers face the contradictions and effects of a tradition that had codified demeaning representations of women.

The texts produced by these three nuns reflect the authors' intense awareness about their prospective audiences. Writing specifically for their sisters and female friends, Sor Violante and Sor Marcela exalt female solidarity, employ various techniques to criticize the world of men, and take up topics related to women and religiosity. The validation of female friendship in their work echoes the emphasis on women's interpersonal relationships and support for each other within convent culture. Ana Abarca de Bolea, in writing for a broader audience, challenged the treatment of women in secular literary tradition. The differences among these nuns' texts confirm that convent literature should be examined with an eye to the circumstances under which such texts were produced, as well as to the intended audience of each piece. In spite of those differences, we also should note that the texts echo the emphasis on women's interpersonal relationships and affective lives that appears in the work of Azevedo, Caro, Carvajal, and Zayas.

The erudition of women like Sor Violante, Sor Marcela, and Ana Abarca de Bolea confirms that women religious drew on numerous intellectual and spiritual traditions when they took up the pen. Their literature gives us access to the reactions of educated women to the pressures and rewards of piety and femininity in early modern Spain. Functioning as part of their own communities and, occasionally, as members of the literary culture, nuns found readers within and outside convent walls. As the examples of Sor Violante and Sor Marcela suggest, they responded to the dicta that excluded women from positions of power within the church by showing themselves capable of intelligent thought. Ana Abarca de Bolea's work confirms that nuns responded to intellectual debates, as well as to the denigration of women in the larger culture. Validating women's communities and spirituality, these and other nuns wrote texts that represent sophisticated responses to secular and religious traditions that treated women as inferior to men.

6

Nuns as Mothers

Biology and Spirituality

We who live in the secular world often imagine life in convents as mysterious and far removed from everyday experience. It often is easier to imagine the lives of people like Eleno/a de Céspedes and Bernarda Manuel or the fictional characters depicted in women's literature than to imagine convent life in centuries past. Literary and historical texts can help bridge this gap, but since many convent records have been destroyed over the centuries, even these sources can be hard to uncover. Research on the diverse types of surviving texts can help us flesh out a full picture of convent life. As we have seen in the cases of Sor Marcela, Sor Violante, and Ana Abarca de Bolea, the prose fiction, poetry, and drama produced in convents gives us insight into the recreational activities, devotional fervor, and quotidian difficulties of the cloister. Such literature also reveals the direct and unique engagement with gender issues offered by educated religious women who wrote for each other and for the outside world.

A complement to literary representation of convent life can be found in letters, financial records, and other official documents that hold the key to understanding fiscal, social, and political histories of given orders and institutions. The genre of the vida—the auto/biographical writing popular across orders—holds a special place in religious history, however. Without the texts of Saint Teresa and her followers, including Ana de San Bartolomé (1549–1626) and María de San José (Salazar) (1548–1603), for example, we might still know the details of Carmelite reform, yet we would know very little about the experiences of the women who implemented, defended, and even disparaged that reform.[1] Such vidas, which include autobiographies, male-authored biographies, and dictated life stories, add an experiential dimension to our understanding of gender and religion in the early modern period. Informed by formulaic themes, structures, and language, the vida nonetheless represents one of the few genres in which women could legitimately participate as authors and as subjects. Indeed, very few men wrote their own life stories, perhaps because they had other venues for expression and exercise of power available to them.[2] Vidas represent a major portion of the texts by and about women religious, offering insight into the lives of their subjects, as well as the motivations of their authors.

Most frequently, the vidas of religious men and women aimed to document, glorify, and even justify the spirituality of author and subject. As suggested by the references to poverty and self-mortification in the works of Marcela de San Félix, the pressures of femininity and religiosity were different for women than for men in Counter-Reformation Spain. Women enjoyed some independence in the convent, of course, but they also lived under the control of male religious authorities. The gender hierarchy of the Catholic church created complex relationships between nuns and confessors. Most nuns who wrote or dictated autobiographies did so upon the request of their confessors, thus producing what we know as *escritura por mandato* (writing upon command). As Alison Weber and other scholars of nuns' life writing have shown, the production of a vida required that women who wrote or dictated their stories strike a balance between writerly authority and appropriate humility.[3] The prevalence of the trope of humility in women's vidas testifies to the pressures placed on religious women, many of whom were called upon to write about their extraordinary spirituality in a climate suspicious of those who claimed to have a unique, unmediated relationship with God. Explanation and justification fill the vidas of female religious, who were literate, active leaders who did not conform to standard expectations for their gender.[4]

In Counter-Reformation Spain, with the Inquisition serving as the religious arm of the law, women's spirituality in particular was seen as increasingly threatening. Nuns-turned-authors had to downplay their singularity and remain properly humble.[5] Writing a life story required a balancing act between obedience and authority, between highlighting and justifying unusual spirituality. The many trials of those accused of false spiritual enlightenment attest to the high stakes risked by those who failed to achieve this balance.[6] As in witchcraft and sorcery trials, women were prosecuted more frequently than men. This imbalance points us once again to the increased vigilance of women and to the risks run by those who refused to comply with dominant definitions of religiosity and femininity in early modern Spain.

The vida of the beata Sor Catalina de Jesús y San Francisco (1639–77) outlines the challenges of justifying unorthodox femininity. The text also provides an intriguing example of the rhetorical and psychological complexity involved in the production of writing about a nun who, in her secular life, failed to conform to society's expectations for women. This hybrid text, written by a priest who was also Catalina's son, adds new valence to the term *escritura por mandato*. Father Juan Bernique reveals in the first pages of *Idea of Perfection and Virtues* (*Idea de perfección y virtudes*, 1693) that his mother prophesied that he would be her biographer. When Juan was nineteen, he read the vida of María de Pol to his mother and was intrigued by "the mystery that [Pol's] own son had been the chronicler of his mother's virtues." Catalina responded that the "the same thing would happen" with her son, to whom she referred as "her historian."[7]

This prophecy may not have come to fruition if Catalina had not collaborated in recording her experiences over the years. As Bernique explains, his mother complied with her confessor's mandate to write her vida. She burned the text, only to write another at a later date. Nuns commonly wrote and destroyed their autobiographies. Writing, after all, constitutes an act of pride and thus directly conflicts with the emphasis on humility in Catholicism. This contradiction helps explain why priests or nuns themselves destroyed many texts written by religious women over the centuries. Bernique's relationship to his subject makes his a complex text indeed, for in addition to being the beata's biological son, he also relied on Sor Catalina's life writings and letters to treat the more delicate topics in the text. In this sense, Bernique acts as both editor and author: His glosses of his mother's autobiographical and epistolary correspondence occupy at least 80 percent of this unusual four-hundred-page text.[8]

Bernique gives little information about his source material. To my knowledge, no related documents survive. He explains in the prologue that *Idea of Perfection* faithfully quotes the autobiographical fragments; he sets them off in quotation marks to distinguish them from his own musings on his mother's life. As Jodi Bilinkoff has shown, the mix of the autobiographical with the biographical is not uncommon in early modern spiritual biographies, and Bernique's control over his mother's material echoes a power imbalance found frequently in the production of religious biography. As Catherine Mooney explains in a study of hagiographies from medieval Europe:

> Among the insights regarding the composition of hagiographic texts is the well-known fact that men, and clerics in particular, exercised nearly complete control over the textualization of women's utterances. Women's words almost invariably reach us only after having passed through the filters of their male confessors, patrons, and scribes.[9]

Whether men exercised "nearly complete control" over women's writing is certainly subject to debate, for the strategies used by religious women to seek authority, justify their experiences, and avoid persecution attest to the control that women exerted over their self-representation.

Idea of Perfection is an unusual text not because of the mix of letters with a biographical narrative but because the psychological tension between mother and son adds a layer of complexity that bears on the consideration of gender in the religious landscape of seventeenth-century Spain. Indeed, the filter of the male voice—which also is the son's voice—cannot be denied in *Idea of Perfection*, where the issue of control becomes the key to understanding the psychologically compelling aspects of the text. Even if Bernique worked from a full set of documentation, including letters and salvaged fragments of an autobiographical vida, the editing and emendations provide clues to his desire to control the presentation of his mother's legacy to the world. While readers might speculate on the complexities of Bernique's motivations, he explains himself up front in a simple manner, saying he cannot bear the thought of allowing Catalina's "good works to remain buried in the shadows of oblivion," so he will let others judge "whether [his] mother deserves applause for being a strong woman."[10]

By taking up the pen, Bernique followed the example of countless other religious men who have chronicled women's religious experiences throughout the centuries. The motivations behind such texts are difficult to decipher, as they range from an interest in recording extraordinary spiritual experiences to the more calculated, political purpose of associating one's name with a woman who might be a candidate for beatification or sainthood. Jodi Bilinkoff describes the conflation of representation and self-representation at work in vidas: "The genre of spiritual biography provided confessors with a useful vehicle, not only for presenting the lives of their female penitents, but also for representing themselves."[11] Priests sought to glorify women's religiosity through overdetermined narratives that showed their subjects as destined for great religious acts from a very young age. They also took great care to distance themselves from anything that approached heresy. In this way, they served as interpreters who attempted to glorify their subjects and, simultaneously, to avoid suspicion of complicity in prideful or blasphemous acts.[12]

The motivations of confessors must be taken into account when reading any biographical vida. In this case, the familial relationship of Bernique to his subject begs scrutiny, particularly since the priest emphasizes his devotion to the "truth" of his text. At the beginning of *Idea of Perfection*, Bernique promises that he will not add anything to his mother's own account of her life, "which faithfully I have transferred from the papers and original letters that she wrote when surrendered to total obedience and that have come into my possession."[13] We must keep in mind, though, that he did not publish or transcribe these letters in their entirety. The lack of comparative documentation makes it impossible to know what he left out of Catalina's vida. By the same token, the text allows ample opportunity to question what Bernique thought he would gain by publishing a heavily edited text in which he had control over his mother's narrative of her life.

As it stands, Bernique's text represents the only written record of Catalina's life. It is a hybrid of religious autobiography, biography, and glosses.[14] His presentation of his mother's words sets them apart so readers could recognize their authenticity. The authenticity remains obscured, however, since none of the original documentation is available for consultation. We have no way of knowing if the words Bernique quotes were penned by his mother, but a few points lead us to believe that they are at least based on her writings. To note, the style and substance of the quotations seem to coincide with those of other religious women's writing. Perhaps more important, Bernique includes details of Catalina's rejection of his father, sex, and child rearing that may have been difficult for him to confront. Based on what we know about Bernique and his mother, he would have had little reason to invent these details. Indeed, the sharp contrast between the mother's and son's words creates an intriguing psychological dichotomy in the text.

A brief summary of Catalina's journey to religious life gives insight into the tensions present in the vida. Whether the text faithfully represents her life or not, the tensions described exemplify the difficulties faced by independent, strong-willed women in the seventeenth century. Raised by her aunt, the young Catalina was forced to marry against her will around the age of fifteen. Class played as much of a part in the marriage as gender expectations, as the self-supporting aunt could not afford to support her grown niece. Catalina had two daughters and a son before becoming a widow at age twenty-two. With three children under the age of six, the only socially acceptable and economically viable option for a woman in Catalina's position would have been remarriage. Yet, as Bernique explains:

> Her [spiritual] plans impeded her compliance with the pressing obligation of raising her children. . . . But she worked herself up into such fervor and her desires became so strong that she arranged clandestinely to enter into the convent of Saint Claire as a Discalced nun [and] as a fugitive from the deceptions of the world, disregarding the obligation to attend to her children.[15]

The description of one's mother as a fugitive who fled from her maternal obligations certainly does not qualify as high praise. While Bernique occasionally condemns Catalina's performance as a mother and wife, he never fails to glorify her spirituality. As he later explains, his mother acted against the advice of her family and her confessor when she entered a Franciscan convent and, at age twenty-six, took vows. The son's narrative of these decisive years in his mother's life chronicles the protests of Catalina's caretakers and his own disapproval of her views toward motherhood, but it also highlights the saintly impulses behind her decision. In Bernique's version, his stubborn, somewhat negligent, but always piously portrayed mother persisted in following God's will. According to his depiction, nobody could keep her from making this righteous decision.

As this episode suggests, Sor Catalina's vida puts forth a clear picture of female sanctity. Currents of tension underlie the veneer of piety, however. In narrating the tensions, the text delineates the familial and religious pressures facing women in the seventeenth century and sheds light on women's struggle for authority in the institutions of both the family and the church. The combination of autobiography and biography adds a psychologically complex dimension to the text. On the one hand, Juan Bernique seeks control over the memory of his mother. Acting in the capacity of priest and advisor, he carefully crafts a text that exalts Sor Catalina's spirituality and accounts for her extraordinary experiences. Yet his glosses on such issues as his mother's performance as a wife and his father's martyrdom reveal that Bernique could not escape his identity as the abandoned son. Insofar as the dynamic between maternal independence and the son's abandonment plays itself out in *Idea of Perfection*, the text literalizes a paradox of women's spirituality: While religious women left behind the ties to sexuality and reproduction that defined secular women, the experience of religiosity often involved an equally intense emphasis on the physical self. Like other nuns, Sor Catalina devoted herself to overcoming her physical self in order to unite with God, but it is only through the product of her flesh—her son—that we know the story of her life.

The goal of idealized representation lies at the heart of the genre of the vida, in which hagiographers take on the task of producing an authoritative narrative of the subject's journey toward spiritual perfection. The struggle for authority in *Idea of Perfection* manifests itself in two inseparable narratives. The autobiographical excerpts trace a woman's battle for independence, while the biographer's interpretive glosses work through the psychological drama of a son who attempts to explain this independence. Precisely because the journey involves the rejection of conventional motherhood and marriage, the strategies mother and son used to justify Catalina's choices and exalt her spirituality constitute one of the most compelling aspects of this unusual text. In the interplay between autobiography and biography,

Idea of Perfection manifests a fight for legitimacy that centers on femininity, motherhood, and saintliness.

SACRIFICE AND REJECTION: THE EARLY LIFE

Juan Bernique published *Idea of Perfection* when he was in his mid-thirties, sixteen years after his mother's death. In the first part of the text, which is dedicated to Sor Catalina's early life, Bernique details many of his mother's negative characteristics. He adopts a critical stance toward her vain behavior and her reading practices, for example. Alternately, he celebrates her "native inclination" toward chastity, portraying her as a girl who "abhorred the state of matrimony as something contrary to her plans."[16] This fits into the larger project of religious biographies, in which authors seek to present cogent stories of their subjects' triumph over human imperfections. Like other spiritual biographies, *Idea of Perfection* details the subject's faults but also alludes to her inclination toward chastity and her religious calling from a very young age.

As in other religious women's stories, marriage emerges as a frightening proposition for the young Catalina. Pressured by her caretaker (a rigid aunt) to marry one of her many suitors, Catalina writes about feeling so put off by sex and men at age fifteen that she became ill:

> Everyone plotted against me using all of the means that one can think of to make me marry. I entered into marriage with such disgust and hatred that I cannot even truthfully say where this came from because by then I had forgotten my desire and plans that I had had to maintain my chastity and become a nun. I became afflicted with such fevers; I don't know if I was able to verify that they stemmed from my suffering.[17]

Eventually Catalina married the forty-year-old Don Juan Bernique. The suitor's financial solvency almost certainly influenced the marriage contract, but the text indicates that he was chosen because he would be more a teacher than a husband to the rebellious young woman.

Father Bernique's interjections throughout this section of the narrative reveal as much about his own views toward women's place in society as they do about Catalina's resistance to being a wife and mother. He begins the chapter on his mother's marriage with a short dissertation on the need for women to either join a convent or marry, since women cause so much trouble for tutors and parents. To reinforce this assertion, Bernique cites the saying, "Either a castle or a husband [is needed] to guard a woman."[18]

Catalina states that she could not stop crying on her wedding day. Bernique focuses on his father's reaction to this public spectacle. The son's interpretation emphasizes that Don Juan's relationship with his wife never improved. In Bernique's view, his father lived as a martyr in the marriage, but he handled the situation with aplomb. Since the son had no firsthand knowledge of the wedding, problems of representation and interpretation become particularly notable here. Bernique faces the challenge of defending both parents, crafting a story based purely on secondhand information, and remaining faithful to a narrative of an unhappy union. As with the rest of the text, the discussion of Catalina's early life attempts to balance criticism with praise. Amid the exaltations of the father's martyrdom, for example, Bernique contemplates the challenges of controlling women, noting that men must "have an awareness of their wives' fragility." Bernique adds, though, that wives who are vain spendthrifts create an "insufferable burden that requires notable suffering just to maintain the peace one so desires in marriage."[19] Such commentary contains an implicit criticism of Don Juan as a weak-willed husband. On the other hand, the attribution of this weak behavior to Catalina's hard-headedness reveals Bernique's identification with his father. In the end, it seems, neither man ever managed to control her.

The discussion of control demonstrates that the indirect criticism of Juan Bernique the elder is offset by the insistence on his long-suffering relationship with an intransigent wife.[20] Similarly, the criticism of Catalina's mistreatment of her husband is softened by the emphasis on her compliance with certain duties. The son-narrator notes that Catalina tried to adapt to her new circumstances: He emphasizes that she went to mass almost every day to learn "to tolerate the cross of marriage, which for her was a terrible weight to bear," and that, although she did not enjoy raising children, she always fulfilled her obligations on this front.[21] For Bernique, the narrative of the early years amounts to an exercise in self-indictment: If the marriage should not have occurred because Catalina was destined for a spiritual life, then the offspring were products of an unnatural union.

Bernique walks a fine line in these early chapters. Many of the quotations he attributes to Sor Catalina communicate a strong aversion to all aspects of married life; this vehemence finds its match in the biographer's criticism of her "typically feminine" behavior. Often Bernique frames the narrative to show the opinions he shared with his mother. For example, both disparage her vanity and blame her for the visits she received from a suitor during her marriage (*Idea*, pp. 27–30). They agree on the importance of chastity, although they conceive of this in different terms. Mother and son seem to concur that, as Catalina de Jesús is said to have written, women hold the blame for most relationship problems because, "with their clothes, decorations, and desire to look good, they occasion and invite men's daring behavior."[22]

In spite of his agreement with his mother on such issues as her culpability in marital matters, the problems that faced Bernique as a son-biographer remain on the surface of the text, emerging quite obviously in the representation of his mother's attitudes toward sex, the body, and motherhood. Bernique seems not to shy away from these issues, as he includes explicit references attributed to Sor Catalina to explain her dislike of sexual relations and her husband:

> In the time I was married, . . . what sorrows, what challenges, what hatred of my husband didn't I experience? . . . In all of these occasions my inclination, that God had given me, served me well: I hated everything that was contrary to the virtue of chastity.[23]

Bernique sidesteps this allusion to sex by shifting the discussion to a more general commentary on the virtues of discretion and shame in women. Using language similar to that attributed to Catalina, he exalts her decision to live more discreetly following the episode with the unwanted suitor: "This was the only means by which she could avoid blame and protect her chastity and discretion. O how delicate is the jewel of chastity, the very crystal of purity!"[24] As the example of sexuality attests, standard attitudes adopted by other spiritual biographers take on different valences when we remember this man's relationship to his subject. The issue of narrative control remains palpable throughout the text, in other words, as Bernique appears to comply with his claim of faithfully reproducing his mother's words while simultaneously manipulating the text to focus not on the sorrows, challenges, and hatred she felt during her marriage but instead on chastity and obedience.

The topic of sexuality provoked deep ambivalence in Bernique, but the most slippery topic he confronted was the death of his father. In chapter 5 of book 1, Bernique introduces the topic by interpreting his mother's widowhood as part of a divine plan:

> His Majesty disposed to deprive her of her husband, either to alleviate the burden of a status that was so bothersome for her or to completely confound her vanity, making it impossible for her to continue with her worldly follies.[25]

As the narrative unfolds, we learn that Catalina's plan involved nothing less than a death wish for her husband. In Catalina's version of the story (as quoted in the text), San Diego de Madrid's relics were paraded through Torrejón de Ardoz, the town in which she and Bernique lived. Catalina begged the saint to take her back to her hometown of Alcalá.[26] As Sor Catalina is said to have written: "The blessed saint answered my petition so quickly that within a month my husband fell ill and died from that sickness, and then I came to Alcalá."[27]

In sum, Catalina hated her marriage and hated living away from home, so she prayed for her husband's death. One month later, he died. Bernique's death enabled Catalina to fulfill her wish of returning home. Neither she nor her son comments on her role in this death, which they both report as part of a chain of divinely inspired events that led her back to her hometown. Any religious biographer might have had a difficult time filling in the gaps of this part of Sor Catalina's life story, but the task was even more charged for the offspring of the ill-fated marriage.

Bernique adopted a two-fold strategy in handling the connection between his mother's prayers and his father's subsequent demise. On the one hand, he included quotations from Catalina that emphasized her husband's goodness and holiness. Notably, she reportedly wrote that thirteen years after Bernique's death, the man was unearthed mistakenly and the cadaver was "without corruption and with an odor that amazed those who were present; and his clothes were intact, as if they had just buried him."[28] Father Bernique echoes Sor Catalina's imputation of martyrdom to her husband when he mentions that people thought of Juan Bernique the elder as a God-fearing, honest man. Moreover, three times before the chapter's end, Bernique describes his mother's sudden understanding of his father's greatness. In his estimation, the young widow opened her eyes to the truth after her husband's death, finally recognizing her luck.[29]

These examples point to an important aspect of the text: Juan Bernique repeatedly overcompensates for his mother's shortcomings as a wife. In addition to emphasizing his father's perfection and his mother's change of heart, Bernique demonstrates surprising empathy for the burdens placed on women in his mother's position. Rather than continue to moralize about his long-dead father, Bernique turns the narrative over to his mother. The inclusion of a full-page excerpt from Sor Catalina's writings marks a shift in the text, since most quotations included up to this point are quite short. This long passage highlights the problems of marriage and motherhood and downplays any guilt Catalina may have felt over Don Juan's sudden death. Moreover, at the end of a comparative discussion about life as a religious woman and life as a wife and mother, Catalina is said to have written that spiritual marriage far surpasses being married to an "imperfect, coarse man."[30] Bernique's primary motivation for excerpting such a long piece may have related to the perceived need to gloss over the problematic issue of his mother's death wish for his father. However, by creating space for the voice of his subject, this strategy also has the effect of allowing Catalina to articulate her negative feelings.

Moreover, by sticking to a narrative in which divine intervention rescued Catalina from the burden of married life, Bernique creates an opportunity to reflect on the pressures placed on secular women. In Bernique's estimation, widowhood represented both a relief and a burden for this mother of three: "She found herself free of the yoke of marriage, which for her had been so painful, but she also had the work of raising her children, and this overwhelmed her more than a little."[31] The pressure to remarry figures prominently here, as Sor Catalina vacillated between her desire for a religious life and the need to ensure stability for her family. As pressure mounted for her to remarry, she hit upon an idea that might have helped her resolve her conflicting impulses:

> I fought with terrible contradictions and I very much wished to marry and I remember that I had this desire and I am not sure if I asked it of Our Lady, I believe I did, that she give me a chaste husband, and then, upon taking a vow of chastity, I would be able to achieve my desire of continuing in the world (with all of its vanities) and at the same time satisfy my natural inclination, which was to maintain my chastity.[32]

While finding a man willing to enter into marriage under such terms may have been impossible, in theory this creative solution offered the best of both worlds. The emphasis on Catalina's aversion to sex raises the question of authenticity. As in similar texts, it is difficult to sort out the extent to which the aversion to sex reflects Catalina's feelings. With the added filter of the son's control over a narrative aimed at proving the subject's sanctity, we cannot possibly decipher what role, if any, her views toward sex played in her choice of a religious life.[33]

We do know, however, that Catalina's views on sex emerge in *Idea of Perfection* as the cornerstone of a divorce from the flesh. Mentioned repeatedly in the context of chastity and sexual relations, this aversion to the physical self eventually paved the way for Catalina's entry into religious life. Spurred on by her confessor, Father Cristóbal Delgadillo, Catalina engaged in a halfhearted attempt to prepare herself for the convent after her husband's death. During this trial period, she fought to overcome her earthly impulses: She tried to stop reading secular literature, expressed guilt about going to the theater, and took daily communion. Then, after having left Delgadillo and another, far less amenable, confessor, Catalina found inspiration in two religious examples: Saint Teresa's writings, which reminded her of the devotion she felt when younger, and the missionary work of a group of Franciscans, who moved her to reevaluate her devotion when they came to Alcalá to preach.[34] After the encounter with the Franciscans, Catalina began to mortify her body, working without spiritual guidance. As Bernique describes it: "She began to punish her body with extraordinary rigor and severity; but actions regulated by one's own rules very rarely fail to reach an extreme."[35] This routine of self-mortification led Catalina on the path toward spiritual purification. Once under the tutelage of Father Juan Sendín, she learned to devote herself entirely to a religious life.[36]

The pull of the flesh represents the key to understanding the contradictions of Catalina Bernique's early life. Burdened by her disgust for sex and marriage, the young woman nonetheless was tied to her body through her role as a mother. The impulse to overcome earthly vanities through a rigorous routine of mortification can be understood in terms of the desire to leave behind the secular roles that she unwillingly occupied as a young woman. Catalina herself links this desire to her distaste for maternity: After willing her husband's death and becoming more convinced of her spiritual calling, she resented the burden of her children. At first she pinned her hopes on entering the Discalced Carmelite convent in Chinchón, but, as she is said to have written: "I felt great pain because, on account of the inconvenience of having children, I couldn't even enter as a laywoman there."[37] According to Bernique, all Catalina's relatives advised her to attend to her maternal duties and not to enter the convent.

Serving the role of biographer and assuaging his own psychological wounds, Bernique insists that his mother knew God's wishes for her, and that she made the right decision in the end. Moreover, he emphasizes her continued devotion to her children: "She did not fail to assist her children, since the mother's good example is the most efficient doctrine for their education and teaching."[38] Continuing with this compensatory rhetoric, Bernique casts his mother's entry into the Convent of Saint Claire at age twenty-six as a sacrificial act. From this perspective, Catalina showed great humility when she cut her hair, covered her head, stopped wearing jewels, and dressed in the habit of the Third Order of Saint Frances.

The emphasis on sacrifice at the end of this transitional chapter leads us to consider the familial dynamic that plays out in *Idea of Perfection*. Neither mother nor son explicitly mentions what became of the children when Catalina entered the convent. Except for Catalina's appreciation of her new life, which she reportedly described as "unoccupied by children," no details emerge about the children's fate. Given the beata's gratitude toward her aunt, it is likely that this relative became the caretaker of the two girls and the young Juan Bernique. The Poor Claires is a third order, which means that the women did not live cloistered. Indeed, later details about Catalina's life make it clear that she performed many works of charity outside the convent and that she traveled to Madrid with some frequency. Eventually she brought her daughters in to live with her after founding a school for poor girls, Colegio de las Doncellas Pobres, around 1671.[39]

In the discussion of Catalina's first twenty-five years, Bernique's glosses and edited citations emphasize the sacrifices Catalina made, her gratitude for her new life, and her "very tender age."[40] The protectiveness with which he presents this younger version of his mother to the world reveals various psychic tensions. Although he attempts to deflect attention from her neglect of maternal duties, the focus on the themes of sacrifice and youth have the opposite effect. Readers thinking about the relationship between this biographer and his subject cannot help but notice that Catalina's many sacrifices included an abdication of child-rearing responsibilities, an act that her society certainly would have viewed as antimaternal and unfeminine.

Perhaps in recognition of the negative opinion that such a narrative might provoke in the reader, Bernique tells a story of religious conversion and of the sacrifices required by the transition to a religious life. The narrative of Catalina Bernique's religious conversion relies on the central theme of conquering the flesh. While not explicitly stated as such, the battle over the flesh encapsulates the difficulties of young Catalina's life. Distaste for marriage, aversion to sex, gusto for worldly pleasures, and a maternal identity all connected her to her body. Yet only when a regimen of self-mortification began in earnest did Catalina's body become a source of authority. While others—priests, family, and community members—pressured Catalina to take responsibility for her children and remarry to ensure their survival, the young woman fought to connect with the spiritual world. The question of Catalina's social class comes into play once again at this juncture, as she clearly had enough resources to avoid immediate remarriage. Had she belonged to a lower socioeconomic class, for instance, the young widow likely would have faced severe financial hardship rather than the spiritual indecisiveness described in the text.

After many months of religious practice and modified daily habits, the disciplining of the self provided the means by which Catalina Bernique prepared to give herself over entirely to the nonmaterial world. Previously tied to the body through sex and childbearing, Catalina Bernique sacrificed herself physically. By defining her body as a source of authority and as a means to accomplish her goals, Catalina found a socially sanctioned path to liberation from the roles of wife and mother.

REWRITING MOTHERHOOD

According to both mother and son in *Idea of Perfection*, the disciplining of the flesh provided the hook by which Catalina finally entered the spiritual realm. As with the structure of many other spiritual biographies, the remaining two sections of the vida provide lengthy details of Catalina de Jesús y San Francisco's rigorous bodily mortification and, generally, of her work as a religious woman. The story of the rest of Sor Catalina's life predictably delineates her good works and emphasizes her great humility. The text shows her in a new phase, having distanced herself from the role of mother and embarked on a journey of religion and leadership. Yet even after these changes, Catalina remained tied to her previous life and maintained contact with her family. Rather than leave behind her maternal identity, she took on the challenges of spiritual motherhood. During the last two decades of her life, Sor Catalina reached out to young women and girls as advisor, teacher, and guide. While she did not act as the primary caretaker for her own children in the six-year interim of 1665–71, she was not shut off from them as a cloistered nun might have been. In 1671, she took the girls into the school she founded. Over this period of her life, Sor Catalina occupied several positions at once. As mother, niece, reformer, and entrepreneur, she proved herself a fighter—against the pulls of the flesh and the limitations of society—throughout her lifetime. These battles are reflected in the text, where the tensions that result from Bernique's multiple subject positions as priest, biographer, and son center on the family and the flesh as the primary sources of conflict in both his life and hers.

Bernique adopts an elliptical strategy to discuss potentially discomfiting issues. Because the author fails to relate what became of his sisters and himself when Catalina took religious vows, the reader is left to assume that the aunt became the caretaker. Interestingly, Bernique depicts his surrogate mother with a certain tolerance and even affection, while Catalina's anecdotes express ambivalence and irritation toward her aunt, who most directly felt the effects of her niece's refusal to capitulate to social pressures. Bernique does not condemn this woman for forcing Catalina to marry or for continually pressuring her to ease her religious fervor, for example. To the contrary, he mentions the tensions between the two women and justifies his aunt's reactions. The burden of having a beata in the family emerges in Bernique's descriptions of his aunt's experiences. She felt ashamed of her niece's insistence on gathering water at the public well and sweeping the streets to show humility. She also tried to intervene to stop Catalina's severe program of self-mortification, accusing the young woman and her confessor of attempting to kill Catalina.

By Bernique's own admission, Sor Catalina's aunt "complained about everything with a rare impertinence." Bernique's interpretation of the relationship rests on an ideal of familial love. He explains that his great aunt loved his mother tenderly and this, in combination with her old age, accounted for her behavior.[41] Catalina's interpretation diverges sharply from Bernique's benign justifications, however: "I felt much repugnance and aversion toward my aunt, in whom God gave me a challenge that, if I had managed well, would have been enough to become a saint."[42]

Sor Catalina's aunt served as a surrogate mother to her and, presumably, to her children. Bernique's optimistic portrait of this difficult personality reflects his efforts to depict an expansive definition of motherhood that reconciles his mother's abandonment of her children with the model motherhood she enacts as a woman religious. In other words, Bernique had to reconcile Catalina Bernique with Catalina de Jesús in order to reach a saintly portrayal of his mother. Once the vida reaches the stage of Catalina de Jesús's life in the convent, this task becomes much easier. Bernique highlights her talent for fostering good relationships among her spiritual daughters and gives extensive attention to her greatest achievement: the founding of a school for girls.

Book 3 of *Idea of Perfection* concentrates on the sacrifices demanded by the decision to found the school. Bernique praises his mother for filling a need in the community of Alcalá. He points out, for example, that in spite of the abundance of institutions for male education, the community lacked girls' schools.[43] Sor Catalina spent both economic and emotional capital on the foundation; she gave all her worldly goods to the endeavor and fought to overcome her aunt's opposition to the project. The two women's entrepreneurial ambitions become apparent here. Sor Catalina's aunt ran a university-oriented printing press in her home, and she was unwilling to quit her profession and be displaced just to allow her house to be filled with other women's children. Yet Sor Catalina insisted on dismantling the business, Bernique explains, "because a place with many people coming through on a daily basis could not be a good girls' school."[44]

The women eventually reached an agreement by which the aunt would move to the back of the house and the school would open. They worked together to publicize the school as place in which girls could learn to live as good Catholics. Bernique attributes the success of the school to his mother's reputation: "[M]any people impressed by the fame of her sanctity turned their girls over to her so that they would grow up educated with her virtue and good example."[45] The school also accepted orphaned girls, so Sor Catalina spent much of her time in search of support. Even though she had received paying students at the beginning, her goal was to accept no tuition

and run the school as a charity. Pressed by priests and others to take payments for the girls' upkeep, she remained devoted to the idea of a religious
school in which students gained entry based on their religious beliefs and
needs, and not on their ability to pay. Although this commitment necessi-
tated patronage-seeking trips, which Catalina hated, she remained dedicated
to this ideal until the end of her life.[46]

The preponderance of maternal language throughout the sections on religious life forges a strong link between Catalina de Jesús and motherhood.
Bernique mentions that Catalina showed great fervor in bodily mortification but urged her spiritual daughters to use restraint, and he stresses that
this practice exemplified her strong leadership as a spiritual mother.[47] In a
powerful moment, Sor Catalina herself connects maternity to the very act
of writing her autobiography. Recalling a time when she had been asked to
write her life story, she is said to describe a vision that she had of the Virgin
and the Christ child. Jesus first appeared in Mary's hands and then:

> He hung himself on from my neck, and the delight and pleasure I felt in
> my soul were so intense that it is not easy to explain. Our Lady let a ray
> of milk flow from her saintly breasts to my lips, and it seemed to me that
> this was meant as my sustenance, to help me write what they had com-
> manded me to write.[48]

Descriptions of breastfeeding appear commonly in religious women's writing, often with the Christ child dispensing the milk. Here, however, we find
Mary nurturing Sor Catalina, thus bringing further nuance to Sor Catalina's
vision, in which she acts as mother and child, nurturer and nurtured.

Bernique's gloss on the vision adds yet another layer to the issue of maternal identity, as he focuses on the triangle between his mother, the Christ
child, and the Holy Mother. Bernique emphasizes that Catalina could not
express the powerful emotions invoked by Christ's caresses. Then:

> The Virgin gave her enough to reach the summit of her favors, to enjoy
> the purest nectars of her virginal and sacred breasts, either to purify her
> lips and write what [Catalina's] confessor had ordered, as she affirms, or
> so that she recognized herself as an adopted daughter, and as one raised
> at the cost of her care, [the Virgin] made her a participant in these sov-
> ereign, sweet gestures of her fortunate breasts.[49]

This passage identifies Catalina de Jesús as part of a trinity in which she
played the role of mother and adopted daughter. Bernique reiterates the
tranquility Catalina de Jesús experienced in a vision in which she appeared

both as a mother holding a child at her breast and as a suckling child. Bernique's interpretation repeats his mother's conflation of maternal and child-like fantasies. The dual roles of mother and child also reflect Bernique's position: As biographer, he acts as spiritual father, yet he cannot escape the mother/son bond. The parallels evoke an unspoken comparison: Unlike Sor Catalina in her vision, Father Bernique did not experience the nurture of a mother fully devoted to her young.

Sor Catalina's failings as a mother in the secular world are evoked indirectly through numerous examples of metaphorical maternity. In addition to emphasizing her role as spiritual mother to many women and girls, Bernique observes that the maternal bonds between Catalina and others extended far beyond the convent:

> So continuous was her assistance in the hospitals, so frequent her visits to the needy and the sick in the poor sections of town that with her piety she won the name of Mother from those whom she helped with so much charity.[50]

Even the two miracles narrated by Bernique revolve around the protective function of motherhood, as they both relate to Catalina's having twice saved the life of one of her spiritual daughters.[51]

The biography represents Catalina de Jesús as a perfect metaphorical mother. Protective, innovative, nurturing, and ambitious, Sor Catalina worked to expand her influence through both prayer and practice. The poor and the religious benefited from her work. Mary Elizabeth Perry, in a discussion of beatas who performed social work and religious instruction, notes that the women forsook biological motherhood and "assumed the role of universal mother in protecting and nurturing others."[52] While this dynamic held true for Catalina de Jesús, the representation of her life portrays her with a large degree of ambiguity. Her son implies that almost everyone believed that his mother sacrificed her children's needs to her own religiously inspired desires. In particular, he notes that she faced tremendous opposition to many of her charitable activities before she took the habit:

> She suffered much criticism from her aunt and relatives, who disparaged and belittled her charitable work, judging that this kind of piety was more than a little dangerous in a nice looking young woman. But even though this was the pretext, the truth of the feeling was the danger posed to her health and to that of her children, but none of this could stop the flow of her piety.[53]

Bernique's rhetoric here protects the image of his family and of his mother. Specifically, he relates the controversy created by Catalina's work at the hospitals but then justifies his family's criticism with the valid point that she risked her children's health by engaging in this kind of charity. Bernique first validates the opinion of those who were concerned for the children's well-being, then puts an end to the criticism by casting Sor Catalina's behavior as unreproachably pious.

This dynamic of assertion followed by counter assertion exemplifies a compulsive force at work in Bernique's text. The numerous examples of piety, spiritual motherhood, miracles, and commitment to reform show that Catalina de Jesús adopted the role of mother in her religious context once she took the veil at age twenty-six. Bernique does not content himself with this adaptation. He also seeks throughout the vida to redeem Catalina's performance as a biological mother. When detailing her work in founding and maintaining the school, he does not lose an opportunity to emphasize her admirable behavior with regard to her own children. Yet such comparisons often result in ambiguous statements such as this:

> She also enclosed her two girls in [the school] with her in the example of the patriarch Noah, who brought his children onto the ark that he built for the salvation of the human race. Since the first obligation is that to our own [families], it would not be right to raise others' children and to forget about one's own.[54]

Guided by the imperatives of hagiography, Bernique depicts Sor Catalina as performing a valuable service for God and the community. Yet the subsequent moralizing statement on the obligations of parenthood potentially undermines this portrayal, making us wonder if Bernique meant to praise Catalina for taking in her girls or, perhaps at some subconscious level, to condemn her for leaving her children behind in pursuit of what he calls in his title an "idea of perfection." The remark about the obligation to one's own children becomes doubly vexed when we realize that Catalina left her son behind when she took her daughters into the school. The reader cannot help but wonder what became of the son when the family home was transformed into a female community.

The juxtaposition of high praise with ambivalent commentary encapsulates Bernique's treatment of motherhood throughout the text. In describing the difficulties of Catalina's early years, for example, Bernique points out his mother's aversion to feeling tied down by her family duties, then casts her coping skills in a positive light. That is, while marriage constituted an experience of "terrible martyrdom" and "continual violence," Catalina handled the situation by practicing exemplary religious devotion.[55] In turn, this devotion led Catalina to join the Poor Claires. As Bernique's narrative tries to convince us, the decision allowed her to have an impact that was felt widely throughout the community of Alcalá. In comparing Catalina Bernique's life with that of Catalina de Jesús, we can see that the two are most intimately connected through the rubric of motherhood. While child rearing held little appeal for Catalina, the many contours of spiritual motherhood allowed her to expand her scope of influence. In representing Catalina as an educator, leader, and reformer, the text shows the success with which the young widow modified the role of motherhood to fit her own ambitions.

COLLABORATION AND CONTROL

The inclusion of Catalina's autobiographical materials in *Idea of Perfection* raises the question of whether the generic imperatives of religious biography differ significantly from those of autobiography. The production of spiritual biography requires the manipulation of the subject's image. Bernique's decision to excerpt Catalina's writings rather than edit them in their entirety speaks to this manipulation. He chose to include (or give the impression of including) primary sources that would help him provide an outline of the story that he wanted to present to the public. While many of Sor Catalina's excerpts solidify her religiosity, they also present various psychological affronts to her family. As her spiritual biographer, Bernique responded to the mandate to represent Catalina de Jesús as a saintly woman: He was in control of image and text. As a man whose psychic life was tied intimately to his subject, Bernique was on less stable ground. The strategies he used to explain his mother's words and actions point to a struggle for control. The rhetorical struggle reflected in Bernique's glosses suggests that, even after death, Catalina de Jesús managed to have a collaborative, perhaps even controlling, hand in the production of her biography.

Many of the tensions in *Idea of Perfection* relate to the direct expression in Catalina de Jesús's writings. In response to his mother's succinct, no-holds-barred discussions of sex and motherhood, Juan Bernique often resorted to elliptical rhetoric in his glosses. To decipher the interplay between mother and son, we must keep in mind the gendered views of religion in the larger context of pre-eighteenth-century Europe. Mooney's overview of male- versus female-authored medieval hagiography notes one relevant point of divergence between the two: "In those cases where women appear to speak in their own voices, they speak of themselves in decidedly more active and assertive terms than do their male promoters."[56] Certainly, in the case of *Idea of Perfection*, the male and female voices differ in tone and style.

Catalina de Jesús's writings contain an assertive quality that is almost surprising at times. No quotations express regret about the choices she made in leaving her life as a mother and wife, for example. To the contrary, she is said to have written about the benefits of religious life over marriage and to have exhibited great impatience with religious women who fail to appreciate their situation:

> I cannot stand it when I see nuns complaining about silly little things: that they're missing this or that, that their schedule got changed, that they had to eat later or earlier, . . . and other things of this nature. If they had the burden of marriage, they would experience having to do all this and much more, and how they would have to obey, if not willfully then by force, and with less merit and less consolation because there is no enlightenment like there is in that which is done for God.[57]

In addition to giving us insight into the quibbles and complaints of convent life, Catalina here details the advantages of not being married to a man and of the relatively light workload of a nun.

Bernique glosses this passage of two-and-a-half pages: In his estimation, these words were written to console women who choose religion over marriage.[58] Yet Catalina de Jesús is said to have more than passionately defended religious life; she also denounced the burdens of marriage and motherhood:

> What an intolerable thing is it to suffer the burden of having and raising children? What exercise can there be in the spiritual life that is as painful as this? I confess that everything I have suffered since God called me to him has seemed small compared to the intolerable trials of marriage. My confessor used to think that the time that I spent praying at night was a lot, and he let me know this and I laughed and I don't know if I told him, How many more bad nights did I spend raising my children? I used to sleep less and I walked around more fatigued and without the relief that God gives to those who spend the night keeping Him company.[59]

In this excerpt—perhaps from the autobiography that she did not burn or from a letter to her confessor—Sor Catalina confronts the problems that face mothers and wives. Her quotes here claim that marriage to God is far superior to marriage to an "imperfect, coarse man." In moments such as these, Catalina de Jesús so clearly articulates the burdens placed on women by marriage and motherhood that she temporarily manages to denaturalize these hallowed institutions.

In many other moments, however, the nun relies on elusive rhetoric to

explain her experiences. This elusivity relates to two commonplaces of religious writing: the humility trope, by which writers claim an inability to
express themselves; and the language of mysticism, in which one attempts
to articulate the ineffable joy of union with God.[60] Interestingly, Sor Catalina used a combination of these when attempting to discuss the difficulties
not of mysticism but of married life: "One faces so many challenges [in mar-
riage] that I find myself lacking words to explain them."[61] Words had not
failed her to this point, and such elusivity contrasts wildly with the straightforward quality of many of her autobiographical fragments.

Elliptical language also infuses the chapter that catalogues Sor Catalina's brushes with sin. Admitting to her struggles with vanity, chastity,
and obedience, she notes on various occasions that she cannot adequately
explain her gratitude to God.[62] God called attention to her vanity, for
example, by giving her such a strong palsy that she had to take medica-
tion to ease its effects. During her marriage, her chastity was tested by a
male acquaintance who visited her to discuss spiritual matters. It turned
out that the visitor had ulterior motives, but because he had connections
to her household, Catalina could not dismiss him out of hand. Sor Catalina writes with much humility about these episodes, yet it is important to
note that she emphasizes these as minor errors in judgment rather than
full-blown sin. On the matter of her body, she writes: "On one occasion
complacency overcame me and left me completely bathed in vanity, staring
at my feet." As to the man with improper intentions, Sor Catalina notes: "I
recognize that I have done nothing."[63] In an effort to avoid further uncom-
fortable situations, though, she vowed to never speak of spiritual matters
with anybody but God.

In contrast to the presentation of Sor Catalina's words as downplaying her weaknesses, Bernique finds much to moralize about in this text.
In terms of her vanity, Bernique notes that God kept his mother in line by
"punishing even the slightest fault."[64] With regard to the male visitor with
questionable motives, however, Bernique muses about the challenge posed
by Sor Catalina's vow to speak only with God, since women "desire to speak
with everyone at all times about spiritual matters."[65] At the end of the chapter that catalogues Catalina's battles against temptation, Bernique notes that
spiritual pleasure can lead to physical pleasure, and that this link "is more
common in the feminine sex where, due to much fragility and natural weakness, this occurs more easily."[66]

Such moralizing comments, which are sprinkled throughout the text,
form part of a group of strategies Bernique uses to gain control of his
mother's life. On a general level, these narrative techniques relate to the challenges of writing spiritual biography. Like any such author seeking a cogent

representation of sanctity, Bernique rewrote the life story of his subject to fit reader expectations. Yet the highly personal nature of his relationship to his subject infused his interpretations, particularly of the issues that most deeply affected him. Specifically, Bernique's editing, interpretive, and moralizing techniques reveal the psychological challenges posed to this son/biographer. Bernique's emotional issues emerge in his interpretive glosses and the form in which he presents his mother's words to the reader.

In book 2, nearly one hundred pages after the lengthy explanations of Catalina's marriage, widowhood, and self-transformation, Bernique invokes his mother's married life in the middle of an otherwise unrelated discussion of her vanity. Once again striving to explain Sor Catalina's disinclination to marry, Bernique attributes her difficulties to her pride and self-esteem, from which "originated the great unease that she experienced while married, because any yoke of subjection and surrender was intolerable for her."[67] Bernique, who in Book 1 discusses marriage as contrary to Catalina's nature, comes back to the topic in this chapter on her faults and spiritual challenges. Religion taught Sor Catalina what marriage could not: Her confessor instructed her in proper humility when he told her to sweep the streets by day and to fetch water in the town square with a bucket on her shoulder by night. Bernique applauds the pedagogical impact of these actions, explaining that while Catalina caused a stir among her family members, others learned from her humble behavior (*Idea*, p. 93).

Bernique's analysis of Catalina's marriage provides an excellent example of his vexed relationship to text and subject. Since no quotations from Catalina support any aspect of the narrative on her vanity and humility, the connection between spiritual and marital submission rests solely in Bernique's hands. By making the leap from Catalina's humility to her failure to submit to her husband, the son reveals his own preoccupation (obsession, perhaps?) with explaining his parents' unhappy marriage.

In addition to his moralistic stances, Bernique engages in a much less subtle assertion of control of his mother's words and life story. In most of the text he uses quotation marks to set off Catalina's words, which he sometimes introduces by saying that they are taken from letters to confessors. Occasionally, Bernique abandons this formal apparatus, leaving readers to wonder about the sources of his materials, as well as the legitimacy of the words. The appropriation of first-person discourse represents the most egregious slippage between the voice of the subject and of the biographer. Of the soul searching and physical pain in Catalina's life, Bernique explains: "Her affliction was so great that it made her burst out these words: End my life, dear Lord, and do not keep torturing me with your absence."[68] Notably, no italics or quotation marks set these words off from the rest of the text, suggesting that they belong to Catalina but leaving one in serious doubt that she wrote them.

In the next chapter, Bernique progresses to a more direct form of rhetorical appropriation. Chapter 10 of book 2 discusses the difficulties Catalina de Jesús had with the Inquisition. Called in for questioning and held under house arrest for three weeks, Sor Catalina lived in fear of the tribunal, and acquaintances often asked her, "Sister, when will they take you to the Inquisition?"[69] While serving as a stylistic technique here, this indirect discourse carries over into Bernique's treatment of his mother. In some instances, Bernique relies on memory to relay his mother's words, repeating, for example, her advice about piety.[70] In others, he appropriates his mother's voice without citing a source. Bernique claims, for example, that during the time she feared the Inquisition, his mother prayed:

> Dear God, she said to him, it is not possible for me to just accept this. If I were alone without my children, relatives, and young girls depending on me, and without the exterior decoration of the habit of my father Saint Frances, then I would throw myself with great gusto into sacrificing myself [to the Inquisition].[71]

Bernique does not cite a source for these prayers, nor does he place them in italics as he does the rest of Sor Catalina's texts. It is hard to believe that this passage and others like it amount to more than narrative embellishment.

Bernique employs this embellishing strategy several times in the middle section of the vida. The terror caused by the Inquisition's interest in Sor Catalina provides the occasion for this appropriative rhetoric. This might be attributable to a lack of documentation about this period in the beata's life, as it is likely that she felt too fearful to commit her thoughts to paper while the Inquisition breathed down her neck.[72] While *Idea of Perfection* details Catalina's fear of the tribunal, it gives little attention to her possible offenses. Like many uncloistered religious women—including those in tertiary orders like the Poor Claires—Catalina found herself under suspicion, possibly for the work she did in her school or for her spirituality.[73] In the former case, Sor Catalina would have been under fire to defend the school's pious, doctrinal approach to girls' education; in the latter, the Inquisition would have questioned the heterodoxy of her spiritual experiences. To my knowledge, no record of the inquisitorial inquiry remains, so its focus remains unclear. Evidently she succeeded in convincing inquisitors of her innocence, for the school remained open and Catalina remained free until her death in 1677.

The Inquisition's inquiries attest to the threat that independent women like Catalina posed to their society. Living without the protection that marriage afforded other women of her time, Catalina de Jesús forged a life in which she was neither of this world nor of a cloister. She fought familial battles to accomplish her spiritual goals of taking vows and establishing a religious school for girls. She ignored the advice of her family and took religious vows; she disregarded warnings about disease and continued to work with the sick in the hospitals; she wrote with great directness about the conflicts she had with her aunt and her confessor. The details of her clashes with family members and confessors confirm that Catalina de Jesús was a headstrong woman who, in spite of an unhappy marriage in her early years, redefined the course of her life upon becoming a widow.

We know these details, of course, only because Catalina Bernique's son deemed it appropriate to write his mother's life story. However, we can see that the control that Catalina de Jesús exerted over her identity and legend extended well beyond her death. While she did not present her autobiographical text to the world, she did collaborate in the production of her *vida*. She wrote her autobiography twice, yet burned it only once. She wrote detailed letters to confessors about her daily life, and she prophesied that her son would become her historian. By making the proclamation about her son's future role years before her death, Catalina de Jesús virtually insured that someone invested in her memory would write her spiritual biography.

In life, Catalina de Jesús was a force with which inquisitors, confessors, and family members had to contend. In death, she continued to loom large in the imagination of her only son. Burdened by the authority that Catalina de Jesús accumulated as a mother, spiritual leader, and, finally, as a prophet, Juan Bernique complied with the onerous task of convincing readers that this woman who rejected motherhood was indeed an exemplary biological and spiritual mother. Perhaps Bernique had an awareness of the different forces pulling on him as he wrote *Idea of Perfection*. Consciously or not, he incorporated the ambivalence of his subject position into the biography. In one telling moment, he even seems to give voice to the struggle of the son/biographer when he writes that one cannot be truly religious "with one eye looking toward God and another attending to the world and all its vanities."[74] As a woman with three children, Catalina de Jesús did attend to the world. As a middle-class woman of relative privilege and strong will, she managed to change the course of her life by adopting the roles that spiritual motherhood afforded some women of her time.

While we would expect a spiritual biography to exalt the otherworldliness of its subject, the identity of the author and the strategies of representation in *Idea of Perfection* actually tie Catalina de Jesús to her very worldly existence as a mother, reformer, and educator. The psychological complexity of this vida relates to Catalina's calculated collaboration in the production of her life story. An ambitious woman who broke out of the roles that society prescribed for her, Catalina de Jesús found an ingenious means by which to collaborate in her own self-representation: She mandated that her son produce the story of her life. Juan Bernique controlled the representation of his mother's sanctity, and his psychological issues pepper the text with ambiguity and complexity. In the end, he served as the filter through which the world could know his mother. Catalina's prophecy was ingenious precisely because it recognized the difficult task of fitting her life story into a standard spiritual narrative. In order for a positive image of Catalina de Jesús y San Francisco to be preserved for history, several issues had to be cast in a positive light. Her hatred of marriage, distaste for biological motherhood, and rebellion against family pressures required explanation. While a story of female sanctity might accommodate a woman's hatred of sex and marriage as part of her religious destiny, the issues of abandoned children and disobedience to one's husband demanded a more sophisticated narrative treatment.

Bernique handled this task well, all the while doing double duty as biographer and son. As a biographer, he produced a clean narrative of sanctity. As a son, he was forced to explain the life choices that his mother had made. In that she took control over the narrative of her life, Catalina abdicated the responsibility that others might have put on her to explain and justify her decision to become a religious woman. Catalina de Jesús made specific choices, many of which were available to her because of her class privilege and, therefore, the lack of serious economic hardship that likely would have focused her attention on meeting basic needs. As with Céspedes and Manuel, the textual evidence of Catalina de Bernique's life depends on presentating an individual's negotiation of limited definitions of gender. Like Manuel, Sor Catalina helped shape the representation of her life story by writing her own versions of it and ensuring that those texts remained in the hands of those who sat in judgment of women's femininity and spirituality. As in the fiction of Mariana de Carvajal and, likewise, the defense of Bernarda Manuel, the role of motherhood plays an important role in Sor Catalina's auto/biography. Yet unlike many other records of women's life stories in early modern Spain, Sor Catalina's vida reveals a self-conscious restyling of a woman who rejected the roles of wife and mother in the secular world, only to rewrite those for her own purposes in the convent. The level of control exerted by this woman religious comes through as one of the most important aspects of the text.

By prophesying that her son would be her biographer, Catalina strategically pressured him to work through the psychic implications of her unorthodox rejection of secular femininity. Rather than leave her reputation in the hands of those who might have written her life story to conform to the model of femininity she had rejected, Sor Catalina chose a biographer over whom she exerted control. Juan Bernique's version of the life story of Catalina de Jesús articulates the pressures of femininity and justifies the rejection of secular motherhood.

In life and in death, Sor Catalina de Jesús rewrote femininity to fit her spiritual and personal needs, as she refused to conform to society's prescribed gender roles. Sor Catalina's biography reveals the conflicting imperatives that faced women, as well as the difficulties that faced relatives of women who failed to conform to social expectations. Laying bare the pressures on a young woman who sought to free herself from the secular world, *Idea of Perfection* delineates the consequences of the restrictive gender codes of early modern Spain.

PART IV

Women's Networks
Leadership and Community

7

Single Women

The Price of Independence

While early modern culture legitimized the roles of nun, wife, and mother, some women neither entered the convent nor married. Others became single through separation or abandonment. These phenomena created two categories of single women: the "never married" and the "ever married."[1] As suggested by the stories in this and the next chapter, marital status in the era inextricably connects to women's educational, economic, and social history. The economic circumstances of single women differed, yet they often managed to be self-sufficient. Many lived among and with other women and even forged professional idetities. Precisely because single women often created economic and social niches for themselves, their stories contain remarkable information about the strategies and networks that unmarried women developed to survive in a culture hostile to their very identity. Because of the women's frequent marginality, many of their stories do not figure in the annals of history. Yet when these can be recovered—through legal, inquisitional, or personal records—we gain access to the economic, social, and religious networks such women sustained. We also can better understand that the texts produced by and about single women—including nuns, beatas, prophets, and practitioners of black magic—document strategies used to justify unorthodox choices and beliefs.

In combination with a generalized view of women as secondary citizens, society's idealization of chastity and motherhood meant that single women often were viewed with a large degree of suspicion. Whether they were ever married (such as widows and abandoned wives) or never married, single women were exposed to disapprobation and scrutiny because of the absence of male protectors in their lives.

Society's anxiety and watchfulness varied with regard to single women of differing categories. People viewed nuns as doing God's work and took comfort in knowing that men oversaw convents. Yet if nuns ran afoul of the church hierarchy, they, too, might find themselves facing the disapprobation of a society that had little tolerance for autonomous, unattached women.[2] While many upper-class nuns enjoyed special privilege afforded few others, numerous cases of nuns tried for suspect religious practices confirm that the convent walls did not guarantee protection from the Inquisition.

Beatas were likely to raise suspicion precisely because they lacked the protection afforded nuns living in convents. While they voluntarily took vows and often had nominal affiliations with religious orders, these independent women posed a threat to a society that endorsed female submission and enclosure. The beata Catalina de Jesús, for example, experienced this suspicion when the Inquisition placed her under house arrest. Even more marginal to mainstream society, prophets and those who practiced black magic often were unmarried women who gained popular and inquisitorial attention for circumventing conventional belief systems.

Single women, particularly those of the lower and middle classes, faced heightened watchfulness in early modern Spain. Due to the intensity with which negative views toward autonomous women permeated Spanish culture of the period, single women's life stories reveal the risks involved in unorthodox femininity. Whether they were nuns or laywomen, entrepreneurs or servants, prophets or sorcerers, aristocratic or poor, women who did not marry or remarry often found themselves on the margins of society. Lacking the economic support of a male head of household, many faced financial hardship. Forbidden from running businesses or seeking legal recourse, they lacked the legitimacy afforded women in traditional family units.

The last two chapters of *The Lives of Women* focus on single women and the communities they created. These chapters offer new ways to think about Hispanic women's history by focusing on women who positioned themselves as leaders, advisors, and reformers. Ranging from nuns and sorcerers to aristocrats and the poor, these active women flaunted prohibitions on female autonomy. A lack of primary sources means that other women who similarly challenged the misogynist status quo—such as prostitutes, gypsies, and healers—do not figure in these analyses, but such women's stories also might be examined in terms of individuals and their female-centered networks. Through the reconstruction of the advisory and leadership roles women played in their respective communities, Chapters 7 and 8 thus bring individual tales to the level of the community. The analyses demonstrate that, in a society in which all major institutions—family, religion, politics— lay in the hands of men, women of various class backgrounds managed to position themselves as educators, leaders, and reformers. This final section thus highlights women's leadership and educational activities and identifies the strategies single women used to create, sustain, and defend spheres of influence.

COMMUNITY AND SPIRITUALITY

Sor Catalina's story in Chapter 6 gives us a sense of women's extensive community involvement. Women ran schools, convents, and small businesses. They functioned as community leaders, educators, and reformers. They worked as vendors, seamstresses, and healers, and often pieced together a living based on a combination of these activities. Yet, as female spirituality became increasingly suspect in the wake of the Counter-Reformation, independent, high-profile, or otherwise extraordinary women were more likely to run into trouble with the authorities. Spain did not persecute witches on a grand scale. Nonetheless, Inquisition trials for witchcraft and sorcery disproportionately involved women.[3] Like numerous Illuminist and converso cases, sorcery trials document the threat posed by alternative beliefs. Both types of cases, and the documents produced about them, show that the marginalized in fact often lived at the center of extensive community networks sustained by individuals who subscribed to those beliefs.[4]

The dangerous combination of popularity with heterodoxy stands out as the common denominator in the stories of four single women who occupied important roles in their communities in seventeenth-century Castile. The strategies used by each woman to insert herself into the dominant culture met with varied results. The unorthodox spiritual expression of María de Orozco y Luján (1635–1709) marked her as an outcast when she was young, yet she eventually managed to craft a pious identity. On the other hand, the trial of Teresa Valle de la Cerda, an aristocrat who founded a convent and then was tried by the Inquisition, exemplifies the dangers of building an unorthodox spiritual community. Like Valle de la Cerda, the uneducated Lucrecia de León followed a trajectory that led her from popularity to condemnation. León, whose dreams became the grist for political scandal, enjoyed a cult following until the Inquisition put an end to her prophetic career. León's downfall stemmed from the public and political nature of her prophecies. Similarly, the witchcraft trial of María Romero illustrates the tenuous position of women who ran businesses based on black magic. The Romero case exemplifies the risks run by those who made their living casting spells and reading cards. Together, the stories of Orozco, Valle, León, and Romero reveal the community ties formed by single women whose unorthodox beliefs and behaviors helped them find a place in society and, simultaneously, put them at risk of inquisitorial prosecution.

These single women enjoyed varying degrees of independence, security,

and popularity. At one point or another, they all suffered consequences for
their nonconformity. Focusing on interpersonal relationships, the following
analysis reconstructs the roles each woman played in her community and
the difficulties each faced in her search for legitimacy. This discussion of the
individuals' economic, political, and social savoir faire brings into view the
roles of unorthodox, unattached women in the seventeenth century. Each
woman examined here has a specific story, yet all the stories represent the
challenges that single women posed to the status quo. Through these individual stories, the chapter throws into relief the strategies by which women
whom society defined as marginal in fact asserted their independence and
authority and, through their spiritual and economic activities, helped others
do the same.

THE MARGINS OF PIETY: BEATAS AND NUNS

In addition to trial records as sources about women's lives, the biographies
and correspondence of individuals who escaped inquisitorial persecution
provide rich information about the survival strategies and daily lives of
women whose beliefs put them dangerously close to the edges of society.
The story of María de Orozco, for example, who was shunned and then revered for her unusual spirituality, comes to us through two biographies and
nearly three thousand letters.[5] One anecdote from her teen years illustrates
Orozco's battles with heterodoxy: While preparing a meal in a girls' school
run by the Discalced Carmelite nuns of Guadalajara, Spain, Orozco saw a
ball of dough fly out of a frying pan. The hot grease severely burned her face
and fingers and blinded her in both eyes.[6] After Orozco recovered from the
injuries, questions about her demonic associations led to her ouster from
the school. Years later, she was turned out of a convent for similarly disrup-
tive behavior. Although Orozco was rejected and ridiculed by institutionalized religion, she eventually earned the respect of those around her and
became a respected beata.

Sixteenth- and seventeenth-century definitions of spirituality adversely
affected women who had enjoyed relative freedom with regard to mystical
and unconventional religiosity before the Counter-Reformation.[7] Thus it is
not surprising that the Inquisition looms large in texts that deal with unconventional female spirituality. One of the biographies of María de Orozco
alludes to a generalized fear of the Holy Office. When Orozco lived in a
Discalced Carmelite convent, a church official came to investigate reports of
the novice's spirituality. He declared the situation dangerous and explicitly
warned of future problems with the Inquisition (*Vida*, fol. 5v).

These examples show that, as a beata, Orozco formed part of a sector of the population whose powers of faith, prophesy, or healing attracted the attention of those concerned with orthodoxy.[8] There was a fine line between being viewed as an enthusiastic Catholic and as in collusion with the devil. Furthermore, religious practice that served a person well in one context could result in persecution in others. The arbitrary nature of these distinctions sometimes made it difficult to avoid conflicts with the authorities. It is clear, for instance, that the combination of unusual spirituality with power or popularity often resulted in inquisitorial investigations.

Orozco's biographers seem to have recognized the dangers of their subject's spirituality. One of her biographers, who also had been her confessor, seeks to cast blame for Orozco's difficulties with the church. Lamenting the absence of enlightened advisors in Orozco's early life, the biographer narrates an incident in which the devil undressed the young girl and held her hostage. Confirming Orozco's spiritual blessedness, a miracle occurred and she found herself dressed and ready for prayer when another sister entered her room after the devil had left. All of this might have gone unnoticed were it not for the devil's reappearance in the choir, where he beat Orozco until she screamed. This raucous behavior left the other nuns thinking "that it was not the best idea to have Orozco in their company."[9] On another occasion, the devil undressed Orozco and placed her in an outdoor pool. This time he set her free just in time to appear dressed and ready for confession. A third disruption occurred when the devil tortured and spoke through her for several hours, leaving her bruised and unable to eat.

Writing many years after the events, Orozco's biographer attributed the problems created by these incidents to the young woman's lack of spiritual guidance. He blamed her ouster from the convent on the inexperienced priest who had little practice detecting the devil's presence. Another priest likewise concluded at the time that nothing definite could be determined about Orozco's spirituality.[10] Few others had such sympathetic views. Orozco's family went so far as to blame her for causing her mother's mental illness and for shaming them all.

It is difficult to interpret such experiences within a modern framework, but we might speculate that the challenges faced by María de Orozco may have included mental illness such as was suffered by her mother. Without such an explanation, it is difficult to explain Orozco's volatile behavior and the instances of undressing or screaming. Her experiences were so odd that not even her contemporaries could find any credible explanation for them. Orozco may have suffered from schizophrenia, an illness that would account for her erratic behavior and paranormal experiences. This interpretation of Orozco's life story also incorporates the judgments of her contemporaries, who were quick to assign demonic possession to women's unusual experiences. The speculation also highlights a triumphant aspect of Orozco's life. In spite of her struggles with conformity and orthodoxy, María de Orozco managed to earn a saintly reputation as a beata affiliated with the Discalced order.

Orozco's biographies and letters detail the daily struggle of a woman of the middle classes to establish the sanctimonious reputation that, in 1683, would allow her to affiliate with the religious order she idolized.[11] The transformation from reviled outsider to revered holy woman relates as much to religiosity as to femininity. Orozco and her biographers fashioned a public image of a woman whose devotion to God led her to pass up opportunities for marriage and conventional home life. Although for many years she found herself on the outside of communities of women and of her own family, she forged an identity that allowed her independence and religious recognition.

The astounding amount of material on Orozco focuses on her lifelong singularity. Francisco Bravo Tamargo's 1719 biography details her difficult birth, a surprising recovery from a fall, and the miracle of her instantaneously acquired ability to read and write.[12] By the same token, all four biographies detail Orozco's rebellious, nonconformist impulse. Much like the adventurous young Teresa of Avila, who wanted to escape with her brother to a faraway land, Orozco used to wear her brother's shorts and climb trees. Described as an energetic girl with a "manly spirit" (*ánimo varonil*), Orozco had a precocious, troublemaking streak.[13]

Tales of a difficult life are the backbone of hagiography, and there is no shortage of them in Orozco's vidas and her own letters. References to poverty appear frequently in her letters, for example. Given that Orozco never married, did not belong to the upper class, and managed two households with little money, the emphasis on scarce economic reserves makes sense. Like other hagiographic texts, her vidas and even her letters detail her ongoing physical ailments. This focus might be a reflection of a narrative strategy aimed at portraying Orozco as a martyr. It might also reflect the real physical ailments that resulted from her self-mortification or poverty. Orozco's physical and emotional difficulties began in childhood. In particular, a year spent with an abusive half-sister and her husband left a mark on the six-year-old. As one biographer describes it, the sister whipped Orozco with sharp cords, made her drink dirty water, and in spite of the child's age, punished her for crying.[14] Isabel Barbeito Carneiro describes an incident in which the beata's uncle approached the young woman with the intent of sexually assaulting her.[15]

Ousted from a convent and a religious school, alienated from her family, and ill-treated by those around her, María de Orozco nonetheless developed strategies by which she managed to earn a saintly reputation. She cultivated a virtuous existence in which she refused all feminine accoutrements (including makeup) and embraced what she described as an ugly physical appearance. Moreover, various biographies portray Orozco's virtue in direct relation to her refusal to marry. As she rejected more and more men, Orozco's reputation as a virtuous woman improved. Having used the pressures of femininity to her advantage and thereby manipulated her public image, she found herself in a position of power for the first time ever. She turned down marriage proposals, refused to enter the new Carmelite convent founded in 1684, and dedicated herself to religious work.

A nominal affiliation with the Carmelites provided Orozco a route to economic and spiritual independence. Although she complained of poverty in the almost daily letters she wrote to confessors over the years, she managed to support her household and her sister's by doing laundry for the Discalced Carmelites. This labor represented only a portion of Orozco's daily life. The documents also tell of assisting her sister in childbirth, helping a divorced niece, and performing numerous miracles. The narratives of miracles in the various biographies on Orozco raise the question of heterodoxy and inquisitorial vigilance. Inquisitors often investigated women for suspect religious practices. Yet Orozco's case provides an example of how the decreased vigilance of beata life allowed Orozco more room for mystical spirituality than she ever found in a religious house. The thousands of pages about María de Orozco's life confirm that a religious laywoman could enjoy a large degree of independence in early modern Spain. This independence was made possible by the cultivation of community trust; it was sustained by an extensive network of women who benefited from Orozco's services.

In addition to painting a portrait of an elaborate community network that sustained her, Orozco's letters reveal a woman tormented by physical and psychological pain. Uncertain if she ever was baptized, convinced that she was crazy, and plagued by severe physical ailments, Orozco continued to feel challenged even after the Carmelites accepted her as a beata. Her letters record struggles with illness, poverty, and devotion. Details about daily upsets and personal difficulties in the letters provided Orozco's biographers with fodder for elaborate narratives about her devout religiosity.

Self-mortification is a common theme in biographical tales of miracles and piety. Orozco's mortification practices—which probably explain many of her physical ailments—suggest that she cultivated austerity as part of her public identity. One repeated anecdote tells of a time that she ate blood sausage and, to repent for her gluttony, punished herself by licking cat excrement that she found on the ground. One vida reports that afterward "she felt content, but her stomach started to hurt so much that she threw up." The Virgin Mary then intervened with a special powder to cleanse the sin.[16]

Protected by the Virgin, this penitent Orozco is a far cry from the young woman shunned by her convent sisters as she recovered from burns inflicted by the devil.

One can detect the balancing act of the hagiographer in these anecdotes. The heavens continued to reward Orozco for the unique spiritual devotion that humans—family members, confessors, and nuns alike—feared and punished in her earlier years. Blaming inexperienced priests and communal lack of judgment for Orozco's rejection by the church, her biographers found many explanations for the young woman's problems. All her experiences, from speaking in voices to speaking to the Virgin, are held up as true because Orozco is described, among other things, as a bad liar. Her confessor indicated that, whenever Orozco lied, her face turned red. As a consequence, she always admitted her errors immediately (*Vida*, fol. 9v).

When considering Orozco's life story in light of the larger picture of gender and spirituality in early modern Spain, we can see that she used her status as an outsider—as someone feared and hated—to secure a more stable position as a sanctioned laywoman. The cruelty of her abusive sister, her unsympathetic parents, and even her Carmelite sisters contributes to a portrait of a misunderstood outcast. Orozco persevered in her search for a sanctioned religious role in spite of the obstacles placed before her by the church. In terms of both sexuality and spirituality, she seems to have turned otherwise negative traits into assets. Her spirituality, which caused commotion in her youth, served as her primary source of strength and authority in later life. In addition to her spiritual perseverance, Orozco managed to turn what many biographers describe as her distinct lack of physical beauty into an asset that enhanced her piety. The issue of Orozco's less-than-perfect physical appearance arises often in her vidas. One biographer, Bravo Tamargo, describes the flying dough incident as a victory on the part of the devil:

> [S]o that the whole world would take up arms against her, [he] returned her to the world looking horrible to strangers and acquaintances alike on account of her expulsion, her ugliness, her blindness, and her complete uselessness.[17]

Although Orozco recovered from her burns, she seems to have cultivated a particularly humble, even antifeminine, appearance. As Barbeito Carneiro points out, repeated physical descriptions—which include a dirty face, a plump body, and severe braids—suggest that Orozco emphasized characteristics that did not coincide with dominant standards of beauty.[18]

The presentation of a desexualized self to the world probably helped Orozco avoid marriage. Throughout her life she insisted that her devotion to God obligated her not to marry, but the cultivation of undesirability might have helped legitimize her life choices in the eyes of society. Evidence for the calculated cultivation of such claims appears throughout the documents, as exemplified in the following statement from a vida:

> [She] used to respond with grace to those who approached her with marriage proposals, saying: "You should know that he who marries me will take with him a good prize—a woman with four marks against her, the worst in the world: [I am] old, ugly, sick, and poor."[19]

Whereas early in her life María de Orozco had few opportunities to realize her goal of being a Carmelite nun, by her later years she had found a legitimate place in the church hierarchy that, in effect, allowed her the freedom that her particular manifestation of spirituality required. Nonconformist to the end, María de Orozco capitalized on the traits—of unusual spiritual experiences, lack of standard physical beauty, and fierce independence—that otherwise proved harmful for many women in her society. Turning these characteristics into assets, María de Orozco transformed herself. The young girl repeatedly accused of having pacts with the devil grew into a woman with a holy reputation who served her community. Stepping back from the margins, where she was accused of demonic association, Orozco settled on a more moderate, only nominally affiliated place from which to devote herself to a religious calling.

Given Orozco's experiences in two religious communities, it seems logical to conclude that the lack of institutional oversight in her later years afforded a freedom of spiritual expression that she might not have enjoyed in the convent. Indeed, while convents provided many women with opportunities for education, community, and self-governance, they were not immune to the anxieties about heresy and heterodoxy that colored Spanish life in the period. The documentation related to the activities and condemnation of Teresa Valle de la Cerda (b. late 1500s) attests to the dangers faced by women who practiced unorthodox spirituality within religious communities during the time of the Inquisition.

Teresa Valle de la Cerda belonged to one of Spain's most influential families in the seventeenth century, yet her class status protected her only to a certain degree from inquisitorial inquiry. Indeed, Valle was found guilty of dealing with the devil and of prophesying only a few years after she founded the Benedictine Convento de la Encarnación (popularly known as San Plácido) in Madrid in 1623. Her trial involved testimony from other priests and nuns whose religious practices had drawn the attention of the Holy Office. At the end of the proceedings, the Inquisition deprived Valle of privileges related to the active and passive vows taken by Benedictines and put her under house arrest in the Convent of Santo Domingo in Toledo. Valle's trial record, correspondence, and autobiographical texts offer insight into the risks taken by women who expressed their spirituality in unorthodox ways. Complex relationships between nuns and clerics emerge as the central focus of the case, suggesting that the benefits of communal living were occasionally offset by the dangers of colluding with or falling under the influence of confessors and other church officials. Finally, the documents reveal the survival strategies used by Valle to distance herself from her community and thus avoid punishment by the Inquisition.

The religious practices in the Benedictine convent led to accusations of prophesy, Illuminism, demonic possession, female sermonizing, and inappropriate physical relationships between confessors and nuns. The convent, which appears to have fostered unconventional Catholicism, enjoyed the support of politically important men. During her term as abbess, for example, Valle corresponded with men as high ranking as the king's favorite, the Count-Duke of Olivares. When the Inquisition opened its investigation into San Plácido, Valle maintained contact with Olivares, keeping him up to date and agreeing that, if things got much worse, she would call in the convent advisor, her confessor Father Francisco García Calderón.

Teresa Valle's letters point to the class connections and political savoir faire that must have served her in founding the convent and later possibly helped her avoid more severe punishment from the Holy Office. Writing to Olivares and García, she discussed the investigation with great caution, calling the priests sent to conduct the inquiry "very good and very sane" and expressing approval at their proceedings.[20] In contrast to the careful rhetoric about inquisition officials, Valle bluntly described the monastery's monks as being "as fierce as the devil" because of the low esteem in which they held García. She initially begged García to stay away in order to avoid problems with the other male religious. As the situation grew more serious, she arranged for Olivares to grant García the necessary dispensation to visit the monastery.

Written during what must have been chaotic and frightening times, Valle's correspondence reflects a certain levelheadedness. She may have felt protected by her class status, but anything she wrote could have been used as evidence. In spite of this potential threat, Valle appears to have used letters to reach out for guidance and assistance. The semi-public nature of the letters perhaps accounts for the mix of emotions we can detect in them.

Understandably, Valle's anxiety increased as the investigation progressed, and the lack of support from García seems to have contributed to her sense that things were falling apart. Although she reported severe headaches by July 1628, she also articulated anew her faith in God, and she maintained her correspondence up to the time of García's imprisonment in Madrid. The close confessor-nun relationship revealed in these letters contrasts with the self-defense strategies later employed in her autobiographical statements, or memorials, in which Valle gradually shifted the blame for the women's behavior away from herself and onto García.

The memorials Teresa Valle prepared for the Inquisition record the strategies she employed as she sought to defend herself and her sisters. Written between 1629 and 1637, the statements had the explicit purpose of explaining and justifying the spiritual practices of Valle and the other nuns in the San Plácido convent. One statement, from 1629, deals with the foundation of the convent and with the women's activities therein. Valle emphatically defends García's piety, yet she does not hesitate to recount her disagreements with him (Valle, pp. 166–69). Like other religious women—most famously Saint Teresa—Valle uses the trope of humility as one method of downplaying her knowledge of the theological issues at stake in the trial. Presenting herself as a woman of "little capacity" for complex matters, Valle employs colloquial phrases such as "chicuelas" and "chiquillas"—little girls—to refer to the nuns (Valle, pp. 168–69). As in other instances of women's self-deprecation, Valle's depiction of herself as ignorant in fact had little to do with her abilities to comprehend church politics and theology. Valle reveals a disparity in her claims when she mentions a time when a male cleric said he had "not understood a word" of one of García's sermons. The nun writes that, in spite of her ignorance of such matters, she nonetheless interpreted the sermon for the cleric (Valle, p. 170).

In the 1629 memorial, Valle had yet to decide that she needed to denounce García and distance herself from the suspicious goings-on in her convent. The humility trope reflects the self-image she wanted to present. In other instances, Valle chose to recount strange occurrences in her convent and defend them in simple terms. These passages suggest that Valle underestimated the Inquisition's interest in prosecuting demonic possession. Here, for example, she defends the existence of the demons that influenced the women's behavior:

> It would be impossible for anyone who saw [everyone's actions] to have any doubt about the demons, just as it is impossible that twenty-two women of such different backgrounds and personalities could fake things so alien to themselves and to most people in the world.[21]

This defense relies on personal experience and on straightforward logic. By highlighting the differences among the nuns and the commonalities of their actions, Valle tries to validate their ecstatic experiences.

Valle discusses the demons in detail, giving their names and recounting some of their appearances. Apparently, the demons inhabited many of the nuns' bodies, but nobody considered them evil. To the contrary, the demons stirred religious fervor in men and women alike. When one nun, doña Gregoria, was overtaken by a demon, he spoke through her about God's expectations for religious women. Valle also describes the reaction of a priest, who claimed that the demon "had such an effect on him and his soul had received so much light that never before had he been moved more to serve God."[22]

In addition to reporting a male cleric's powerful reaction to the women's demonic encounters, Valle further tries to legitimize the events by insisting that some of the women had strange experiences even before coming to her convent: "It is also clearly true that this evil did not have its start in the convent" since before the foundation of San Plácido, God was served by letting the demons enter the women.[23] Valle and many of the other women had similar experiences before coming to San Plácido: Some had inexplicable childhood illnesses, others screamed like dogs, others did "crazy things" (*locuras*). This behavior had been attributed to the women's demonic associations long before they came to the convent (Valle, p. 174).

In the 1629 memorial, Valle also responds to accusations of inappropriate touching between García and the nuns. Her principal strategy consists of a defense of García's doctrinal solidity. She defends all of the nuns, too, indicating that none of the women thought the kisses and hugs indecent: "And so I consented to them with Father Francisco, thinking of him as my father and being quite sure of his sanctity." Holding hands with García or other confessors was of no consequence whatsoever.[24] On the other hand, she dismisses accusations of having kissed García on the lips, and she offers up the names of clerics who would vouch for the innocence of the relationship. Finally, Valle attacks those nuns who, out of jealousy, were unhappy that García "did not give them many caresses."[25]

The last line of defense that Valle uses for herself in fact turns out to be the most important: She claims a loss of memory that makes it difficult for her to recall exact details. While she dismisses out of hand all accusations of inappropriate touching, she also says that if such touch occurred, she does not remember it specifically. Similarly, she expresses appreciation for the permission the inquisitors gave her to write her defense, because in speaking her "memory falters," but writing permits her the time she needs to gather her thoughts and remember the whole truth.[26] Valle concludes with an assertion common among defendants: "I do not remember anything else at this time." [27] This statement left open the option for future revisions and new information.

The subsequent memorials contain many more admissions of guilt and far fewer defenses of the practices in the San Plácido convent. The 1629 statement admits three errors, all of which relate to having believed in the demons that plagued her and her sisters. Acknowledging that she should have consulted with church experts, Valle explains why she failed to advise outsiders about the demons. Her justification—that García, the abbott of Ripoll, and a duchess all believed in the demons—relates to her previous representation of herself as a naive woman who trusted those around her. Quite rationally, she suggests that if these three people all acknowledged the existence of the demons, then why should she have notified anybody else? The second of Valle's memorials in Barbeito Carneiro's *Jails and Women* (*Cárceles y mujeres*) implicitly recognizes the naïveté of such logic. While Valle depends on such reasoning to convince inquisitors to let her go, she also takes responsibility for the sins of the entire convent. She admits that, as the women's leader, she should have known to guide them better. These admissions and justifications reflect Valle's repentant, occasionally defiant, tone.

By February 1630, Valle had decided to distance herself definitively from García. In a brief statement, she expresses regret over having allowed García to touch her. Sorry for her association with him, for participating in his *locuras*, and for not consulting with outsiders, she again takes responsibility for putting the others on the road to perdition. Repentance, blame casting, and humility failed to serve Valle, however. She and her sisters were convicted in 1630, with the most common sentence being house arrest and the deprivation of both active and passive vows. Seven years later, Valle turned in one last memorial. This document contributed to the overturn of her conviction and to the exoneration of almost everyone involved in the San Plácido scandal. At this point, all the blame was shifted to Father García Calderón, the priest who had served as confidant and advisor to Teresa Valle and the others.

Valle's final memorial relies on several strategies to discredit the proceedings that led to her initial conviction. Valle laments the dishonor that she suffered on account of her conviction. While she claims to have written this statement out of obedience to her superiors, most of the prose is devoted to denouncing Father García and the nuns who spoke against Valle in the trial. Previously reluctant to use the *tacha* system to discount witnesses, here Valle invokes her right to have the testimony of several nuns barred because of the enmity between her and them. She also points out the flaws in the reasoning that led to her condemnation. The Inquisition had suggested that she invented the demonic stories out of vainglory and a desire to win over

others. Yet, as Valle explicitly writes, out of thirty nuns, twenty-five were affected by demons, and three of the others were her friends. So, she asks,
"Who were the women that I was trying to win over?"[28]

The difficult position of the penitent seeking relief from punishment is
palpable in this memorial. Valle needed to maintain a fine line: She had to
defend and justify herself, but with so much testimony already on record,
she ran the risk of completely contradicting previous statements. This balancing act resulted in a document that, while humble and painstakingly
penitent, also has a straightforward, almost exasperated tone. For instance,
Valle operates within a framework that gives credence to the demons that
possessed her, yet she tries to show the flaws in logic that led to her being
blamed for the demons' comments. Specifically, she confronts the inquisitors
with the question of separating the possessor from the possessed: "If the
demon said it, then how am I to blame?"[29] Resonant of Bernarda Manuel's
plea for compassion in her Judaizing trial, this strategy mixes claims on piety
with challenges to inquisitional logic.

In a similar vein, Valle frankly admits guilt with regard to her physical relationship with García, yet she continues to defend the orthodoxy of
his beliefs. Anything less would amount to an admission of heterodoxy, of
course, but it is interesting to note that she does not denounce García repeatedly. Instead, she explains the situation from the perspective of a woman
who gave herself over fully to her spiritual advisor. Valle admits that she saw
García enter the cloister to eat with the nuns, that she shared his chewed
food, and that she allowed him to touch her hands and face. She also admits
to seeing no harm in these actions. Moreover, she defends García's sincerity
and kindness, stating that she never thought ill of him or of his treatment of
any of the nuns.

As Barbeito Carneiro points out in her edition of Valle's writings, by
1637 the nun had completed the bulk of her sentence.[30] While potentially
useful as a means to lift the sentences immediately, the final memorial
sought the vindication of Valle and her convent. It was successful on both
counts. We cannot know for certain what factors came together to make the
Inquisition exonerate the nuns after Valle wrote her final testimony. However, the four memorials that form a crucial part of the trial also provide a
record of the multiple strategies of self-authorization and self-justification
used by Teresa Valle de la Cerda during her partly successful battle with the
Inquisition. Valle provided inquisitors with a complex portrait of a woman
who was simultaneously ignorant and knowledgeable, trusting and self-
protective, evasive and straightforward. Like María de Orozco, she paid a
high price for her spiritual practices. Both women positioned themselves as

independent women whose strategies enabled them to vindicate themselves without fully renouncing the experiences that put them on the margins of Spain's Catholic society.

THE PRICE OF INDEPENDENCE: PROPHETS AND SORCERERS

The cases of Orozco and Valle demonstrate that beatas and nuns did not enjoy immunity from the pressure to conform to mainstream Catholic practices. Even so, those who remained without institutional or political protection found themselves much more intensely exposed to the scrutiny of the Inquisition. For each single woman who successfully attained an independent existence based on a sanctimonious self-presentation, there were countless others whose spiritual practices put them in more immediate danger of persecution.

The prophecy trial of Lucrecia de León (1568–?) highlights many of those dangers. León's story is an astonishing account of the political and social risks taken by a young woman who, because of her highly publicized dream life, became known for her powers of prophecy. León began having prophetic dreams while still a teenager. Eventually she allowed clerics to write down the vivid scenarios, which included predictions about the defeat of the Spanish Armada and indictments of Philip II's personality and policy flaws. Such politically charged messages led to León's arrest in 1588. To the dismay of the Spanish, the English defeated the Armada after León's release. With her prediction come true, León's popularity soared.

Richard Kagan has told León's story deftly in *Lucrecia's Dreams*, noting that the Armada's defeat led to Lucrecia's integration into court and salon life, and even to the establishment of a confraternity based on dreams she had about Christian soldiers. Describing León's political audacity, Kagan notes: "By placing the blame for Spain's troubles squarely upon Philip's shoulders, Lucrecia's dreams articulated what many Spaniards undoubtedly felt but were afraid to say aloud."[31] When she was arrested again on charges of sedition and treason in May 1590, León had 415 dreams on record. She claimed to be illiterate and defenseless, a woman misled by men like Alonso de Mendoza, a church canon and a defender of León's prophecies.

Lucrecia de León's trial record is remarkable for the information it contains about a savvy woman's attempts to convince the Inquisition of her naïveté. To avoid torture, for instance, she claimed that she was persuaded to allow her male protectors to write down her dreams "so that they could say that I dreamed them when I really had not." Days later, however, she recanted this blame-filled statement and reported that she had indeed had some dreams, but others had been greatly embellished by Mendoza and Fray Lucas de Allende. The inquisitors were not convinced, particularly since León had received and presumably read letters from her lover, Diego de Victores Texeda, while in prison.

As the trial progressed over the next few years, León frequently contradicted herself. She pled ignorance with regard to the political importance of her prophecies and pled innocent with regard to their transcription and distribution. These claims to innocence were undermined both by the protection she received from Mendoza and by the affair with Victores. Moreover, while in prison, Lucrecia continued to tell her dreams to other prisoners. She also gave birth to a child, a result of her relationship with Victores. Nonetheless, throughout the trial she clung to a presentation of herself as young, naive, and exploited. Kagan summarizes León's defense with an eye to her strategies of self-presentation:

> Her argument, expressed repeatedly during the course of the trial, that she was a weak woman manipulated by strong men suggests that she was fully prepared to exploit sixteenth-century conceptions of women as a means of strengthening her defense.[32]

This portrayal evidently helped León in her trial, since the tribunal could not come to a unanimous decision. In July 1595, she was found guilty only of making heretical statements and given the lightest possible sentence—one hundred lashes, banishment from Madrid, and two years' seclusion in a religious house.[33] Compared to the possible sentences she faced for treason and sedition, León's was lenient. We know little about León after she served time in two hospitals in Toledo. Kagan speculates that Mendoza may have found work for her, but we do not know what happened to the prophet and her child.[34]

León's social role matched that of a political critic who dared to voice opinions that others kept to themselves. In this sense, León functioned as a spokesperson for those disenchanted with Philip, so it is not surprising that she developed a cult following. Apparently she filled a need in late sixteenth-century Madrid, as many followed and endorsed her powers of prophecy and thus found a way to remain close to the Crown and still criticize the monarchy.

The sorcery trial of María Romero (c. 1674–?) documents the complex social roles fulfilled by yet another subset of threatening women. While León's trial allows us to peek into court society and glimpse the threat a purportedly illiterate woman's dreams posed to a weak monarch, Romero's case reveals the intricate counseling and protective functions of women who earned their living by casting spells. As a woman separated from her husband and supporting herself with a business in black magic, Romero was a likely target for the Inquisition.[35]

As with other accused witches and sorcerers throughout Europe, Romero posed a double threat to the status quo. Her claim to supernatural powers made her a threat to the church, and her economic independence made her a threat to a society that believed that a woman required the guidance and support of a man. Yet, like many others who engaged in black magic, Romero made a successful living by providing services to abused, abandoned, dissatisfied, and sick women. As Guido Ruggiero has eloquently stated about cases similar to Romero's, the testimonies "open the complex, rich, and often virtually poetic world of love magic, dominated largely by women and women's networks."[36]

The economics of intimacy come to light in both financial and emotional terms in these cases. For instance, Romero's clients paid her one to six reales per spell, often paying more money to start the process again if the first round failed to produce results. During the trial, some of her clients testified against her and expressed anger at having paid for ineffective sorcery, but depositions about domestic abuse and sexual affairs reveal that Romero's neighbors and acquaintances regularly turned to her for help.

Details of Romero's and Gómez's remedies and spells fill the pages of the trial record. The most common spell recommended by Romero used men's pubic hairs. The women brought the hairs to Romero, who placed them in a piece of bread and then finished off the mixture with nine pins and drops of green candle wax. The chants that Romero taught other women appear here as well. Invoking the Virgin, the devil, and various saints, the chants were said in conjunction with a variety of activities that included throwing salt and lighting candles. Ground potions frequently figured among Romero's cures as well. In one exchange with Mariana Díaz del Valle (b. 1600s), herself later arrested by the Inquisition, Romero accepted two reales and offered a powder the color of ground pepper to keep Díaz's husband from continuing to sell off their possessions and to stop his violent behavior.

As in other sorcery and witchcraft proceedings, the testimonies of witnesses from lower classes reveal women in search of control in a culture that gave them little say in matters related to sex and marriage. Díaz had come to Romero asking if "there might not be a cure to keep my husband from destroying me."[37] The powder, which Díaz had strewn throughout the

house and on her husband's clothes, apparently had no effect. Thus Díaz
became one of many disenchanted customers who testified against Romero.
The group also included Juana Gómez (b. 1600s), who seems to have been
Romero's business partner. Originally, the Inquisition charged Romero and
Gómez, both of whom were described by one witness as being "great trick-
sters" with "bad habits."[38] The women were accused of various acts of sorcery, including throwing cards, casting spells, predicting the future, and having pacts with the devil. In the end, inquisitors merely penitenced Gómez,
which meant that her punishment was much lighter than Romero's sentence
of two hundred lashes, six years' banishment from Madrid, and two years'
mandatory hospital service.

The testimonies against Romero contain language that captures the importance of women's role in black magic in early modern society. In recalling their interaction with the defendant, many said that she asked "what
was afflicting them," and the women sometimes described themselves as
"afflicted."[39] For Gómez, the dysphoria involved a relationship with a disin-
terested soldier. Several other women also needed help in maintaining their
affairs with men, including some priests. Díaz testified that she had wanted
to leave her husband because he was destroying her financially and because
"she could not tolerate his bad temper."[40] Romero had advised Díaz not to
leave, because such an action would make her look guilty of treachery or bad
wifely behavior. It was at this point that Romero offered the powder as a
remedy for Díaz's strained domestic situation.

Díaz's testimony reveals the double bind of those facing the Inquisition. Díaz had to offer some evidence against the defendant without indict-
ing herself at the same time. Walking this fine line, Díaz insisted that she
told Romero she did not want to hurt her husband in any way, but that,
upon receiving assurance as to the safety of the powder, she gave it to him.
The remedy failed, however, as fifteen days later the man remained at home.
Díaz also admits that she asked Romero for help in drawing lovers to her.
On one occasion, Díaz paid over six reales for powders that would make her
lover, Fray Pedro Santos, continue his relationship with her. Romero created
a potion that contained menstrual blood and wine, but this seems only to
have had the effect of angering the cleric, who wrote two wrathful letters to
Mariana. Indeed, that none of the spells worked probably explains Díaz's
willing depositions against Romero.

Other women similarly requested help in controlling men's behavior and
emotions. The testimony of Zebriana de Escobar contains the most overt
description of violence in the trial. When Romero asked Escobar, in November 1701, what was "eating her up," Escobar replied that her lover had
"sworn on the cross of his sword that he is going to give me a punishment

that I will remember for the rest of my life."[41] At this point, the widow already had been beaten by her lover. Romero offered a remedy that involved chants and a green candle as an antidote to the problem. During the trial, Escobar repeated many of the chants and prayers that Romero taught her. Escobar's testimony portrays a psyche in conflict. She wanted her lover to stop beating her, but at the same time she wanted to use spells to incite his desire. The lack of control this widow had in her relationship with Dionisio de Mendoza is palpable in her depositions. Like many other women who sought to assert themselves over their partners and lovers, Escobar wanted to improve her situation by stopping the violence and stabilizing the relationship.

That women like Escobar relied on Romero for aid points to the important social function of women as practitioners of black magic in early modern society.[42] María Romero offered psychological solace, but she also helped her clients take action through spells. Based on the testimonies, we can see that once the women began to feel desperate about their partnerships and marriages, they turned to Romero and Gómez for guidance and action. The various depositions also reveal the means by which women reached out to each other for help and support. For example, Escobar met Romero when she went to her daughter's house for a visit. Since the others noted that Escobar looked like she had "too much sorrow," they inquired about her state of mind. Romero entered into a business arrangement with her, and Escobar ended up testifying one year later about the remedies Romero had given her.[43]

While it comes as no surprise that people in the seventeenth century made connections through neighbors and acquaintances, the details about these networks in Inquisition trials testify to the ways in which women depended on each other for consolation, education, and economic gain. Romero listened to women's problems and taught a select few how to throw cards and say chants. She took money in exchange for remedies meant to influence men's behavior. She provided people with a sympathetic ear and with tools to help them improve their lives.

In conjunction with the references to economic exchange and domestic violence in the Romero trial, the testimonies of women who sought to repair and strengthen their relationships with men folds into the reconstruction of women's survival strategies and social networks analyzed in previous chapters. The sorrow and affliction described by Escobar and Díaz suggest that many of the women who turned to María Romero felt they had nowhere else to go for help. Involved in affairs with priests or in violent domestic partnerships, women with few economic resources paid for the services of someone who could help them gain control over their lives. Perhaps chants and spells would not have been the remedy of choice for some, since many described the panic they felt when they thought the remedies may have adversely affected the health of the men whose pubic hairs were used in the spells. Others simply felt duped when the remedies failed. Still, enough people had faith in black magic that many women like Romero were able to earn a living casting spells and reading cards.

STRATEGIES FOR SURVIVAL

Like the documents about María de Orozco, the trial records of María Romero, Teresa Valle, and Lucrecia de León reveal the complex social networks of unmarried aristocratic, midde-, and lower-class women in early modern Spain. Such texts also give us insight into the survival strategies of women whose marital status, spirituality, economic activity, and personality made them targets for suspicion and even persecution in the period. In recording the struggles of women, the texts also suggest that the search for authority and survival varied greatly according to social context and individual background.

María de Orozco managed to attain legitimate spiritual independence after years of turmoil and rejection. By cultivating a sanctimonious identity, she avoided marriage and gained the approbation of the church. The cultural capital ascribed to female chastity helped her toward legitimacy. On the other hand, Teresa Valle's defense of physical contact between nuns and inquisitors did not convince the tribunal that it had incorrectly condemned such practices. Eventually, Valle had to modify her defenses of caressing and handholding and acknowledge the inappropriate nature of many activities that occurred in her convent. Still, she never fully renounced her belief in the righteousness of many of the San Plácido events.

The price that Orozco and Valle paid for uncommon spiritual practices ranged from shunning and disparagement to incarceration and house arrest. Lucrecia de León and María Romero fared worse in their battles for an independent existence. León acquired a cult following based on her dreams about Spain's poor leadership and impending decline. Such popularity made it difficult for her to convince the Inquisition that she had been a pawn in the hands of the male clerics who transcribed and publicized her dreams. León's and Valle's cases both demonstrate that defendants found it hard to strike a proper balance between knowledge and naïveté when they faced the Inquisition. After serving several years of her sentence, Valle finally managed to convince inquisitors that her sin was one of obedience, of placing faith in a misguided confessor. León's self-portrayal as an innocent failed to convince the Holy Office.

Romero represents a large class of people who lived without a safety net in early modern society. Her husband had been gone for a year at the outset of the trial, indicating that for all intents and purposes she lived as a single woman and paid her own bills. A letter from the hospital in which she served her sentence indicates that Romero was poor and practically "disabled in both arms, without any means to feed herself and incapable of earning her own money."[44] Like León, Romero presented a burden to the institution to which she was sent to serve part of her sentence. Taken out of the milieu in which she acted as counselor and purveyor of spells, Romero no longer functioned effectively. Among lower- and middle-class women in need of advice and assistance in domestic affairs, María Romero and others like her performed necessary social services with varying degrees of success. Regardless of whether individual spells and chants had any noticeable effects, the activities of Romero and her peers help us understand the ways that women turned to each other for help in resolving domestic crises.

When read together, Orozco's texts and the Inquisition cases of Valle, León, and Romero capture a range of survival strategies related to women's existence in early modern Spanish society. These documents provide details about the challenges of women's daily lives, suggesting that we might find new ways to write histories of domestic violence, sexuality, and even social interaction. The stories of these four women—a beata, a nun, a prophet, and a purveyor of black magic—provide us with another way of understanding that, in a society attempting to excise all heterodoxy, those with suspect beliefs, profiles, and practices lived a precarious existence. By capitalizing on dominant ideologies about femininity, single women like Orozco carved out a niche as beatas. Others, like Valle and León, attempted to cast themselves as victims of their own femininity. León in particular tried to make herself out to be a woman too trusting of the clerics who had guided her. Yet both Valle and León demonstrated fully functional leadership, which later made it difficult for them to pose as innocents in their trials. Out of this group, María Romero was most exposed to the Inquisition's machinations. Without a husband or any other male authority figure nearby, Romero was forced by the inquisitors to take full responsibility for the threat that her independent existence and unorthodox practices posed to the status quo.

The stories of Orozco, Valle, León, and Romero differ in their details and in the class backgrounds of their subjects, yet together they represent many common experiences of women who forged independent roles for themselves in early modern Spanish culture. The records of the individual lives of beatas, charismatic nuns, prophets, and practitioners of black magic highlight the difficulties faced by women who existed without the protection of men. The combination of heterodoxy with independence often caused more problems for single women than for men or married women.

The single women whose stories we have heard struggled with the psychological toll of being outsiders, the fear of inquisitorial prosecution, and the challenge of defending themselves in a society that encouraged female submission. Their experiences suggest that women paid a high price for living independent lives and making unorthodox choices. The texts that record their experiences reveal complex strategies that helped some women on the margins to survive and even thrive in early modern Spain.

8

Toward a History
of Women's Education

The endeavor of recovering women's textual history necessarily involves an investigation of literacy and education. To date, no research synthesizes the roles women played in the educational sphere, yet we know that they advised nuns, priests, kings, and queens, as well as educating their family members. Women's roles as educators extended from the informal to the formal, from the domestic to the political. As we will see in this final chapter, women positioned themselves within the church and in the larger culture as educators and reformers.

As the previous chapters suggest, literacy and education have particular importance for Spanish culture of the early modern period, when the book market took shape, literacy rates rose, and convent foundations gave more women access to education than ever before. Indeed, the explosion of women's writing in Spain's long seventeenth century leaves us wondering to what extent educated women had an awareness of others like them. Many scholars, including Electa Arenal, Amy Katz Kaminsky, Stephanie Merrim, Elizabeth Ordóñez, and Stacey Schlau, have speculated on the degree to which women forged such communities within convents or literary circles, yet we still do not know whether a community of women writers existed. On an even broader scale, we have yet to reconstruct the connections among the larger pool of literate women of this period. It is difficult to say whether each operated in a vacuum, reinventing responses to a culture that insisted on their inferiority.

We have ample evidence to prove that convents provided continuity among generations of educated women. Formally and informally, these institutions gave women access to the activism and intellectualism of other nuns, saints, and martyrs. The women who gained an education outside convent walls did so in spite of the mandate to provide women with only enough education to make them good wives—certainly not good scholars, activists, or writers. Yet even within these parameters, the slave who was born Elena de Céspedes learned to read and learned a trade, even before her transformation to a male identity. The Portuguese native speaker Bernarda Manuel wrote well enough in Spanish to defend herself in writing to the Inquisition. Upper-class writers María de Zayas, Ana Caro, Angela de Azevedo, and others were steeped in knowledge about the literature of their time, although it remains unclear to what extent they were familiar with female authors from Spain and the rest of Europe.

The diverse texts we have seen in *The Lives of Women* provide just a small sample of the many ways in which we might access past women's experiences, thoughts, and words. The impressive amount of evidence for literacy and advanced education among women of varying class and ethnic backgrounds begs fundamental questions about women's access to formal and informal education. Research in this area is often limited to guesswork, however, since traditionally we have had little access to primary texts that accurately document women's educational levels. Furthermore, literacy is notoriously difficult to gauge and often is measured merely by whether women signed their own names to wills and other legal documents.[1]

Textual evidence suggests that women acted as advisors, consultants, and teachers in domestic, inquisitional, and political contexts. Inquisition records point to numerous ways in which women educated each other and established networks of support. Research on conversos has shown that women acted as educators at the familial level, as many defendants claimed that their mothers taught them to read and write. Moreover, it is common for religious women's vidas to refer to their mothers as the family educators.[2]

Writing the history of women's roles as advisors, educators, and leaders marks a crucial step toward a full understanding of gender and culture in the European past. By broadly defining education to include informal and formal mechanisms of women's education of and support for each other, I argue here that women in the seventeenth century laid the groundwork for direct involvement in the public sphere, and that we can recuperate women's educational history by turning to evidence of informal instruction and support found in advice and behavior manuals, religious instruction, fiction, and even Inquisition archives. This approach posits that women in the early modern period regularly engaged in a broad spectrum of educational activities and that they received education in more forms than has been previously acknowledged. The analysis also provides a starting point for more thorough accounts of women as educators and beneficiaries of education in the history of Europe and the Hispanic world.

EDUCATIONAL HISTORY

Women's education in Europe has an uneven past. While we can identify moments in which individuals enjoyed opportunities for learning and professional training, the education of almost everyone but upper-class men was neglected until the twentieth century. In the Spanish context, as elsewhere, there have been propitious periods for women's formal instruction. In the ninth century Hispano-Moslem culture of Córdoba, for example, some women had relatively extensive access to education.[3] Many centuries passed before women again had similar opportunities. Renaissance humanism gave rise to pockets of highly educated women throughout Europe. The reign of Queen Isabella in late fifteenth-century Spain, for example, produced a positive climate out of which emerged Beatriz Galindo (1475–1534), whose erudition won her the nickname *La Latina*. Although Venice, as one instance, saw a significant increase in the numbers of educated women during the sixteenth century, Spain had only a handful of well-known women writers from the period, including Beatriz Bernal (b. 1500s), Luisa de Carvajal y Mendoza (1566–1614), Luisa Sigea (c. 1530), and Saint Teresa (1515–82). Women such as Isabel Liaño (b. 1500s) and Oliva Sabuco (1567–?) outside the convent and numerous women within also formed part of the small cohort of Renaissance writers in Spain.[4]

By the seventeenth century, dozens of European women participated in public debates about gender. Moderata Fonte in Italy, Marie de Gournay in France, Mary Astell in England, Anna Maria van Schurman in Germany, and María de Zayas in Spain were among the writers who protested women's subordination in this period. Little was done in any of these countries to rectify the situation, however. In the 1700s, Enlightenment thinkers promoted educating the masses, including women and the nonaristocratic classes. Yet even as late as the 1930s, the severe disparities between male and female education led Margarita Nelken, a radical member of the Spanish Republican parliament, to oppose female suffrage on the basis that women were so ignorant that they simply would vote as their husbands or confessors directed.[5] The Franco period brought setbacks to the progress women and others had made in the relatively liberal years preceding the Civil War. Finally, post-Franco Spain saw the implementation of a liberal constitution that included an egalitarian model for universal education.[6]

This overview suggests that much of Spain's educational history mirrors that of other Western countries. The connections between the twentieth and seventeenth centuries were more marked than in other parts of the world, though, since Franco's propaganda machine publicized the Renaissance incarnation of the submissive wife as the feminine ideal. Most famously espoused by Fray Luis de León in *The Perfect Wife*, the notion that women should receive training to make them efficient household managers, obedient domestic partners, and good Christians permeated Renaissance humanist discourse. Centuries later, this ideology appealed to Franco's retrograde sense of social order.[7]

In the early modern period, innumerable male writers weighed in on the topics of women's spiritual and domestic instruction. In addition to *The Perfect Wife* and Juan Luis Vives's *Instruction of a Christian Woman* (*De Institutione Feminae Christianae*, 1524), other notable prescriptive texts for women include Juan de la Cerda's *The Political Life of All of Women's Estates* (*Vida política de todos los estados de las mujeres*, 1599) and Juan de Espinosa's *Dialogue in Praise of Women* (*Diálogo en laude de las mujeres*, 1580). These and other authors offered their opinions on how best to instruct women. The specific details of their plans varied slightly. Vives, for example, embraced a more solid instruction than other men of the time, while Antonio Herrera de Salcedo (*Mirror of the Perfect Wife* [*Espejo de la perfecta casada*, 1637]) did not believe women should learn how to write. As Pilar Tenorio Gómez summarizes, most moralists wanted women to be "silent, humble, virtuous, obedient, and above all, married."[8]

Renaissance moralists focused on the creation of a helpmate who would take charge of household affairs and raise good Christian children. In a sense, this marked a step forward from the late Middle Ages, for at least women were considered fully human and therefore worthy of education. Nonetheless, as Stephanie Merrim has noted, this educational project had serious limitations. Vives, Erasmus, and others promoted instruction for the upper-class woman to increase her level of literacy, "while emphatically restricting to the private realm of the household her sphere of action."[9] Bound by considerations about class and spheres of influence, prescriptions for instructional reform left out many, but unfailingly endorsed the subordination of all women.

What did women make of this obsession with their proper training and behavior? Traditionally, our understanding of women's reactions has been limited to a few literary and nonfictional texts. Discussions of behavior manuals and other prescriptive texts rarely include female voices, although Zayas's call to the "vain legislators of the world" certainly has drawn the attention of modern readers. Zayas's texts, published in 1637 and 1647, marked a turning point in Spain's feminist history. Until that point, much of the discussion on women had been bound by the *querelle des femmes*, a debate that provided room for misogynist and antimisogynist discourse. While the *querelle* created opportunities for many intellectuals to debate women's worth, it also produced highly structured texts that tended to offer flat and often formulaic defenses of the authors' positions. As Stephanie Merrim has summarized, the debate authorized feminist defenses of women, but only the most talented of writers truly exploited this potential.[10]

In 1647, upon the publication of the second half of her novella collection, Zayas became the first Spanish woman to transcend the mere rhetoric of the *querelle*, and her writings herald a new direction in Hispanic and European history. By the end of the seventeenth century, larger numbers of women across Europe and the Americas articulated their anger about the state of female education.[11] In addition to the writers mentioned, Sor Juana Inés de la Cruz in Mexico and Hannah Wolley in England stand out for their advocacy of women's right to justice and education. Indeed, these and other writers are familiar to us today because they transcended the mere rhetoric of the debate on the woman question and spoke out in original and convincing ways against social injustice.[12]

Religious women's writing constitutes a body of literature that is less overtly political, but no less insistent, in its pedagogical and reformative messages. For historical reasons, convent writing provides an obvious point of entry into the development of women's education. After the exclusion of women from universities in the thirteenth century, convents were the first institutions to offer structured education for women. Nuns who wrote about spiritual life frequently devoted their attention to the importance of moral, spiritual, and literary instruction. A prevailing belief in the superiority of religious life often infuses these texts, reinforcing the authors' choice to live as brides of Christ. In convents across Spain and the Americas, nuns wrote about religious education and practice. Saints' lives and auto/biographies by and about women religious also aimed to teach readers the finer points of piety. The pedagogical purpose of such texts should not be overlooked, as it suggests that much information has yet to be incorporated into discussions of women's educational history.

Informal education—including counseling and mentoring—also plays a key role in the records of women's lives. From vidas to letters to Inquisition cases, women repeatedly emphasize the importance of female friends and advisors. The role that María Romero played in attempting to resolve domestic problems forms an important part of a history of women's reliance on each other for guidance. A glance at a few nuns' autobiographies also reveals the wealth of information about women's interpersonal relationships and educational development that can be mined in women's texts.

For example, a 1633 autobiography by Sor Teresa de Jesús María (1592–?) suggests that the nun's affective world centered almost exclusively on convent life. Whereas Sor Teresa states that she did not mourn her father's death and did not wish her widowed mother to enter her particular convent, she emphasizes the nurturing roles that other nuns played for her. The mutual guidance that Sor Teresa and another Carmelite gave each other strikes a chord in our search for records of educational experiences. The author notes that, as she assisted one of her sisters toward spiritual perfection, the two women helped each other achieve a state of spiritual bliss. Sor Teresa experienced a state of extraordinary resplendence, which in turn lifted her friend to intense spiritual heights for several days.[13] This anecdote captures the interdependence that fueled the spiritual lives of Carmelites. Like the hundreds of poems written by Carmelites to their founding mother, Teresa of Avila, this story of nuns' mutual instruction suggests a starting point for the reconstruction of women's formal and informal educational experiences.[14]

Other texts by religious women place equal emphasis on the role of guidance and instruction among nuns. The prolific writer Madre Hipólita de Jesús y Rocaberti (b. 1600s) mentions in her autobiography that for five full years she spoke only to a confessor and "a teacher whom I regarded as a substitute for my mother."[15] The role of mothers—metaphorical and biological—in the instruction of girls figures prominently in many texts produced in convents. Sor Estefanía de la Encarnación (1597–1665) articulates the conflicted nature of her relationship with her mother in her 1631 autobiography, for example; the nun proudly recounts that her mother consulted her in all matters even when she was just a child. In spite of the fondness with which she recalls these details, Sor Estefanía also relates her dismay over the rejection she experienced after her little brother was born. In retrospect, she postulated that her mother acted appropriately in favoring the younger male sibling.[16] The nun's reaction to the cultural practice of valuing boys over girls testifies to the emotional effects of prejudicial child rearing. Sor Estefanía expresses resentment over the preferential treatment given to her brother, yet she also justifies her mother's reaction, characterizing her own feelings as petty and peevish.

In addition to providing a record of one woman's reaction to the gendered experiences of early modern culture, Sor Estefanía's biography reveals the key role that female-to-female education played in her life. Having received a solid educational foundation from her mother and a male teacher as a child, Estefanía discovered her gift for painting and used this to instruct at least one other woman in the plastic arts. A gifted artist, the young Estefanía had been compared to the famed painter Sofonisba Anguissola and, while in her teens, was hired to instruct the noblewoman Beatriz de Villena in how to draw. The discussions of these experiences in the autobiography suggest that Sor Estefanía valued learning and teaching throughout her life.[17]

Another documented case of a mother who cultivated learning in her daughters is that of Cecilia de Morillas (1539–81), who has been described by Stacey Schlau as "an intellectual and humanist in her own right."[18] Educated by her father, Morillas in turn instructed her nine children in the fine arts, as well as in the study of several languages. Morillas's artistic and intellectual talents attracted the attention of King Philip II and other royals. Two of Morillas's daughters became nuns who worked, wrote, and translated together in the Convento de la Concepción in Valladolid. The stories of María de San Alberto and Cecilia del Nacimiento (1539–81) are extraordinary insofar as they capture a lifelong intellectual collaboration between sisters, as well as an entire family's indebtedness to an intellectually powerful mother.[19]

As these examples suggest, traces of women's educational networks can be found in Inquisition, convent, and literary texts. As we have seen, Inquisition records help us reconstruct various ways that women relied on each other for counseling and assistance. Others have used Inquisition documents to study Jewish and Moslem culture, suggesting that women played a major role in educating their families and maintaining religious traditions in spite of prohibitions to the contrary.[20] Literary fiction often depicts women relying on each other for guidance and support. Whether produced in convents or extramuros, female-authored nonfiction includes a subgenre of advice manuals aimed at religious instruction, behavioral modification, and societal improvement. As a genre, advice manuals by women have rarely been studied. These manuals provide a powerful counterpoint to the seemingly endless advice that men gave daughters, wives, and widows in the period. They constitute a rich source of information about the means by which women influenced each other and sought to make changes at domestic, local, institutional, and national levels. Sor Estefanía's autobiography provides excellent examples of the rich historical information we can glean about women's lives in their writing.

In reading for educational and advisory roles played by women, we can find direct evidence of responses to the gender codes that sought to domesticate and control women in early modern Spain. The texts reveal the extent to which women advocated change, sought to establish networks of influence, and reached out to each other. They also reveal the appeals to public authorities for help in bettering the social conditions of women. Writing to nuns, monks, politicians, and kings, women appealed to a broad range of communities and individuals for help in improving women's lives in the seventeenth century.

CONVENT INSTRUCTION

Poetry, fiction, and nonfiction written in convents serve as excellent sources of information about the moral and practical instruction nuns provided for each other. From basic convent management to complex spiritual questions, these texts deal with quotidian issues and abstract ideas that affected religious women. It is fascinating to read these details in such a variety of genres. The short plays by Sor Marcela de San Félix and the auto/biography of Sor Catalina de Jesús capture the diversity of convent texts—the authors use different media to speak explicitly of the difficulties of religious life. Considered together, many texts produced in convents can be viewed as constituting their own educational enterprise of woman-to-woman instruction. Fiction and nonfiction produced by nuns often share a concern for improving a religious community by instructing others on proper behavior and spiritual perfection.

The degree to which convent literature provides instruction and guidance suggests that a reconstruction of women's educational history needs to begin with a consideration of the educational function of convent texts. Nuns gave advice to each other and to those outside their convents. Constanza Ossorio (c. 1565–1637), in her posthumously published *Grove of the Celestial Spouse* (*Huerta del celestial esposo*, 1686), demonstrates great confidence in her judgment and influence when she addresses monks in many chapters. She tells them how to act when reprimanded, how to speak, and what to read. She instructs monks to fall to their knees when they have erred, always to speak of God, and to show a happy face to the world. Ossorio sees nonreligious writing as dangerous; she warns against egotism and curiosity in one's reading practices "because new reading engenders new ideas, and this quells the devotion of the soul."[21] The rigidity with which the Cistercian nun views reading and ideas might surprise us, since she herself was a writer with a strong educational background. Moreover, such unapologetic advice issued to men is surprising given the church hierarchy, as well as the humility with which many nuns expressed themselves.

The Cistercian nun has similarly strict advice for her sisters. She devotes a chapter to "how nuns should behave in the bedroom" ("Como se han de haber las monjas en el dormitorio"), in which she lays out explicit instructions for proper sleeping arrangements:

> It is also a very indecent thing that the religious woman should give herself entirely over to sleep, like a beast, with her hands parted ... and this is why they tell us to sleep with our clothes on, so that we cannot touch our nude bodies with our hands.[22]

Physical and mental restraint figure prominently in Ossorio's text. Concerned with imposing order, Ossorio used writing as a vehicle for articulating the rules and regulations of Cistercian life.

Valentina Pinelo (b. 1500s) expresses similar concern for the behavior and spiritual health of her religious order. Pinelo describes herself as ignorant in her *Book in Praise of the Excellent Qualities of Saint Anne* (*Libro de las alabanzas y excelencias de la gloriosa Santa Ana*, 1601), yet she has much to say on the topics of martyrdom, spirituality, and monasteries.[23] She, too, includes advice for nuns and monks. In Pinelo's estimation, the primary weapon needed for solid spirituality is prayer. Her advocacy of raising children in convents rests partly on an endorsement of the superior education provided to girls in religious contexts. Pinelo notes that in the external world, boys have teachers and girls have nursemaids. By setting up this comparison with the outside world, she highlights the superior access to education that girls have in convents. They learn to write, to speak with measured words, and to act with proper self-discipline. The author was proof of these benefits, as she lived in Seville's Convent of San Leandro from the time she was a small child.[24]

Pinelo exhorts the pleasure of watching children grow up as servants of God. Calling them "little plants in God's gardens," she describes youngsters learning the central practices of Catholicism (e.g., self-mortification, prayer, and confession) from an early age.[25] The use of a gardening metaphor for spiritual nurturing, used most famously by Saint Teresa, appears frequently in religious writing. Sor Angela María de la Concepción (b. 1600s) devoted an entire book to the concept. *Spiritual Watering of New Plants* (*Riego espiritual para nuevas plantas*, 1686) is a Trinitarian treatise on how best to instruct nuns in the "continuous war" they fight in their quest for spiritual perfection.[26] The metaphors of growth and gardening underpin this spiritual instruction manual:

> And so we are new plants. May we ever have renewed fervor for taking up arms to tame our passion and embrace all virtue, for with this we will achieve triumph and we will present a victory to God.[27]

Discussions of nurture and war permeate the text, infusing it with a combined sense of urgency and enthusiasm for the work of women religious.

Spiritual Watering reads like a passionate sermon, and the intimacy with which Sor Angela addresses other nuns adds an intriguing component to the text. She mentions the "manly spirit with which nuns have enlisted under the banner of the Holy Husband" and she speaks with fondness to her sisters, calling them "my dears," "dear sisters and daughters," and "beloved servants of

God."[28] Her choice of narrative voice adds a further intimate component to the text, as the use of the first-person-feminine plural *nosotras* emphasizes that the author and her readers are engaged in the same spiritual struggle.

The intimate, encouraging language of Sor Angela's suggestions for nurturing women spiritually finds a counterpart in Madre María de San José's similarly gentle but decidedly firm *Instruction of Novices: Dialogue between Two Nuns Named Gracia and Justa on the Prayer and Mortification with which Novices Should Be Brought Up* (*Instrucción de novicias: Diálogo entre dos religiosas que Gracia y Justa se llaman sobre la oración y mortificación con que se deben criar las novicias*. 1602). Written as a novel in dialogue, the text combines elements of drama and prose to create an outline of proper spiritual instruction for Carmelite novices. The prolific Madre María (1548–1603) wrote educational, poetic, and epistolary texts related to religious life, most during the last eighteen years of her life when, as head of the Reformed Carmelite convent in Lisbon, she was imprisoned and several times forced to report to the Inquisition. Finally, as Electa Arenal and Stacey Schlau explain, Madre María was so devoted to the Carmelite reforms implemented by Teresa of Avila that she suffered for her order. In the end, "she died in internal exile in her native land, persecuted and ostracized."[29]

Having traveled with Saint Teresa and participated in the early foundation of the order of the Discalced Carmelites, María de San José (Salazar) shared with her predecessor a firm belief in the religious education of nuns. In *Instruction of Novices*, the character Gracia informs Justa of the rules that guide the treatment of novices. The text contains advice for male and female religious on how best to nurture their spirituality and offers wonderful insights into the types of women who aspired to become nuns. Three kinds of people populate convents, according to Gracia. Some have perfect character, others are neither bad nor good, and others have "perverse inclinations and indomitable spirits." Melancholic women should not consider a religious life, and this text advises that those who have personalities unfit for the habit should be encouraged to return home and not be put through the tests involved in the training of all novices.[30] Madre María comments on the need for nuns to maintain levels of formality, to avoid gossip, and to use good hygiene. She also notes that monks are not exempt from these high standards of behavior.

Madre María identifies the literary education of women as a key component of religious life. Having grown up in an aristocratic household, she received such a superior education that Saint Teresa referred to her as a bookworm (*letrera*).[31] Madre María firmly believed that women religious must pursue an education, and *Instruction of Novices* disparages those who neglect their studies in favor of other kinds of devotional practices. The reenactment of the education of a novice provides the dramatic structure for the text. Three novices present themselves to Gracia, each representative of one of the three personality types laid out in earlier descriptions of convent populations. Each young woman must defend her intentions, which leads the melancholic third novice, Irene, to reveal that she was drawn to religion because she "feared for her sins."[32] Ill-suited for the strict life of the reformed Carmelites, Irene represents the type of novice that should be weeded out.

The distinct characters and dialogue structure make this an intriguing text in the development of women's drama in the period.[33] Moreover, the dramatization of learning and teaching brings the issue of women's education front and center. The educational processes involved in turning novices into nuns formed an important part of convent life. This text highlights the cooperation necessary for such institutionalized instruction, as the knowledgeable Gracia teaches Justa how to instruct the novices in Carmelite religiosity. In turn, the young women learn the expectations that others have of them. Gracia lays out the unique aspects of Carmelite religiosity, including the various components of prayer. The Latin prayers listed at the end of the work provide a study manual for novices and a guideline for their teachers.

With *Instruction of Novices*, María de San José gave her order an outline for religious education, more explicit in its discussion of women's teaching and learning than the other texts we have reviewed. She also offered a model for female-to-female education in which cooperation and devotion are the cornerstones of a successful instructional program. Like Ossorio's *Spiritual Grove*, Pinelo's *Book of Praise*, and Sor Angela María de la Concepción's *Spiritual Watering*, *Instruction of Novices* provides information about the advice that religious women gave to others. The prevalence of such advice highlights the important role that education played in cultivating and maintaining proper religiosity among the Catholic orders. While priests enjoyed influence and prestige, women's religious writing confirms that nuns looked to each other for the nuts-and-bolts details about convent spirituality and domesticity. For many, to be a nun was to be both a teacher and a learner. Texts produced for consumption by nuns and monks confirm that mutual responsibility and obligation lay at the heart of religious life for women and men.

ADVICE FOR THE SECULAR WORLD

During the early modern period, nuns and aristocratic secular women developed elaborate strategies to offer advice for the secular world. Historian Magdalena Sánchez has reconstructed the story of how three Habsburg women influenced the policies of King Philip III, for example. Sánchez's

The Empress, the Queen, and the Nun puts into relief the strategies used by Philip's mother, wife, and sister to participate in the political decisions of the House of Austria in the period 1598–1621. Similarly, Helen Nader's essay collection on the Mendoza women illustrates the active roles the female members of that powerful family played throughout the early modern period.[34] Such studies demonstrate the concerted efforts made by high-ranking women to secure, stabilize, and increase familial wealth and prestige.

Unlike the high-ranking aristocrats discussed in recent scholarship, most women did not have direct access to the monarchy. Nonetheless, nuns and aristocratic secular women put pen to paper to influence their society. Many offered social and political critiques. Their reform and behavior manuals outlined basic educational and moral instruction and explicitly advocated social reform. Two countesses—María de Guevara and Luisa de Padilla— wrote extensively on the state of affairs in mid-seventeenth-century Spain, for example. Magdalena de San Jerónimo strove to influence social change through her plan for female penal reform. While their approaches varied considerably, the authors seem to have shared a basic belief in the validity of their ideas. That each wrote a text dedicated to social reform suggests they hoped or perhaps believed that their ideas might influence society at large. Addressing themselves to the men who controlled the political and legal spheres and to those who needed to improve their treatment of women, these three authors laid out programs for change. Consequently, their texts afford us access to the public policy and social recommendations of highly educated women in seventeenth-century Spain.

Luisa María de Padilla Manrique (1590–1646), the Countess of Aranda, had many such recommendations. Indeed, this noblewoman from Burgos wrote several tomes on such lofty topics as chastity, truth, and nobility. She devoted most of her attention to problems with the aristocracy, writing four books on the virtues, problems, and ideologies of the Spanish nobility. The third book in this series, *Tears of the Nobility* (*Lágrimas de la nobleza*, 1639), laments the disordered affairs and unacceptable behavior of Padilla's fellow nobles. Each chapter focuses on a specific problem, including cursing, laziness, and gambling; the mistreatment of servants; and bad parenting. Proclaiming that nobles do a poor job of raising their children, Padilla offers a list of historical and mythological examples to bolster her argument for strict child rearing.[35] Like Madre María de San José and others before her, Padilla believed in the instructional power of history.

While Madre María recorded the history of Carmelite reform and delineated an educational program for her sisters, Padilla wrote that her words would act "as reminders to the wise" and would "bring enlightenment to the ignorant."[36] Padilla clearly states in book 4 of this series that she expects her books to help people "see the path of virtue" and "flee from vice."[37] Most fascinating about Padilla's litany of advice in this fourth book, *Idea of Nobles and Their Undertakings* (*Idea de nobles y sus desempeños,* 1644) is that Padilla chose men as her primary audience. Covering everything from what a noble child should learn in the first years of life to how to be fair in government, Padilla outlined the fundamental information a nobleman needed to be both decent and successful. In sum, she positioned herself as a seventeenth-century Emily Post, offering in her hefty tomes the outline of a proper education for nobles. The confidence with which Padilla addressed noblemen suggests that, like the nuns who advised monks, she felt comfortable asserting her authority. What is more, Padilla felt confident enough in her knowledge of society to give advice about positions of power from which women were excluded entirely.

María de Guevara (d. 1683) chose a similar audience for her social critique. As the Countess of Escalante, Guevara had access to the highest echelons of society. Her 1664 *Disenchantments at Court and Valiant Women* (*Desengaños de la corte, y mujeres valerosas*) laments the general disarray and degradation that afflicted the court during the reign of Philip IV. Guevara had many of the same complaints as Padilla about the Spanish aristocracy. Her first chapter laments the malice, envy, and avarice of the court, for instance. She recommends that the court be diminished in number, arguing that this change would eliminate at least some social problems. Moreover, Guevara gives voice to women's plight, openly criticizing the consequences of men's philandering:

> Many men are simply lost and they lead their wives to perdition with dirty illnesses with which they lose the succession [of their family lines]. And he who has such illness has children who are so sick that they die with their first breath.[38]

This discussion of the infertility, deformity, and other problems caused by such diseases as gonorrhea and syphilis captures the straightforward tone of Guevara's discourse. It would not be surprising to read an indictment of the "dirty illnesses" of the lower classes, for example, in texts written by a noblewoman, but in this instance, Guevara avoids such overt elitism. Instead, by linking the promiscuity of her fellow nobles with the ill health of the entire aristocracy, she makes a convincing argument for social responsibility.

The indictment of men in chapter 1 gives way to a celebration of illustrious women in chapter 2. At first the connection between the two topics seems obscure, but Guevara's affirmation of women's superior intellectual abilities makes clear that the author holds men responsible for much of the disorder and destruction in the world. She asserts, for example: "It is beyond a doubt that if women known for their spirit and valor were allowed on governing boards that they would be viewed as positively as the keenest advisors."[39] Guevara focuses on the invention of modern weapons to illustrate her dissatisfaction with men's courage and general leadership skills; modern weaponry only encourages cowardice, according to Guevara's schema. Her argument rests on the stories of those who did not need firearms to prove their bravery. The courage of women such as Antona García, who defended her city with a kitchen tool, and of women who maimed themselves to avoid capture or attain their husbands' release support Guevara's point about women's resourcefulness and strength.

Guevara does not set out to disparage all men. Rather, she aims to improve gender relations and to motivate noblemen to meet their obligations. Her approach is direct in this regard. In addition to insisting that men treat women with respect, she declares that men who do not take women's advice are crazy.[40] Guevara has advice for kings in chapter 4 and, later, for men who run their own estates. At times, *Disenchantments at Court* reads like a retirement brochure, as it covers questions of financial planning, household management, and charitable giving. Guevara emphasizes lords' responsibility to their vassals, particularly with regard to the surrounding community. A lord should support his local church, sponsor festivals, and look after the poor. This outline of the responsibility of the rich to the poor appears amidst advice for military action and guidelines for gender relations. Guevara covers a host of issues that, in their totality, constitute a basic moral instruction manual for aristocratic men. If a nobleman followed all of Guevara's advice, he would have a smoothly run estate, a copacetic marriage, and a clean spiritual slate. In other words, he would be a respectable citizen by most standards.

María de Guevara emphasized the need for strict yet empathetic governance of one's house and one's country. Her insistence on balancing rigidity with compassion echoes a text on prison reform from earlier in the century. In 1608, Madre Magdalena de San Jerónimo (b. 1500s) published *Explanation and Structure of the Galley and Royal Prison* (*Razón y forma de la galera y casa real*).[41] In the prologue, Madre Magdalena explains that her program for reform had been judged as "too rigorous and severe, particularly for something invented by a woman against women."[42] Clearly the author did not allow such concerns to dissuade her, for she presented her plan to the king for his consideration. The problem, as Madre Magdalena saw it, was that human beings constantly create the need for new incarceration practices. In her humbly named "little treatise" (*tratadillo*), Madre Magdalena advocated the establishment of penal institutions in which to punish "female vagrants, thieves, sorceresses, go-betweens, and other similar women."[43]

Madre Magdalena sought not only penal reform, but also a new program of education for the female prisoners. Twenty years of experience working with delinquent women led Madre Magdalena to observe that such women, who infect men with disease and encourage sinful behavior, are "miserable enemies of God who contaminate the Republic."[44] To deal with them, the reformer proposed implementing highly structured female prisons, which she called galleys (*galeras*). These combination prison-workhouses would have their own secret jails, chapels, and torture chambers. Madre Magdalena emphasized the importance of daily work, as well as the presence of implements of torture. She laid out the terms of women's punishment as well. More rigid than the author of the 1598 reform manual upon which her own program was based, Madre Magdalena advocated that women new to town be required to register at the prison and to obey a curfew of 9:00 P.M. in summer and 8:00 in winter. Three levels form the backbone of the punishment scale, which progressed from incarceration to branding the flesh to execution by hanging.

Madre Magdalena positioned herself as an expert on female delinquency and social reform. She was right in predicting that others would judge her harshly, as her intolerance for crime and her suggestions for behavioral control were severe, even for the times. Knowing that she diverged from the prevailing opinion that women deserved more leniency than men, she relied on her credentials to convince readers that her program could be so successful that, ideally, women would be dissuaded from engaging in crime and sin and no prison at all would have to exist.[45] By the time Madre Magdalena published her text, the Madrid prison had opened, providing her with a successful example to bolster her penal plan. Evidently she argued with some success, for a 1608 text described an institution called a *galera* that followed the working-reform model proposed by Madre Magdalena.[46] Apparently the religious woman/jailer/reformer convinced the Crown to bankroll the institution.

Although Magdalena de San Jerónimo wrote about topics different from those dealt with by Luisa de Padilla and María de Guevara, all three women addressed the same audience. They weighed in on public policy and gender relations with such authority that kings, lords, and prison wardens alike could find guidelines for behavior and decision making in the women's texts. In their choice of readership and topics, the authors broke with the prevailing ideology that relegated women to the domestic sphere. Moreover, their social criticism turned contemporary writing by men on its head. Many behavior manuals by men lamented women's laziness, promiscuity, and corruptibility, yet Padilla's series on nobles and Guevara's *Disenchantments at Court* pointed the finger at men's irresponsibility and cowardice as major sources of social ills. In a different way, Magdalena de San Jerónimo's plan for penal reform flew in the face of gender expectations. As Madre Magdalena anticipated, her plan did not jibe with most views on the treatment of delinquent women. Contrary to what one might expect from a woman, Madre Magdalena had harsh recommendations for control of behavior, punishment for repeat offenders, and general living conditions of the delinquents. In a fundamental sense, all three of these women wrote against the grain. They took on social issues that desperately needed attention, and they did so by addressing those most likely to influence change. By speaking to an audience of men, Padilla, Guevara, and Madre Magdalena appealed to those who could implement solutions.

NETWORKS OF INFLUENCE

Instructive and advisory texts reveal that women played key roles in educating and advising each other in a time when male authorities spent much energy outlining proper female behaviors. As we have seen, Inquisition records and convent documents confirm that women of all classes engaged in educational and counseling activities in the early modern period. Even the brief mention of interactions among female friends in the trials of Bernarda Manuel and Eleno/a de Céspedes alludes to the ways in which women leaned on each other for guidance and support.

If we take instructional literature as a loosely defined category of texts in the period, we can see that nuns wrote dissimilar texts whose shared purpose was education. Even when we look only at convent texts, we can see that nuns wrote with different purposes in mind. Sor Marcela de San Félix wrote plays for festivities, yet her texts were no less instructional than Madre María de San José's manual on novices. Speaking to their sisters, these nuns chose the vehicles of drama and prose to reinforce the ideologies and practices of their orders. Living in the world of the aristocracy, on the other hand, María de Guevara and Luisa de Padilla reached out to the public in their socially critical books. Specifically concerned with capturing the attention of men, these authors derided the degradation of the aristocracy and offered advice for improving political, social, and domestic conditions.

Produced in different arenas and for different purposes, all these texts aimed to educate readers. In keeping with the impulse in the larger literary culture to educate while entertaining, women writers produced texts that had instructional messages for other women and, often, for men. In spite of the wide range of opinions offered, it is clear that they form a body of literature written by women for the explicit purpose of instruction and education. Each author, in her own way, was a moral guide. Like María Romero,

Teresa Valle, and Catalina de Jesús, these women positioned themselves as counselors and leaders. Whether they made their communities in convents or in society at large, they acted as advisors and educators.

The consideration of a broad spectrum of texts through the lens of women's educational history allows for an analysis of religious, class, and ethnic difference. It also allows us to reconsider the dicta proffered by men to women in the period. Male humanists, politicians, and church leaders outlined proper female behavior through their laws, sermons, pamphlets, books, and decrees. Guevara, Padilla, and, through her fiction, María de Zayas, responded by laying the blame for social degradation squarely on the shoulders of men. Madre Magdalena responded by outlining penal reform that she deemed appropriate for female delinquents. In convents, women's daily activities and their prolific writing proved that claims of inferiority did not apply to them. Capable of running institutions, creating and implementing rules, and instructing each other in all matters great and small, nuns were living examples of the wrong-headedness of those who described women as the weaker sex. Women living in and out of convents developed specific strategies for combating the ideologies that defined them as inferior and incapable.

If we jump ahead to the eighteenth century, it becomes clear that the 1600s provided women with opportunities to solidify and expand their roles as advisors and educators. By the eighteenth century, women occupied a more prominent role in the public sphere in Spain.[47] More women wrote for the public book market than in the previous century, for example. In particular, women wrote and translated advice books, took part in debates on female education, and participated in literary culture by running salons (known as *tertulias*). Through such organizations as Madrid's Economic Society, educated middle- and upper-class women oversaw the vocational education of their working-class counterparts. The integration of early modern women's writing and life stories provides a background for the more public activities of eighteenth-century women. The ties between the two eras are well worth noting. The texts examined throughout this chapter support the existence of extensive networks and elaborate strategies for advocacy and leadership among women. Seventeenth-century women challenged conceptualizations of gender, and they participated in decision making in the public and private, secular and religious spheres.

Literary, Inquisition, and convent texts document women asserting their independence, helping each other, and contributing to the greater social good. Such texts confirm that, in spite of being excluded from educational institutions, women developed systematic and sometimes professional means by which to offer advice and instruction to others. In their daily activities, their life choices, and their writing, women from varied class backgrounds acted as advisors, teachers, and reformers in the seventeenth century.

The archives are teeming with stories of women who occupied leadership roles in all realms of Spanish culture. As each new story comes to light, we move one step closer to knowing how women experienced the culture of early modern Spain. In a time of increased access to literacy, travel, and social mobility, women found ways to insert themselves into the newly stratified, urbanized society. Examining their stories gives us an opportunity to see the communities, beliefs, and practices sustained by women, and to better understand, from a distance, the relationship between gender and culture in a historical moment that, not unlike our own times, saw tremendous social change. The stories throughout *The Lives of Women* suggest that a complete history that includes men and women in this foundational moment of Europe's past can be written. Educators and reformers, widows and businesswomen, wives and nuns all must form part of this new history, for their experiences provide a counterbalance to traditional views of the culture of control of Spain's early modern period.

CONCLUSION

erhaps because some consider Spain slightly backward—a poor step-child to the rest of western Europe—people often express incredulity when they discover that Spanish women wrote in the sixteenth and seventeenth centuries. Did women in Spain actually write then? Did they use pseudonyms? Did they all live in convents? Women, in and out of convents, did write. What's more, their words are recorded in hundreds if not thousands of texts, waiting to be recovered from their slumber.

When I began this project, I did not know so many records of these women's words existed. Nor did I expect to find so many similarities among the fictional texts, autobiographies, and legal records. To my surprise, the repetition of the themes of motherhood, friendship, sexuality, and community pointed to common priorities among women of different backgrounds. Religion emerged as an important facet of women's lives, but not all of the texts dealt with spirituality. Still, secular and religious women alike emphasized their identities as mothers, wives, advisors, and friends. No matter what kind of text I studied, I found that women focused on the interpersonal, affective aspects of life.

The textual evidence examined in this book suggests that women experienced the world differently than men in the early modern period. Gender was such a compelling factor that, in spite of great differences among women, many had similar reactions to a culture that tried to control and domesticate them. This is not to say that there was no variety among women or their experiences. Class, ethnicity, marital status, and religion functioned as key markers of difference in the 1500s and 1600s, just as they do today. From the perspective of class, the aristocracy clearly enjoyed more privilege than any other group. Aristocratic women's superior education was matched only by that of some nuns, whose convent training included both moral and literary instruction. Like other women, noblewomen were schooled in the domestic, so-called womanly arts, but because of their enormous privilege, most also acquired the coveted skill of literacy. María de Zayas, Luisa de Padilla, and María de Guevara had in common their similar class positions, as well as their impressive educational backgrounds. As members of a class that advocated a sense of obligation to itself, its land, and its society, they tried to incorporate the concerns of women into these priorities. These writers added gender obligation to the framework of noblesse oblige, producing texts that blatantly challenged the status quo.

Zayas, Padilla, and Guevara all directed themselves to male audiences, denouncing the general state of affairs and calling for social change. Fiction writers Mariana de Carvajal, Ana Caro, and Angela de Azevedo also belonged to this group of upper-class female authors. Often less confrontational than Zayas and her cohort, these authors nonetheless wrote texts focused on women's love and friendship, providing a wholly distinct perspective on gender and society than we find in men's texts from the period.

The privileged status of the aristocratic women who wrote bold commentaries about Spanish society leads us to contemplate the important role played by class in the reconstruction of women's history. Helen Nader, in her introduction to *Gender and Power in Early Modern Spain,* has gone so far to assert that the women of the powerful Mendoza family operated in a matriarchal culture that coexisted with the patriarchy. Analyses of aristocratic women's writing and agency do suggest that such women exercised more power than ever before understood. Such findings also remind us that, just as reading only men's words limits our understanding of history, considering only women of great class privilege—such as Zayas, Guevara, and the Mendozas—would likewise yield a compromised view of gender in early modern Spain. Based solely on upper-class women's acerbic criticism or political influence, we might think that all women enjoyed unchecked freedom of speech and action. Similarly, based on the implementation of Madre Magdalena's idea for a reform prison, we might think that female advice often was heeded at institutional levels. Yet these women were the exceptions.

The voices of prostitutes, prisoners, and other women are absent from this book, as they are from other books on the period. This notable absence speaks to the ongoing challenges of recovering women's history: We know that few women were literate, even fewer wrote, and an even smaller number saw their work in print or in circulation. Perhaps even more important, we know that the men to whom Zayas referred as the "vain legislators of the world" in fact did not make any significant changes for women, who continued to be excluded from legal and educational processes for three more centuries.

Since scholars traditionally have relied on texts produced for the book market or for the political sphere, documents by and about those who did not form part of the upper echelons of society add new dimensions to our understanding of the early modern period. The psychologically complex auto/biography of Sor Catalina de Jesús captures many of the pressures of women's existence in the period. The young Catalina belonged to a relatively privileged class, yet concerns for her economic welfare led her family to force her to marry and, upon her husband's death, to try to force marriage on her again. Sor Catalina's story highlights many of the economic, spiritual, and emotional difficulties faced by women in the period.

Many religious women did not hail from upper-class backgrounds. Their writing represents a body of literature that promises to enhance our understanding of the relationship between religion, gender, and class. Some religious women we did not consider here, such as Isabel de Jesús (1586–1648), left only dictated texts. As we have seen, the letters and vidas of women such as María de Orozco, who struggled for recognition and legitimacy, also add to the body of literature by and about those of varying circumstances. In conjunction with the writings of upper-class nuns, the letters and life stories of these women can help us understand spirituality, authority, and education from the perspective of women religious.

As the examples we have seen suggest, Inquisition archives contain a wealth of information about the pre-eighteenth-century Hispanic world. As each new generation of scholars visits the archives, we learn more about the workings of the institution and its effect on individuals and society. Bernarda Manuel's self-defense provides fascinating details about mental illness and domestic abuse, as well as women's relationships with friends and family. Trial records of unusual figures such as Eleno/a de Céspedes and Lucrecia de León fill out our knowledge of the ways in which the lower and middle classes navigated social restraints. Céspedes and León sought to create niches for themselves in a society that wanted to purge itself of all signs of difference. While Céspedes drew attention to him/herself by moving up through society's ranks, changing genders, and practicing various professions, León colluded in publicizing her politically explosive dreams. María Romero lived more squarely on the margins than any of the other defendants whose cases we examined. As a member of Madrid's lower classes, Romero occupied a tenuous social position. She filled an important role in her local community, yet practiced a form of healing viewed as dangerous by the authorities. In the end, all these people fell victim to rigid ideologies enforced by the Inquisition. The often poignant narratives of their lives found in legal defenses and depositions provide intimate, detailed information about women's daily existence.

Contrary to what the trials of these and other lower- and middle-class defendants might suggest, class privilege did not immunize one from prosecution by the Inquisition. Teresa Valle de la Cerda maintained correspondence with high-ranking government and church officials, yet this did not prevent her conviction or punishment. Valle's discussions of physical intimacy, power politics, and ecstatic spirituality offer a record of convent culture from a woman's perspective. Her texts offer a fine example of the insights that women's words offer about the intimacies and power struggles of early modern life.

Literary, convent, and Inquisition sources have put into relief the early modern dynamics of gender, sexuality, ethnicity, and religion. All these sources contain information on the pressures that women lived with and the strategies that they used to cope with such pressures. By examining a variety of sources, we have glimpsed women's open discussions of sexuality and covert religious practices. We discovered details about domestic abuse and mental illness from the perspective of a terrified wife. We glimpsed the psychological consequences of forced marriages, and the rewards and difficulties of religiosity.

The experiences of these individuals tie into the larger picture of the overlapping politics of gender, ethnicity, and class in early modern Spain. Prescriptive texts purport to tell us what choices were available to women, but documents that record women's words reveal the ways in which women worked within and, sometimes, around such options. In spite of the emphasis on control, women circumvented many prohibitions on sexuality, spirituality, and autonomy. Numerous texts confirm that many women compensated for their lack of access to formal education by serving as educators, advisors, and confidants.

The reconstruction of advisory and educational networks in the last two chapters exemplifies the research that we still need to do to enrich our understanding of gender in the early modern period. This analysis demonstrated that the baroque emphasis on moral instruction in fact pervades texts written by and about women. Looking to the educational intent and value of women's texts, the final section of the book argued that we need to reconceptualize our definitions of education. We need to include the mechanisms by which women inserted themselves into the history of education by acting as advisors, teachers, and instructors to other women and men.

The frequent mention of sexuality and touch in Inquisition records and literary texts suggests that a more complete history of intimacy might be written if we return to the archives. In a similar vein, a history of domestic violence has yet to be written for the Hispanic world. Documents like that of Bernarda Manuel provide a clear record of such violence. More can be learned by studying legal records as well as ecclesiastical petitions for separation, which sometimes detail domestic violence.

Lucrecia de León and Bernarda Manuel's ability to read and write raises the topic of literacy training. If these nonaristocratic women could read and write, there must have been others like them. How many others, and who exactly educated them? The frequent mention of mothers as educators, as in the case of Sor Estefanía de la Encarnación and numerous Inquisition records, piques the curiosity and suggests that the maternal role in education has yet to be explored sufficiently. Moreover, the existence of educated women at all strata of society raises the question of women's relationship to the written word and the book market. We still do not know, for example, whether men or women were the primary consumers of female-authored fiction in the seventeenth century. Nor have we studied the expressions of women—both negative and positive—with regard to their identity and their lot. Did mothers encourage their daughters to read Zayas and Carvajal? Did this reading form part of their moral as well as literary instruction? Did cloistered women read their secular counterparts? Did nuns express dismay as well as pleasure regarding their position as subordinates in a male-oriented church structure? These are only a handful of the questions raised by the compelling stories of women found in historical and creative texts from Spain's early modern period. The sheer variety of sources and stories confirms that we still have much to learn about women in the European past.

One does not undertake historical work without the firm belief that the past has something to teach us about the present. In studying the lives of women from early modern Europe, we can gain perspective on complex issues—our views on gender, race, and ethnicity, for example—that continue to challenge us today. The early modern period resonates strongly with our own day and age. Modern definitions of citizenship and social organization that took hold in Europe continue to affect nations in the twenty-first century. Elitism and discrimination of all forms were institutionalized during this formative period by the government and, in Spain, by the Inquisition. Women were considered secondary citizens by almost every definition, yet the strategies of survival and resistance practiced by women of various backgrounds, classes, and ethnicities point to a collective sense of validation and purpose. Denigrated by the larger society and excluded from full participation in the emerging nation-state, women found ways to assert their authority and cultivate their talents. The dynamic relationship between women and the larger culture bears witness to the challenges that nondominant groups continue to face in today's world.

While life in the twenty-first century is different from life in inquisitional Spain, entire groups of people throughout the West still confront discrimination and disenfranchisement on a daily basis. Immigrants, Moslems, and people of color continue to fall victim to racist and xenophobic policies throughout the developed world. By advancing our understanding of the relationship between women, minorities, and the dominant cultures of the past, we can learn how individuals have responded to the exclusionary policies and value systems that pervade modern societies. Whether found in legal records, convent documents, or fictional texts, individual stories offer insight into the coping mechanisms of those who faced discrimination based on their gender, class, sexuality, and ethnicity. The stories of early modern women suggest that many individuals developed sophisticated—albeit not always successful—strategies to overcome their exclusion from justice, education, and other points of access to the public sphere. Many women in the early modern period articulated their priorities, spoke with authority, and legitimized their gender-specific experiences. They accepted and also circumvented the options available to them. Some struggled to survive and others struggled for social change. Collectively, theirs is the story of women in early modern Spain.

GLOSSARY

auto de fe. Ceremony in which those tried by the Inquisition had their sentences read. Autos de fe sometimes included public execution but more often involved displays of penitence.

beata. Religious laywoman, often affiliated with a religious order.

comedia. Classical Spanish play in three acts with three thousand lines of text.

converso, conversa. Convert from Judaism to Christianity or the descendant of such a person.

Crypto-Jew. Converso/a who practiced Judaism covertly.

fray. Title for a religious brother.

hagiography. Representation (in art or in writing) that aims to glorify the spiritual perfection of its subject.

Holy Office. Official name of the Inquisition, so called because of the Catholic origin of the institution.

limpieza de sangre. Literally "purity of blood," in reference to a "pure" Christian lineage. Statutes were passed in the sixteenth century requiring such purity for many offices, positions, and privileges.

memorial. An autobiographical statement made by a defendant in an Inquisition trial. Usually a verbal statement, but some individuals wrote their memorials.

Morisco. Convert from Islam to Christianity or the descendant of such a person.

querelle des femmes. Renaissance debate over the worth of women or, literally, "the woman question."

sanbenito/sambenito. A penitential garment that bore a representation of an individual's heresy.

sor. Title for a religious sister.

tacha. System by which defendants before the Inquisition could attempt to exclude witnesses hostile to them.

vida. Spiritual biography or autobiography.

BRIEF BIOGRAPHIES

Abarca de Bolea, Ana Francisca (1602–late 1680s): A Cistercian nun from Zaragoza, Abarca took vows in the Real Monasterio de Santa María in Hueca in 1624. A poet and writer of prose fiction and nonfiction, Abarca was very active in the literary culture of her region.

Angela María de la Concepción (Sor) (b. 1600s): Founder and prioress of Convento de las Recoletas Trinitarias in Toboso, Sor Angela María wrote the spiritual treatise *Riego espiritual para nuevas plantas* (1686).

Azevedo, Angela de (c. 1600–?): Born in Lisbon, Azevedo moved to Madrid with her parents and served in the court of Philip IV as lady-in-waiting to Queen Isabel de Borbón. She wrote plays with secular and religious themes. Upon widowhood, she entered a Benedictine convent with her only daughter.

Bernal, Beatriz (b. 1500s): This native of Valladolid was the author of the chivalric novel *Don Cristalián de España* (1545), originally published anonymously. Bernal married and had a daughter who later became instrumental in republishing the book under her mother's name.

Caño, María de (b. 1500s): Wife of Eleno/a de Céspedes, who was a licensed surgeon and a hermaphrodite, Caño was accused, and later exonerated, of having married a woman during Céspedes's Inquisition trial in the 1580s.

Caro Mallén de Soto, Ana (c. 1600–?): Author of secular and religious plays, Caro was born in the south of Spain, possibly in Granada, and is on record as having received payment for her writing in Seville. It is not known if she ever married.

Carvajal, Mariana de (c. 1610–?): A mother of nine children, whose financial situation was difficult after her husband's death, Carvajal published a novella collection in 1663.

Carvajal y Mendoza, Luisa de (1566–1614): A member of the powerful Mendoza family, Carvajal traveled to England in 1605 with the goal of converting Anglicans to Catholicism. She wrote poems, an autobiography, and more than one hundred letters before dying in England in 1614.

Catalina de Jesús y San Francisco (Sor) (1639–77): Born near Toledo in central Spain, the young Catalina was raised by an aunt in Alcalá de Henares. Probably for financial considerations, she was required to marry Juan Bernique. After bearing three children and becoming widowed, Catalina Bernique joined a third-order Franciscan convent in Alcalá, where she took her religious name and later founded a school for poor girls.

Cecilia del Nacimiento (Sor) (1570–1646): Born Cecilia Sobrino Morillas, Cecilia took the veil with her sister, María de San Alberto, at the Convento de la Concepción in Valladolid in 1588. Together the women wrote, translated, and exercised leadership as Discalced Carmelites.

Céspedes, Eleno/a de (c. 1545 or 1546–?): Born a morisca slave girl and named after her owners, Céspedes married, gave birth, and developed a protrusion that eventually led to her transformation from woman to man. Tried by the Inquisition in the 1580s, Céspedes was sentenced to ten years of service in a hospital and was forced to live as a woman.

Cueva y Silva, Leonor de la (b. 1600s): Born in Medina del Campo early in the seventeenth century, Cueva y Silva wrote plays and poetry. It is not known if she ever married.

Díaz del Valle, Mariana (b. 1600s): Prisoner of the Inquisition and witness in the sorcery trial of María Romero in 1702, Díaz was married to a volatile man and paid Romero to provide her with remedies to stop the violence and to attract lovers.

Enríquez de Guzmán, Feliciana (b. 1500s): Probably born before 1580 in Seville, Enríquez wrote a two-part play with elaborate requirements for staging. The playwright married twice, experienced financial problems upon the death of her second husband, and had no known surviving children.

Escobar, Zebriana de (b. 1600s): Witness in the sorcery trial of María Romero in 1702, Escobar was a widow who had been beaten by her domestic partner. She testified to the Inquisition that she paid Romero for remedies to stop the violence.

Estefanía de la Encarnación (Sor) (1597–1665): Born Estefanía Guarre de la Canal, Estefanía became a nun at the convent of Santa Clara in Lerma. Artist and author, she wrote several texts, including a beautifully illustrated autobiography.

Francisca de Santa Teresa, (Sor) (1654–1709): Born Manuela Francisca Escarate in Madrid, Francisca took the veil at the Convento de las

Trinitarias Descalzas in that city in 1673. Like her sister and literary predecessor Sor Marcela de San Félix, Sor Francisca wrote poetry and plays that, for the most part, remain unedited to this day.

Galindo, Beatriz (1475–1534): Galindo served Isabel la Católica as a lady-in-waiting and as a Latin tutor. A Renaissance humanist par excellence, she wrote commentaries on classical authors. She married once and, in her widowhood, oversaw the construction of a hospital for the indigent in Madrid. The hospital is known today as *La Latina*, Galindo's nickname.

Gómez, Juana (b. 1600s): Gómez was a business partner of María Romero, and both were tried by the Inquisition in 1702. Both women seem to have practiced love magic in seventeenth-century Madrid, yet Gómez was only penitenced, not banished as Romero was.

Guevara, María de (d. 1683): As the Countess of Escalante, Guevara wrote an instructional text on court life dedicated to Philip IV's son, Prince Carlos. She also wrote a biography of her family in the form of a petition to the king for financial support.

Hipólita de Jesús y Rocaberti (Madre) (b. 1600s): Prolific author of numerous spiritual and moral treatises, Madre Hipólita was a Dominican nun in Valencia.

Juana Inés de la Cruz (Sor) (1648–95): After serving as a lady-in-waiting in the court of the Marquise and Marquis de Mancera, the young Juana entered the Convento de las Carmelitas Descalzas in Mexico City. In 1669 she took the veil at the Convento de San Jerónimo, where she lived until her death. She was an enormously talented author of plays, poetry, and prose. In conjunction with Teresa of Avila, Sor Juana is one of the most influential women writers of the early centuries of Hispanic writing.

León, Lucrecia de (1568–?): León predicted the 1588 fall of the Spanish Armada, a prophecy that helped lead to her Inquisition trial in 1590. Found guilty of making heretical statements, she was given the lightest possible sentence—one hundred lashes, banishment from Madrid, and two years' seclusion in a religious house. Some 415 of her dreams were recorded before León disappeared from the record.

Liaño, Isabel de (b. 1500s): In the biography in verse on Saint Catherine of Siena that she published in 1604, Liaño claimed to be writing for women only. Little is known about Liaño's life, but she does not appear to have come from aristocratic stock.

Magdalena de San Jerónimo (Madre) (b. 1500s): Little is known about the early life of Magdalena, who lived and worked in Valladolid, Madrid, and Brussels. She corresponded with high-ranking aristocrats such as Isabel Clara Eugenia and Luisa de Carvajal y Mendoza. She also wrote an influential treatise on women's prisons.

Manuel, Bernarda (c. 1616–?): A Portuguese-born immigrant to Seville who married Antonio Gómez Borges and had five surviving children at the time of her Inquisition trial in 1650, Manuel, accused by her husband, was tried and convicted for Judaizing.

Marcela de San Félix (Sor) (1605–88): Born Marcela del Carpio in 1605, Marcela took vows in 1622 at the Convento de las Trinitarias Descalzas de San Ildefonso in Madrid. A fine playwright and poet, Sor Marcela perhaps inherited her artistic talents from her father, the great dramatist Lope de Vega, and her mother, the famous actress Micaela de Luján.

María de Agreda (Madre) (1602–65): Franciscan nun, mystical author, and frequent correspondent of Philip IV.

María de San Alberto (Madre) (1568–1640): Born María Sobrino Morillas, María took the veil at the Convento de la Concepción in Valladolid with her sister, Cecilia del Nacimiento. Together the women wrote, translated, and exercised leadership as Discalced Carmelites.

María de San José (Salazar) (1548–1603): A prolific nun who participated with Teresa of Avila in the founding of the Discalced Carmelites, Madre María wrote educational, poetic, and epistolary texts related to religious life, including a treatise in dialogue, *Instrucción de novicias* (1602).

Meneses, Leonor de (c. 1620–64): Born in Lisbon, Meneses published a novella collection in 1655 under the title *El desdeñado más firme*. It is unknown whether she lived in Madrid and Paris, as clues in her text suggest. Meneses married twice and died in childbirth.

Morillas, Cecilia (1539–81): Mother of María de San Alberto and Cecilia del Nacimiento, this native of Salamanca had a versatile intellect, which she used to educate her nine children in fine arts and humanistic studies. She was known as a singer, painter, illuminator, maker of silk flowers, and intellectual.

Muñoz, Magdalena (b. 1500s): Placed in a convent in the town of Ubeda in southern Spain as a girl, Muñoz was declared a man in 1605 and subsequently left the convent to live at home.

Orozco y Luján, María de (1635–1709): Born in Guadalajara, Spain, Orozco was expelled from a convent and a girls' school before officially becoming a *beata* in 1683. Her life story is chronicled in several biographies and some three thousand letters.

Ossorio, Constanza (c. 1565–1637): The posthumously published *Huerta del celestial esposo* (1686) by Ossorio, a Cistercian nun, advises nuns and monks on proper Christian behavior.

Padilla Manrique, Luisa María de (1590–1646): Padilla was likely born in Burgos, one of seven children. She married the Count of Aranda in 1605 and it is unknown if they had surviving children. A student of archeology and history, she is the author of numerous instructional texts on the moral obligations of the nobility.

Pinelo, Valentina (b. 1500s): Author of *Libro de las alabanzas y excelencias de la gloriosa Santa Ana* (1601), Pinelo lived in Seville's Convent of San Leandro from the time she was a small child.

Romero, María (c. 1674–?): Tried by the Inquisition in 1702 for sorcery and dealing with the devil, Romero was a practitioner of love magic.

Sabuco, Oliva (1567–?): A philosopher and humanist with an orientation toward science, Sabuco is the author or coauthor of the *Nueva Filosofía de la Naturaleza del Hombre* (1587).

Sigea, Luisa (c. 1530): A Renaissance humanist who wrote in both Latin and Spanish, Sigea served in the Portuguese and Spanish courts, married once, and had one daughter. Her extant texts include poems, letters, and a dialogue in Latin.

Souza, Joana Theodora de (b. late 1600s): Souza is described as a *dama portuguesa* on the title page of her hagiographical play *El gran prodigio de España*. She lived in the Convento da Roza in Lisbon and likely was an active writer in the first part of the eighteenth century.

Teresa de Jesús María (Sor) (1592–?): Sor Teresa, a Carmelite, wrote a text about the friendship and guidance she found among her religious sisters.

Teresa of Avila (Saint Teresa of Jesus) (1515–82): Born Teresa de Cepeda y Ahumada, one of eleven children, she entered a convent in 1536 and founded the first of seventeen Discalced Carmelite convents in 1562. Teresa of Avila is known as a mystic, a reformer, and a writer. Her prolific literary output marks the beginning of women's legitimization as writers in the Hispanic world. Teresa of Avila was beatified in 1614 and canonized in 1622.

Valle de la Cerda, Teresa (b. late 1500s): A member of a highly influential aristocratic family, Valle founded the Benedictine Convento de la Encarnación (also known as San Plácido) in Madrid in 1623. Tried by the Inquisition, she was first found guilty but, along with other nuns, was exonerated in 1638.

Violante do Ceo (Sor) (1601–93): Born in Lisbon, Sor Violante was a bilingual poet who professed as a nun in the Convent of Nuestra Señora del Rosario in 1630. Her poetry collections, which included work in Spanish and Portuguese, were published during her lifetime and posthumously.

Zayas y Sotomayor, María de (c. 1590–?): An aristocratic author of fiction and drama whose popular short stories protest the mistreatment of women in Spanish society, Zayas is not known to have married.

NOTES

A NOTE ON TRANSLATIONS AND CITATIONS

All citations appear in English, with the original Spanish in the notes. For archival materials, I have modernized the Spanish and resolved abbreviations, except where stated. Unless otherwise noted, all translations are mine. For ease of consultation, archival sources are listed by the name of the author or, in the case of Inquisition trials, the name of the defendant.

PREFACE

1. Chapters 1 and 2 follow in the tradition of "microhistory" or "history from below" as exemplified in such superb books as Davis, *Society and Culture* and *Fiction in the Archives*; Ginzburg, *The Cheese and the Worms*; Farr, *Authority and Sexuality*; and Ruggiero, *Binding Passions*. The historiography of microhistory is discussed in Biersack and Hunt, *The New Cultural History*; and in Foner, *Who Owns History?*, pp. ix–24.
2. The *querelle des femmes* is discussed further in Chapters 5, 7, and 8. Also see Constance Jordan, *Renaissance Feminism*, for an overview of women's writing, as well as the tradition of misogynist versus antimisogynist debate.

INTRODUCION

1. "[H]abía oído decir que tenía dos sexos ansí por esto como por haber oído a otras mujeres que se gozaban con sus maridos alguna libertad tenía ésta gana y lo procuraba con cuidado de tentarle sus partes de hombre por ver qué cosa era" (Elena/Eleno de Céspedes, Inquisition Trial, fol. III.41v).
2. After mentioning that she used to let confessors touch her face and hold her hand even before becoming a nun, Valle wrote: "De suerte que ésta es una acción que, hecha sin advertencia y con sinceridad, no la tengo por mala, y es cosa que todos la hacen, y cuanto más santos son, mejor" (Valle in *Cárceles y mujeres*, pp. 182–83).

3. Valle was convicted in 1629 but wrote another communication (*memorial*) in 1638 in a final attempt to clear her name. After nine years under house arrest, she was exonerated by the Inquisition in 1638. Mary Elizabeth Perry has noted that the trials of *beatas* (independent religious laywomen) often mention the question of touch (see "Beatas and the Inquisition," p. 152).

4. María de Zayas y Sotomayor, *The Disenchantments of Love*, p. 224; "[S]upuesto que el alma es toda una en varón y en la hembra, no se me da más ser hombre que mujer; que las almas no son hombres ni mujeres, y el verdadero amor en el alma está, que no en el cuerpo" (*Desengaños amorosos*, p. 317).

5. For historical overviews of the period, see Elliott, *Spain and Its World*; Kamen, *Empire* and *Inquisition and Society in Spain*; and Ruiz, *Spanish Society*.

6. A sample of the recent excellent research on women in the early modern Hispanic world includes Cruz, "Feminism"; Cammarata, *Women*; Dopico-Black, *Perfect Wives, Other Women*; Herpoel, *A la zaga de Santa Teresa*; Merrim, *Early Modern Women's Writing*; Pérez Molina, "Las mujeres y el matrimonio"; Perry, *Gender and Disorder*; Ríos Izquierdo, *Mujer y sociedad*; Schlau, *Spanish American Women's Use of the Word*; and Vigil, *La vida de las mujeres*. Amy Katz Kaminsky gives a summary of Spanish women's history in her introduction to *Water Lilies*, pp. 1–14.

7. Literacy statistics depend on how one defines the type of literacy being measured. Sara Nalle estimates that in the urban areas of Madrid, Avila, Toledo, and Cuenca, "over half of the males were literate" (*God in La Mancha*, p. xvi). Nalle's "Literacy and Culture in Early Modern Castile" asserts that approximately one-fourth of the women in Madrid signed their own names to their wills (p. 69), which of course represents only a very basic form of literacy. For more on literacy, see Cátedra and Rojo, *Bibliotecas y lecturas de mujeres*.

8. See Nader, *Power and Gender*, pp. 1–26. For an overview of women's legal status, see Casey, *Early Modern Spain*, pp. 19–42.

9. For primary texts, see *Escritoras españolas*, a collection of women's writing from the Biblioteca Nacional that is owned by many university libraries in the United States. Other resources include: *Autoras en la historia del teatro*; Barbeito Carneiro, *Escritoras madrileñas del siglo XVII*; Mujica, *Sophia's Daughters*; Schlau, *Viva al Siglo*; and Soufas, *Women's Acts*.

10. In *La mujer y la sexualidad en el antiguo régimen*, María Helena Sánchez Ortega suggests that we have an insufficient amount of information about women's lives and thus need to read between the lines to reconstruct women's cultural history (p. 18). Similarly, Margarita Ortega, in *Historia de las mujeres de España*, laments the "inexistence of source documents produced by women themselves" (Garrido et al., p. 250); and Marina S. Brownlee has described "the miniscule number of active writers" in the seventeenth century (*The Cultural Labyrinth*, p. 7). Yet a growing body of research suggests that documents that trace women's literary and political agency do exist. See, for example, Barahona, *Sex Crimes*; Barbeito Carneiro, *Mujeres del Madrid Barroco*; Bilinkoff, *Related Lives*; Giles, *Women in the Inquisition*; Kagan, *Lucrecia's Dreams*; Nader, *Power and Gender*;

Perry, *Gender and Disorder* and *The Handless Maiden*; Poska, *Regulating the People*; Velasco, *The Lieutenant Nun*; and Weber, *Teresa of Avila*.

11. For these purposes, culture refers not only to the customs, values, and artistic production of an era, but also to the codes of decorum and behavior that influence personal identity. Laws, moralists, and the Inquisition enforced such codes in early modern Spain.

12. Many women authors of the period are available in English translation. See Zayas, *The Enchantments of Love* and *The Disenchantments of Love*; Sor Juana Inés de la Cruz, *The Answer / La respuesta*; Teresa of Jesus, *The Complete Works*; and Erauso, *Memoir*.

13. Key studies on early modern gender and culture in Europe include Brown, *Immodest Acts*; Davis, *Society and Culture* and *Fiction in the Archives*; Kelly, "Did Women Have a Renaissance?"; Marshall, *Women in Reformation and Counter-Reformation Europe*; Traub, Kaplan, and Callaghan, *Feminist Readings*; and Wiesner, *Women and Gender*.

CHAPTER I

1. "[T]an hombre como el que más" (Torres, fol. 258). Mss. 2058 at the Biblioteca Nacional includes a copy of the letter in which this quote appears, sent in October 1617 by Fray Agustín de Torres to the Abad mayor de San Salvador in Granada. Since this is a fair copy of the original letter, I have only added accents and altered the punctuation only slightly. The subsequent summary of the letter, which I do not believe to have been written by Torres, indicates that Muñoz was put in the convent "on account of being a closed girl and not being one who should marry" ("por ser cerrada y no ser para casada") (Torres, fol. 258). "Closed" indicates that her vagina was impenetrable, but since Torres does not confirm this information, I do not take it as part of the original story. I am grateful to David Nirenberg, who generously gave me the reference to this document, and to Daniel Heiple, with whom I had many conversations about homosexuality in Golden Age and present-day Spain.

2. "[S]us fuerças y ánimo y las propiedades y condiciones eran de Varón" (Torres, fol. 258).

3. "[C]onfesó que jamás le avía venido su mes, y por que las monjas no le llamasen marimochacho, que quando se disçiplinava hacía obstentaçión de la sangre en las camisas, diciendo estava con su regla" (Torres, fol. 259).

4. "[L]o vimos con los ojos y palpamos con las manos y hallamos ser hombre perfecto en la naturaleza de hombre" (Torres, fol. 258v–259).

5. "[P]ensó morirse de espanto" (Torres, fol. 259).

6. "[E]l padre está muy contento porque es hombre rico y no tenía eredero y aora se halla con *un hijo muy hombre* y que se puede casar, *ella* tanbién va contenta porque después de doçe años de carçel, sabe muy bien la libertad, y *se halla de mujer varón* que en las cosas y vienes temporales ninguna merced mayor le pudo haçer naturaleça" (Torres, fol. 259, emphasis added).

7. Torres, fol. 259.
8. For excellent, accessible studies on intersexuality and hermaphroditism, see Dreger, *Hermaphrodites*, and Kessler, *Lessons from the Intersexed*.
9. Jones and Stallybrass, in "Fetishizing Gender," and Daston and Park, in "The Hermaphrodite," discuss competing early modern views toward hermaphroditism. Both articles convincingly argue that no single explanation about intersexuality prevailed during the period.
10. Daston and Park, "The Hermaphrodite," detail Jacques Duval's 1612 account of Marie-Marin le Marcis (p. 124). Also see Greenblatt, "Fiction and Friction." For changing uses of the term "hermaphrodite" to refer to masculine women in the eighteenth century, see Trumbach, "London's Sapphists."
11. "[D]esprecio al matrimonio y tener pacto con el demonio" (Céspedes, Inquisition Trial, cover page). Succeeding citations of this trial document appear by folio and page number. Not all folios are numbered, but since the numbers start over twice and are clearly marked, I have marked the numbered folios as belonging to part I, II, or III. Either in lieu of or in addition to page numbers, I give as much identifying information as possible. For ease of reading, I have resolved abbreviations and modernized accents and spelling.

    A transcript of the Céspedes autobiographical statements appears in Kagan and Dyer, *Inquisitorial Inquiries*.
12. The Inquisition case includes folios from the original inquiry in Ocaña.
13. For other perspectives on Céspedes's case, see Barbazza, "Un caso de subversión social"; Escamilla, "A propos d'un dossier inquisitorial"; and Folch Jou and Sagrario Muñoz, "Un pretendido caso de hermafroditismo." Israel Burshatin has written several fascinating articles and a forthcoming book that highlight, among other issues, the racial politics of the case. See "Elena alias Eleno," "Interrogating Hermaphroditism," and "Written on the Body." Perhaps the best-known story of a historical hermaphrodite is that told in Foucault's edition of *I, Pierre Rivière*.
14. For more on this issue, see Chapter 2 in this book, in which the Portuguese-inflected Spanish written by Bernarda Manuel contrasts sharply with the standardized Spanish attributed to her by Inquisition scribes.
15. "Elena de Céspedes / Eleno de Céspedes cirujano / Hermafrodita" (fol. I.1).
16. "Dijo que en realidad de verdad ésta es y fue hermafrodito que tuvo y tiene dos naturas, una de hombre y otra de mujer" (fol. III.7, deposition of 17 July 1587).
17. "Céspedes, Elena y Eleno de, natural de Alama, esclava y despues libre, casó con un hombre y tuvo un hijo después y muerto su marido se vistió de hombre y estuvo en la Guerra de los Moriscos de Granada, se examinó de cirujano y se casó con una mujer" (cover page).
18. The use of pronouns presents a challenge when writing about intersexuality. In her work on the U.S. case of Thomas/ine Hall, Mary Beth Norton in *Founding Mothers and Fathers* employs the gender-neutral abbreviation "T" as a subject and a possessive pronoun. In the case at hand, because Céspedes refers to himself as a man throughout the trial, I refer to him as a man except when discuss-

ing the time in which he identifies himself as female (in his pretransformation period).

19. The summary states that Elena had a son with Cristóbal Lombardo and that the son was alive at the time of the trial (fol. III.78).

20. "[C]uando ésta parió como tiene dicho con la fuerza que puso en el parto se le rompió un pellejo que tenía sobre el caño de la orina y le salió una cabeza como medio dedo pulgar" (fol. III.7, deposition of 17 July 1587).

21. I am grateful to Suzanne Kessler for her helpful comments about the Céspedes case. The references in this paragraph are to personal correspondence from 23 April 2000. In *Lessons from the Intersexed*, Kessler explains that fewer than 5 percent of intersexuals are "true hermaphrodites," defined as cases in which "both ovarian and testicular tissue are present in either the same gonad or opposite gonads" (pp. 13–14). The majority of cases involve an infant with either ovaries or testes (p. 15).

22. "[L]e vino gana de besarla y sin decirle cosa alguna la besó y espantada se dejó ella, ésta le dijo que podría tener con ella cuenta como hombre" (fol. III.6v, deposition of 17 July 1587).

23. "[V]olvió a la dicha Ana de Albanchez y con ella tuvo muchas veces cuenta y actos como hombre y estuvo en su casa sin que su marido entendiese nada como cuatro o cinco meses" (fol. III.7, deposition of 17 July 1587). All other cited details about the physical transformation appear on folio III.7 as well. The length of Céspedes's penis is drawn in the record.

24. "[P]or amenazas que la había hecho el dicho Heredia y otros rufianes sus compañeros por disfrazarse ésta determinó de andar en hábito de hombre y dejó el de mujer que hasta allí siempre trujo" (fol. III.3, deposition of 17 July 1587).

25. On the issue of Céspedes being taken for a monfí, see Burshatin, "Written on the Body," especially pp. 439–41, where the issues of race and ethnicity are taken up in the context of the forced assimilation of Moriscos. According to Cabrillana (*La almería morisca*, pp. 159–79), the presence of the monfí reached its peak between 1561 and 1568, precisely when Heredia and his cohort believed Céspedes to be a monfí. For more on Moriscos in sixteenth-century Spain, see Halavais, *Like Wheat to the Miller*; Márquez Villanueva, *El problema morisco*; Perry, *The Handless Maiden*; and Tueller, *Good and Faithful Christians*.

26. "[Q]ue [Céspedes] era mujer y otros que decían era macho y hembra" (fol. III.6, deposition of 17 July 1587).

27. Speaking of "el dicho miembro y los testículos," "dijo que los iba cortando cada día poco a poco" (fol. I.45).

28. In *Frontiers of Heresy*, William Monter indicates that in 1524 the pope granted the Aragonese tribunal "jurisdiction over the 'unspeakable sin' [*pecado nefando*] in the three main parts of the Crown of Aragon," which were Zaragoza, Barcelona, and Valencia (p. 36). As Stephen Haliczer explains about sodomy and related crimes: "By its decree of October 18, 1509, the Suprema ordered the Castilian tribunals to leave them in the hands of the secular and ecclesiastical courts. In Aragon, however, popular hostility toward sodomites as expressed in the Valencian rioting of 1519 and the presumed connection between sodomy

and the Islamic minority resulted in a request to Pope Clement VII for a brief placing it under inquisitorial jurisdiction (*Inquisition and Society in the Kingdom of Valencia*, p. 302).

29. "[E]ntonces tenía miembro y esto es la verdad" (fol. I.45v).

30. The category of sodomy could include women who used instruments (dildos) to have sexual relations with each other, but far more men than women were prosecuted for this crime, both in the secular courts and in the tribunal. For more on same-sex relations between women, see, for example, Herrera Puga's dated but informative *Sociedad y delincuencia*, pp. 246–69; and Perry, "The 'Nefarious' Sin." For two interesting descriptions of dildos, see Perry's mention of female prisoners who made "artificial male genitalia" (*Crime and Society*, p. 84), and Kagan's discussion of Lucrecia de León, who talked about her preference for dildos made not of sheepskin but "a special kind of wood . . . and a cover of satin or velvet" (*Lucrecia's Dreams*, p. 33n.72).

31. The summary at the beginning of the document says that Céspedes "fue presa en Ocaña y llevada a la Inquisición donde se le acusa y condena por desprecio al matrimonio y tener pacto con el demonio" (cover page).

32. Daston and Park, "The Hermaphrodite," pp. 123–24.

33. Ibid., pp. 124–29. For more on the question of determining the legitimacy of the nonnormative body, see Cohen, *Monster Theory*.

34. Burshatin, "Written on the Body," p. 422. Céspedes's friendship with the Morisca and purported witch Catalina de Haro was used against him as well (fol. I.93, letter dated 13 July).

35. "[S]iempre que se echaba con mujer cumplía con ella y echaba simiente en el vaso de ella" (fol. III.74).

36. "[E]ra la polución en demasía" (fol. III.9). On a different date, he answered an accusation about his failure to ejaculate saying, "no fue por falta de ser hombre sino por alguna de las causas por las cuales dichos hombres caen en esta falta" (fol. III.76v).

37. "[E]s de presumir que ésta no pudo dejar de ver como el dicho Eleno de Céspedes no era hombre y más viéndole sin barbas y las orejas agujeradas como mujer y bajarle su regla y ansí es de presumir pues ésta dijo que trató con él antes de desposarse, que saviéndolo se casó con la dicha Elena de Céspedes sabiendo era mujer como ésta" (fol. III.43).

38. Céspedes raised the issue of hemorrhoids as an alternative explanation to the question of menstruation, saying that when riding a horse, the hemorrhoid sometimes broke and bled (fol. 41v). For a discussion of views toward Jewish men, see Buestein, "Jewish Male Menstruation."

39. Daston and Park in "The Hermaphrodite" make the important argument that views toward hermaphroditism in the medieval period differed from those of the early modern period (pp. 117–18). On the difficulties of determining biological sex, see Epstein and Straub, "Introduction: The Guarded Body," p. 3. Also see Spanier, "Lessons from Nature," for a critique of the ideologies that influence determination of biological sex.

40. For an analysis of the hermaphrodite as a site of fetishization, see Jones and Stallybrass, "Fetishizing Gender," pp. 105–7.

41. Daston and Park ("The Hermaphrodite," p. 119) explain the differences between the two prevailing models of hermaphroditism: Hippocrates and Galen, on the one hand, saw hermaphrodites "as being truly intermediate in sex, neither male nor female, but exactly in between," while an Aristotelian view— which was probably more dominant in the period (see Jones and Stallybrass, "Fetishizing Gender," p. 88)—saw them "as beings with doubled or redundant genitalia."

42. "[E]n este mundo nuevas veces se han visto personas que son andróginos que por otro nombre se llaman hermafroditos que tienen entrambos sexos yo también he sido uno de estos" (fol. III.76).

43. "Dijo que con muchas mujeres ha tenido acceso carnal" (fol. III.7v) and "como andaba con muchas quiso ... casarse y no tener que hacer más que con su mujer y por esto se casó que no pensó que en ello erraba antes pensó que estava en servicio de Dios" (fol. III.8).

44. María "siempre le tuvo por hombre como lo es y lo era este confesante" (fol. I.38v). Isabel Ortiz's protest over the Caño-Céspedes wedding appears on folio III.5.

45. Martínez testified that "no se puede determinar si era sexo feminil" (fol. I.18), and Casas simply said "no viéndola más no se determina sobre ello" (fol. I.18v).

46. The notary Francisco de Gómez Ayala testified to this finding, saying in reference to February 1586 that Céspedes has a "miembro viril el cual tiene bueno y perfecto con dos tésticulos," and adding that Céspedes also had a mark near his anus that could not be penetrated (fol. I.22v, deposition of 19 June 1587).

47. "[L]a ha visto y tiene de presente sexo de mujer y es mujer ... es alguna ilusión del diablo y que la dicha Elena de Céspedes debe de ser el hechicera [*sic*]" (fol. I.44, deposition of 1 July 1587).

48. "Dijo que estaba mala delante de sí y que se le caía el miembro y que la cura que se hacía era para que se tornase a formar" (fol. I.46v).

49. "[C]iertos lavatorios con vino y balaustras y alcohol y otros muchos remedios y sahumerios para ver si podría curar su propia natura de mujer" (fol. III.5).

50. "[Q]ue tenía de proporción y forma de miembro de hombre proporcionado a su cuerpo ni grande ni pequeño que no antes más grande que pequeño" (fol. III.65v).

51. Caño's responses to sexual questions, including whether Céspedes "alabó su miembro de hombre," appear on fols. III.41v–42.

52. Caño says that Céspedes "la llevó su virginidad y que ésta no ha conocido a otro hombre para saber lo que los otros saben" (fol. III.42).

53. "Dijo que como ésta le rogaba tanto y le pedía que se lo mostrase una vez estando sentada encima de la cama el dicho Eleno de Céspedes desvistiéndose andando ésta por el aposento un poco apartada de él alzó la camisa y la dijo que mirase y luego se volvió a echar la camisa y tapar y ésta quiso llegarse a él y mirarle y él no se lo consintió y que fuera de esta vez tampoco se lo vio jamás" (fol. III.41v).

54. "[Q]ue su miembro de hombre se le había comido de cáncer y metídosele adentro [y] que se fuese ésta a la iglesia porque no la prendiesen" (fol. III.42v).

55. "[L]a dicha mujer no podía entender que se casaba sino con hombre, pues la dicha Elena hacía obras de tal" (fol. III.79v, deposition of 19 November 1587).

56. "[V]ivió allí en Yepes más de un año haciendo vida maridable con la dicha María del Caño hasta que por Navidad por no haber cirujano en Ocaña se fue ésta a vivir allí" (fol. III.6). Since they were married in May 1586, they had not been together a full year when they moved to Ocaña.

57. In addition to Halavais, *Like Wheat to the Miller*, and Perry, *The Handless Maiden*, see Pike, *Aristocrats and Traders*, for a general discussion of slaves, Moriscos, and Andalusian culture.

58. Burshatin discusses the effects of a 1567 royal decree related to Moorish culture ("Written on the Body," p. 441). Also see Root, "Speaking Christian."

59. On 27 June 1587, Vázquez examined Céspedes and mentioned his "rostro e habla" and "altura de cuerpo" as being appropriate for a woman (fol. I.27v).

60. "[M]andamos que en pena de sus delitos para que a ella sea castigo y a otros ejemplo para no cometer semejantes embustes y engaños, salga al presente auto de la fe en forma de penitencia con coroza e insignias que manifiesten sus delitos" (fol. III.83v).

61. "[L]a dicha Elena de C. había nacido y era mujer, y que como tal tenía todas las señales de mujer, y que nunca había sido hermafrodito, ni en buena medicina podía ser que lo hubiese sido, ni tenido partes de hombres. Y que todos los actos que como hombre decía haber hecho, fueron con algunos artificios, y que todo era embuste y no cosa natural, ni sabían el artificio con que había hecho el dicho embuste y engaño a las mujeres, a quien decía haber tenido acceso" (fol. III.81).

62. "Artifice" refers to fakery or even possible witchcraft. Moreover, Burshatin ("Written on the Body," p. 450) reminds us that artifice had the meaning of "dildo," which, in the assessment of at least one of the examining doctors, equated the term *burladora* with a woman who impersonates a man during the sexual act.

63. Dreger, *Hermaphrodites*, p. 6.

64. For a study of the one-sex model, see Laqueur, *Making Sex*. See Traub, Kaplan, and Callaghan's introduction to *Feminist Readings*, pp. 1–15, for a discussion of gender in the early modern period.

65. Commenting on Park's excellent essay, "The Rediscovery of the Clitoris," Jones and Stallybrass note: "In France, there was certainly an increasing tendency to absorb the hermaphrodite into the figure of the deviant woman, a conflation which was made more plausible by the medical rediscovery of the clitoris in the mid-sixteenth century" ("Fetishizing Gender," p. 90). The idea was, of course, that a woman with an enlarged clitoris (labeled a *tribade*) could penetrate another woman.

66. As Jones and Stallybrass have noted with regard to the lack in the early modern period of a single universally accepted discourse of gender assignment, the move away from Aristotle and Galen—that is, from one clear understanding

of biological sex—"the production of gender from state to state, class to class, ethnic group to ethnic group" was "differential and local" (ibid., p. 88).

67. "[P]or el discurso de doze años en muchas ocasiones vieron las monjas no ser hombre porque unas vezes cogiéndola dormida, otras por vía de trisca la descubrían para satisfacerse: porque sus fuerças y ánimo, y las propiedades, y condiciones eran de Varón" (Torres, fol. 258).

68. Another intersexed person outed by the power of rumor was the aforementioned Thomas/ine Hall, an inhabitant of colonial Virginia who was manhandled on several occasions by groups of men and women in search of knowledge of Hall's true sex (see Brown, *Good Wives, Nasty Wenches*, pp. 75–79; Norton, *Founding Mothers and Fathers*, pp. 184–93).

69. "[E]l grande estorbo y embarazo que ha causado la entrada de la dicha E[lena] de Céspedes por la mucha gente que acude a verla y a curarse" (fol. III.88).

70. "Pido . . . y suplico a vuestras mercedes que . . . sea de allí sacada para que el dicho hospital se pueda governar y servir con la quietud y concierto que antes se hacía." The second quote is from the next letter, asking once again for Céspedes's transfer: "[P]orque abiendo cobrado nombre de que la susodicha es cirujano y que cura de muchas enfermedades es tanta la gente que acude a ella que no la deja cumplir con quietud su reclusión" (fol. III.86).

71. Burshatin has written that he wants to "interrogate the Inquisition's record of Eleno's hermaphroditism and thereby claim Eleno's voice—one of exemplary *mestizaje* in its articulations of the African, the transgendered, and the subaltern—for the widening conversation of 'Hispanisms and homosexualities'" ("Interrogating Hermaphroditism," pp. 5–6). He also refers to the transgressive irony of the "transgendered 'butch' surgeoness—in proper skirts, presumably—produced by the Inquisitors themselves" ("Written on the Body," p. 436).

CHAPTER 2

1. "[E]l mal de las mujeres" (Manuel, Inquisition Trial, fol. 63). Manuel's writing is transcribed verbatim here and line numbers are given for ease of reference. All other transcriptions of the case are given by folio number in modernized Spanish. Translations from the Spanish are mine. Succeeding citations of this trial document appear by folio and line number in parentheses in the text or, in the case of translations, in notes. In a deposition on 8 March 1650, Manuel gave her age as thirty-four, so she was born in 1615 or 1616. I first came upon references to her document in Barbeito Carneiro, *Mujeres del Madrid Barroco*, pp. 51–55.

2. The terms "converso" and "New Christian" refer to those who converted from Judaism to Catholicism or to the descendants of these converts. "Crypto-Jew" refers to those conversos who continued to practice Judaism to one degree or another, or who were suspected of Judaizing. Being a converso, even if you did not hold to any Jewish beliefs or practices, automatically caused suspicion and, often, prosecution (Melammed, *Heretics or Daughters of Israel?* p. 14).

3. For current debates on converso identity, see "Forum." Also see Nirenberg,

Communities of Violence, for background on the topic and, for an overview of scholarship on the conversos, Contreras, "Family and Patronage."

4. Statistics bear out the Inquisition's rigidity and changing focus in Portugal. In Spain, Judaizers made up 5.5 percent of the Inquisition cases between 1560 and 1614, but 20 percent of the cases from 1615 to 1700. In the Toledo tribunal, where Manuel was tried, Judaizers made up 44.3 percent of the accused (Haliczer, "The First Holocaust," p. 14). The situation turned particularly bad for the Portuguese who returned to Spain in the seventeenth century, as evidenced by appeals to the inquisitor Adán de la Parra in the 1640s to stop accusing all immigrants from that nation of being Crypto-Jews (see Blázquez Miguel, *Madrid,* p. 71).

5. As Ruth Pike points out in *Aristocrats and Traders,* the conversos occupied influential posts in Seville society, "predominated in certain professions and trades," and "were most numerous in the clothing trades" (pp. 103, 143).

6. Regina Graycar observes in "Telling Tales" that, in spite of the attention to violence against women since the 1970s, "women's stories about the violence in their lives remain rarely (and barely) acknowledged in legal discourse. They have difficulty being told and heard" (p. 297).

7. A large majority of conversos convicted during the first phase of the Valencian tribunal (from the 1480s to 1530) belonged to the middle and artisan classes (Haliczer, *Inquisition and Society in the Kingdom of Valencia,* p. 225). Wealth and political ties worked for and against the conversos: Money protected many but also attracted the attention of an Inquisition ever desiring to fill its coffers through confiscated goods (see Kamen, *Spain,* pp. 303–5). For a compendium of conversos tried by the Seville tribunal, see Juan Gil's *Los conversos y la Inquisición sevillana.*

8. Kamen, *Inquisition and Society,* and Elliott, in *The Count-Duke of Olivares,* explain the converso-related policies and negotiations of Philip IV's favorite, who retired in January 1643. In addition to advocating a relaxation in the *limpieza de sangre* statutes (Elliott, *The Count-Duke of Olivares,* p. 119), Olivares tried to involve the international New Christian community in Spanish economic affairs, even securing a "temporary edict of grace from the Inquisition" for the Portuguese financiers he invited to come to Madrid in 1627 (p. 303); also see Kamen, chapter 12, "Last Days of the *Conversos,*" in *Inquisition and Society,* pp. 218–37. For more on Olivares's advocacy for liberal converso policies, see Elliott, *The Count-Duke of Olivares,* especially pp. 117–19, 300–304, and 680. Domínguez Ortiz (*Los judeoconversos,* pp. 80–94) details Olivares's actions and the Inquisition's reactions. Domínguez Ortiz suggests in *Política y hacienda de Felipe IV* that the exodus of the conversos to more prosperous countries began for economic motives but accelerated under Diego de Arce y Reynosos's regime, 1643–65 (pp. 136–37).

9. See Kamen's *Inquisition and Society* for more on the role played by the Portuguese in filling the economic and intellectual vacuum, as well as on the increased discrimination and persecution of the seventeenth century (pp.

224–25). The bibliography on the Spanish Inquisition is vast, and research on converso issues is highly polemicized. Some scholars reject the possibility that any Crypto-Jews existed (see Netanyahu, *Toward the Inquisition;* and Roth, *Conversos*). Others embrace the notion of an essential Jewishness among conversos (e.g., Beinart, *Los conversos*). Compelling discussions of converso culture and persecution appear in Contreras, *El Santo Oficio;* Haliczer, *Inquisition and Society in the Kingdom of Valencia* (pp. 209–43); Kamen, *Spain* (pp. 303–10); Melammed, *Heretics or Daughters of Israel?* (pp. 3–30); Nirenberg, "Conversion, Sex, and Segregation"; Seidenspinner-Núñez, "Inflecting the *Converso* Voice"; and the lively responses to Seidenspinner-Núñez and others in "Forum." For a study of women in converso trials in the earlier years of the Inquisition, see Starr-LeBeau, *In the Shadow of the Virgin.*

10. "[A]ntes de estar desposada me dise a mim hi a mi padre hi irmanos hum cunhado mio hi parete suio que não hera de pareser q[ue] se hisese tal casamento porque anto borges tinia mui mal natural por que la muger com que fora cazado q[ue] com os desgustos q[ue] lhe avia dado se avia morto hi q[ue] cosederasem q[ue] sus dois irmãos abos avião dexado a sus mugeres hi q[ue] não quisemos q[ue] ele fisese o mesmo ao q[ue] io respondi q[ue] por nenhuma manera me cazaria com tal obre" (fol. 33, ll. 10–18).

11. "[O]s q[ue] tratavan el cazamento me presuadira a q[ue] disese q[ue] sim dizedo q[ue] hera moso hi que el cairia na coiza hi trataria a su muger como asen los obres onrados hi asim se izo el casamento" (fol. 33, ll. 19–22).

12. "[H]i a cabo de tres somanas de desposada tuvo mi padre huna carta de hun tio mio em q[ue] lhe ma[n]dava diser q[ue] se sua sobrinha não estava ainda casada q[ue] não casasem com anto borges porq[ue] não matase a sua sobrinha como a la otra mulher porque achegara a trata[r]la de manera q[ue] asta huma espada desnuda punha emtre si hi ela na cama" (fol. 33, ll. 22–28).

13. "[D]e modo senhor que hera taõ grande o temor q[ue] cosebi que nem de dia nem de note tinhia mi corasaõ sosegado hi este temor me duro asta que tive ijos" (Manuel, fol. 33, ll. 29–31).

14. "[N]i su marido la dejaba comunicar con nadie" (fol. 65). Manuel also wrote that for the six-month period she lived on that street, she had a conversation with only one woman, doña Catalina (fol. 37v, ll. 2–5). She talks about Borges following her on folio 38.

15. "[S]e declaró con él de que era observante y creyente de la ley de Moisés en cuya observancia la ha visto éste" (fol. 1).

16. After three audiences with the tribunal, Borges refused to ratify the accusations against his wife, saying "no se acuerda haber depuesto tal y que si a declarado algo contra la dicha doña Manuel su mujer sería estando loco y sin juicio" (Manuel, fol. 4–4v).

17. Melammed, "Crypto-Jewish Women," p. 13.

18. Even though Manuel's husband seems to have been compromised by his paranoia, illnesses, and suspected Judaism, the Inquisition was unlikely to ignore his testimony. To the contrary, the institution relied on its prisoners to turn in

others like them. The lack of standards for witnesses' credibility is well documented. As Beinart explains, it was not unusual for the Inquisition to use testimonies of prostitutes, drunks, the poor, and other marginalized people to im-
prison others (*Los conversos*, p. 148).

19. Manuel describes the memorial in her deposition as "pliegos de papel escritos
de mi letra" (fol. 31). It begins: "[D]iguo sñor [*sic*] que io hei descorido por
mim mente hi que não alo persona alguma que me pudese aser tão gran mal"
(fol. 33, ll. 1–2).

20. Kagan, *Lucrecia's Dreams*, pp. 136–37.

21. Melammed, "Crypto-Jewish Women," pp. 10–11.

22. Haliczer found that 88 percent of the conversos who came forward during the
grace period in Valencia were later tried by the Inquisition (*Inquisition and Society in the Kingdom of Valencia*, p. 225).

23. For a list of typical charges leveled at suspected Judaizers, see Melammed (*Heretics or Daughters of Israel?* p. 97). Commenting on the "monotonous sameness"
of the trial records, Roth (who believes that no Crypto-Jews existed) concludes
that conversos merely confessed to Judaizing because of the fear of death or
torture, and that their confessions were based on information about Judaism
spread by Inquisition manuals (*Conversos*, p. 218). He also asserts that some
of the customs "were nothing other than popular superstitions with no basis in
Jewish law or custom whatever" (p. 219).

24. The repetitive rhetoric of the trials raises more questions than scholars can
answer about the complicity of the masses in the Inquisition's long life span.
Pointing out that inquisitors rarely initiated cases without previous testimony,
Kamen has suggested that the evil of the institution "lay in its availability"
(*Spain*, p. 295).

25. For another defendant's own writing, see Ahlgren, "Francisca de los Apósto-
les." More commonly, women dictated their experiences (see Kagan, *Lucrecia's
Dreams*), as well as chants and prayers (see Costa Fontes, "Four Portuguese
Crypto-Jewish Prayers"; and Sánchez Ortega, *Ese viejo diablo* and "Sorcery and
Eroticism").

26. The web of influence that protected some is visible, for example, in the inves-
tigation records of the mystical author Sor María de Agreda. See Colahan,
"María de Jesús de Agreda," and Agreda's letters to King Philip IV (Agreda,
Correspondencia con Felipe IV).

27. "[C]uando nos casamos él tenía opinión de un hombre de tan áspera condición
y terrible natural que no sólo no me podía atrever a traerle a su voluntad" (fol.
31).

28. "[Q]ue siendo yo una mujer flaca de natural débil había de tener atrevimiento
para persuadir al dicho Antonio Borges ni a otra persona alguna a la observancia de la ley de Moisés, sino tenía tanto miedo que en su presencia no osaba
hablar ni comunicaba con persona alguna más que con muchos criados que
[yo] tenía" (fol. 31–31v).

29. The most obvious influence of Portuguese in Manuel's writing can be found in
her spelling (*diguo* for *digo*, *não* for *no*). She also uses a few Portuguese words

(*ainda* for *todavía* and *minha* for *mía*) and places object pronouns irregularly. For more on women in converso culture, see Melammed, *Heretics or Daughters of Israel?* and also her "Judaizers and Prayer."

30. Anne Jacobson Schutte has asserted that Inquisition documents accurately reflect witnesses' statements ("Inquisition and Female Autobiography," p. 108). For similar assertions about legal documents, see Chaytor, "Husband(ry)," p. 401n1; and G. Walker, "Rereading Rape and Sexual Violence," p. 8. Jean Pierre DeDieu eloquently delineates the limitations of depositions as historical records in "Archives of the Holy Office," p. 168.

31. "[E]s otro testigo falso por que não sei demais ayunos que os que mada la santa fei catolica hi esos los asia poco por sempre estar criado o prinhado" (33v, ll. 10–12).

32. "[H]i por mutos disgustos q[ue] tivese em mi caza sempre me asentei a mim mesa por aqueatar a mim marido [e] hijos" (fol. 33v, ll. 13–14).

33. "[H]i este temor me duro asta que tive ijos" (fol. 33, l. 31).

34. Her children were Inés Manuel, eleven; Juan Méndez, eight and a half; Francisco Gómez, six; Pedro Méndez, three; and Clara, who was breastfeeding and less than a year old at the time of the trial (fol. 19v). The natural fertility cycle would be a child every twelve months for a healthy woman. In Manuel's case, this leaves approximately seventeen months to account for between pregnancies. This time lag might be explained by James Casey's suggestion that the average nursing period was eighteen months (*Early Modern Spain*, p. 217), although the average spacing probably varied regionally and by social class.

35. "[H]i no hes posilve creerse qui isese io aiunos deferentes de lo que mada la santa igleza diante de hun obre tão catolico como ele disia ser" (fol. 33v, ll. 15–17).

36. Haliczer, for example, describes the case of Brianda Gacenta, accused by the Valencia tribunal of "participating in the lashing of a cross with Christ's figure on it." The prosecutor claimed that Gacenta and the others present "took great delight in the cruel passion and torment that the Jews inflicted on his sacred person and proclaimed a strong desire to have been present at the passion" (*Inquisition and Society in the Kingdom of Valencia*, p. 73). Similarly, Joaquín Pérez Villanueva notes that, among the more remarkable examples of inquisitorial zeal in the seventeenth century, a 1632 auto de fe in Madrid involved fifty-three prisoners, seven of whom were burned. Of those accused of Judaizing, two were Portuguese accused of whipping a statue of Christ ("Felipe IV y la Inquisición," p. 439).

37. "[N]ão salia de su casa mas q[ue] a una misa hi a casa de mi padre"; "tal noche como a de navidade nem emdo sola nem em casada nuca sali de mi casa" (fol. 34, ll. 16–18, ll. 1–2).

38. Several witnesses, including the converso prisoners Francisco López and Francisco Duarte deposed in Seville, testified that Borges had spoken of going to Italy through Cádiz, Cartagena, or Alicante, and that they understood this to mean that he wanted to go to practice Judaism freely (fol. 13). In fact, López indicates that Borges wanted to join his in-laws in Pisa, and "even though he

did not say that they were in the Jewish district, this [witness] understood it, and he took it for certain that for the reasons that he has stated about the fact that those of the Hebrew nation don't go to Italy unless it is to Judaize in the synagogues" ("aunque no le dijo que estaban en la judería, éste lo entendió, y lo tuvo por cierto por las razones que ha dicho de que los de la nación hebrea no van a Italia sino a judaizar en las sinagogas" [fol. 11]). Haliczer's observation about travel is helpful in understanding these assumptions: "The Holy Office had helped to sabotage the 1606 act guaranteeing the new Christians freedom of movement by alleging that they only wished to leave the Iberian Peninsula in order to revert to Judaism abroad" ("The First Holocaust," p. 14). For more on the Jewish diaspora and minorities in exile, see chapter 4, "Alternative Religions: *Conversos, Moriscos,* and the Inquisition," in Hillgarth, *The Mirror of Spain,* pp. 160–240. At the start of the trial, Manuel testified that her father had been dead for more than a year, and her mother for more than twenty. Either she was lying to protect them or Borges's mention of the in-laws in Italy was incorrect or meant to mislead.

39. "[M]e dise que se io não quiria ir co[n] ele pa onde fose que iurava a dios que me avia de dexar com mis igos hir el adonde io não supese mais de ele hi se as pocas ganas que io tinia era por que dexava a mim padre que las mugeres onradas despois de casadas não tinham que aser con sus padres senão que tinham obrigasion de irem com su marido aunque fosem a los infernos" (fol. 34, ll. 28–35–fol. 34v, ll. 1–2).

40. "[N]ão dudo se me digua que como se a de creier q[ue] hu obre onrado ijo de buenos padres hi casado de dose anos hi com simco ijos avia de alevantar huna cosa tão grande sem aver ocasio. a isto respodo s[e]ñor que desde o dia que emtro em madrid 1[e] e entrado em su maginasion hum pesamento tão feio como es diser que io le tenio echo agravio en su onor" (fol. 34v, ll. 19–27).

41. "[M]utas vezes vi a morte diante dos oljios" (fol. 34v, ll. 28).

42. "[N]ão pudia tirarme la vida dio em me tratar tão mal de palabra q[ue] não avia nobre infame q[ue] não se me pusese cada ora em a cara" (fol. 35, ll. 5–7). The suggestion in Manuel's testimony that Borges would have killed her had he found proof of her infidelity is hard to decipher. If she is referring to the still-existing law from the twelfth-century *Siete Partidas* that stated a man could kill his wife if he found her in the act of adultery, this statement could be used as evidence that this law was more widely recognized and, perhaps, more commonly implemented than records have led us to believe. See Vigil, *La vida de las mujeres,* pp. 145–55. Perhaps Manuel merely means that, given Borges's violent temperament, he surely would have killed her if he had evidence of adultery.

43. "[D]isendo q[ue] por que avia de tomar a peto suas cosas pues sabia q[ue] el era hun loco hi afirmava com mtos juramentos que ele sabia mto bem q[ue] não avia obre que tivese mulher mais onrada q[ue] ele" (fol. 35, ll. 12–15).

44. Vacillating between verbal attacks and repentance, the cyclical nature of this abuse resonates strongly with Lenore Walker's discussions in *The Battered Woman* of the cycle of domestic violence—or so-called battered-woman's syn-

drome—in which tension builds, an attack takes place, and then the aggressor demonstrates contrition until the cycle begins again.

45. "He de tener poco juicio" could also mean "I must have little sense." Either translation captures the fact that Borges saw himself as acting crazy on certain occasions and, as María Cristina Sacristán points out in *Locura e Inquisición* (pp. 35–38), words related to reason, judgement, and craziness were often used in Inquisition trials related to mentally unstable individuals.

46. "[D]isedo q[ue] aquel punhal era pa mi tirar a vida se acordase di note i me vise em su camara" (fol. 35v, ll. 18–19).

47. She told Borges that "sera bien lhe dijera quem erão os traidores q[ue] lhe querião tirar a vida" (fol. 35v, ll. 31–32). Borges said on a different occasion, "[Q]ue se quiria ir por ese mudo por não morir a manos de traidores" (fol. 36, ll. 3–4).

48. "[E]le não tiria sosega asta q[ue] se vingase de mi" (fol. 36, ll. 14–16).

49. "[L]he dise q[ue] ia lhe perdoava pemsando q[ue] aquela perdão se me pidia por os agravios q[ue] me tinha foito . . . todo aquel dia ando mui contento con el perdon q[ue] lhe tinha dado" (fol. 36, ll. 27–32).

50. "[I]o me alevantei de la mia com arto temor disedome las mismas criaturas no variasen" (fol. 36, ll. 35–36).

51. "[M]atame com este punhal hi pagarei o q[ue] tenho echo . . . pois veio q[ue] o não mereses hi q[ue] estas inosente i milhor es q[ue] tu me mates" (fol. 36v, ll. 8–10).

52. "[I]o lhe disia q[ue] antes q[ue]ria morir a sus manos q[ue] salirme de mim casa pois estava inosente de lhe aver hecho ofensa" (fol. 36v, ll. 22–24).

53. "[L]ocuras tão sin fundamento" (fol. 37v, l. 21).

54. Borges imagined that his brother-in-law had insulted him. For two months after this, Borges kept his hand on his dagger, ready to assault his relative ("estivera con a mano en el puhnal [*sic*] pa lhe quitar a vida" [fol. 37v, ll. 27–28]).

55. "[C]omo hun tigre" (fol. 37v, l. 32).

56. "[A]lguna pesoa q[ue] lhe queria mal lhe queria por fuego a la casa" (fol. 37v, l. 38).

57. "[A]quela era cosa q[ue] io lhe echava por a boca en se dormendo pa o matar"; "aquela ninha avia de ser tão mala muger como su madre" (fol. 38, ll. 7–8, 16).

58. Manuel describes Borges as "mas umano" (fol. 38, l. 21) on the day he saw things more clearly ("bem via ser aquelo una atentasion del demonio que lo ensitava a vengansas con aquellas falsas aparesias" [ll. 23–25]).

59. "[C]uando lo vise con aquelas locuras q[ue] não as tomase de manera a pecho q[ue] viriao[n] mis ijos a quedar sin padre e sin madre por q[ue] aquelo não era mais en su mano. [I] la verda es s[e]ñor q[ue] todos los dotores afirmao[n] q[e] el mal de la perlesia quita mta parte de iuisio por ser prosedido da nuca" (fol. 38v).

60. A final paragraph names possible witnesses for the defense, but this section was added to the original document, perhaps as a transcription of a previous memo.

61. "[L]a quería matar habiendo y diciendo muchas locuras ocasionadas de sus en-

fermedades y mala curación de forma que siempre la dicha d[oña] Bernarda ha vivido con grandes temores de perder la vida" (fol. 39).

62. The relationship between Alfsono Rodríguez Borges and Antonio Gómez Borges is unclear, but a third party, the witness Fernando Rodríguez Correa, confirms that they are related.

63. "[C]on su mala condición, locuras y celos el dicho Antonio Gómez Borges ocasionó la muerte de su primera mujer de cuyo nombre no se acuerda" (fol. 41).

64. "[P]orque era loco y arrojado por lo cual siempre vivía la dicha doña Bernarda con grandes temores de que no le quitase la vida el dicho su marido" (fol. 44).

65. Alfonso Rodríguez Borges said that Manuel "vivía mártir" (fol. 41), while his maid, María de Mora, confirmed hearing her master say this on many occasions (fol. 43).

66. "[S]e declararon la una con la otra de ser observantes de la ley de Moisés creyendo salvarse en ella y que estando en Alicante hicieron ésta y la dicha doña Blanca un ayuno por la guarda de la dicha ley . . . y que no sabe que su marido de ésta ni el dicho Gaspar Rodríguez supiesen que las dos hacían el dicho ayuno porque no se declararon con ellos" (fol. 64v).

67. See Vigil, *La vida de las mujeres*, p. 102–5. The bibliography on early modern sexual and domestic violence is growing. See, for example, Barahona, *Sex Crimes*; Dolan, *Domestic Familiars*; Pérez Molina, "Las mujeres y el matrimonio"; Vollendorf, *Reclaiming the Body*; and Welles, *Persephone's Girdle*.

68. Sánchez Ortega, "Sorcery and Eroticism," p. 67.

69. Kamen has suggested that this fear of outsiders and of the unconventional sustained the Inquisition (*Spain*, p. 294). Vigil has summarized the honor question in terms of women's sexual purity: Family honor rested on wifely fidelity and daughters' virginity (*La vida de las mujeres*, p. 294). Also see Cruz and Perry, Introduction; Maravall, *La literatura picaresca*, pp. 639–97; and Perry, *Gender and Disorder*.

70. Borges tried to see "se pudia sacar algun umo de su mal pesamento mas como donde não a fuego no pode aver umo" (fol. 35, ll. 2–3).

71. "[A]gora digo s[e]ñor q[ue] se su corasion lhe disia q[ue] a ropa susia q[ue] traia al sabado era lipa hi . . . os aiunos verdaderas erão falsos hi todo lo q[ue] era bueno su maginision lhe disia q[ue] era malo *q[ue] culpa tiego io*" (fol. 38, ll. 17–20, emphasis mine).

CHAPTER 3

1. The life stories of these women appear in Mujica, *Women Writers*: Carvajal, pp. 283–91; Meneses, pp. 321–31; and Zayas, pp. 126–36.

2. Only Saint Teresa appears on a significant number of graduate reading lists in the United States (see Brown and Johnson, "Required Reading").

3. See Heller, "Rediscovering," p. 15.

4. "[M]is borrones" (*Novelas amorosas y ejemplares*, pp. 159, 161). Spanish quotes from Zayas are taken from Olivares' edition of this work and from Yllera's second edition of *Desengaños amorosos*. English quotes are from H. Patsy Boyer's

translations: *The Enchantments of Love* and *The Disenchantments of Love*, with "modified translation" used to indicate minor changes to Boyer.

5. My translation of "[un] aborto inútil de mi corto ingenio" and of "obligación precisa es de un pecho noble el suavizar tan penoso desconsuelo" (Carvajal, *Navidades de Madrid*, p. 5).

6. As confirmed by Brown and Johnson's studies, these calls for attention to women's literature strike a chord today (see Brown and Johnson, "Required Reading").

7. Other writers also deal with issues of gender and sexuality. See the following editions and studies of pre-eighteenth-century Hispanic women's writing: Marcela de San Félix, *Literatura conventual femenina*; Arenal and Schlau, *Untold Sisters*; Zayas, *La traición en la amistad*, ed. Hegstrom; Kaminsky, *Water Lilies*; Meneses, *El desdeñado más firme*; Mujica, *Sophia's Daughters*; Schlau, *Viva al Siglo*; Soufas, *Women's Acts*; Whitenack and Campbell, *Zayas and Her Sisters, 1*; and Yllera, *Introducción*.

8. Until recently, most critics disparaged Carvajal's literary abilities (see Amezúa, "Formación y elementos"; and Manuel Serrano y Sanz, "Carvajal y Saavedra") but praised the realist aspect of her texts (see Bourland, "Aspectos de la vida del hogar"; J. Jiménez, "Doña Mariana de Carvajal y Saavedra"; and Rodríguez Cuadros, *Novelas amorosas*, pp. 9–69). Recent studies on Carvajal are more balanced in their consideration of her talents, including Armon, *Picking Wedlock*; L. Jiménez, "Imágenes costumbristas"; Romero-Díaz, *Nueva nobleza, nueva novela*; and Velasco, "Reconsidering Romance." Recent books on Zayas include Brownlee, *The Cultural Labyrinth*; Greer, *María de Zayas*; and Vollendorf, *Reclaiming the Body*.

9. Valis, "Mariana de Carvajal," pp. 251–52. Unless otherwise noted, all Carvajal translations are from this source.

10. Specialists in early modern women's writing might also want to refer to the more in-depth consideration of these issues in Vollendorf, "The Future of Early Modern Women's Studies."

11. On the formulaic style of the novella genre, see, for instance, Goytisolo, "El mundo erótico," p. 71. Rodríguez Cuadros notes that novellas, along with *comedia*, expressed dominant ideologies (*Novelas amorosas*, pp. 24–25).

12. Zayas, *Desengaños amorosos*, p. 118, hereafter cited in text and notes as *Desengaños*.

13. I follow others in the field (such as Mario DiGangi, Jeffrey Masten, Bruce Smith, and Valerie Traub) who use the term "homoerotic" to refer to erotic arrangements among members of the same sex in the early modern period. See, for example, Traub, "The Rewards of Lesbian History" and *The Renaissance of Lesbianism*. For the Hispanic context, see Delgado and Saint-Saëns, *Lesbianism and Homosexuality*.

14. Zayas, *The Disenchantments of Love*, p. 214, hereafter cited in the text as *DL*. "Amarte y servirte hasta merecerte, como lo haré mientras viviere; que el poder de amor también se extiende de mujer a mujer, como de galán a dama" (*Desengaños*, p. 306).

15. Gossy, "Skirting the Question," p. 24. Also see Boyer, "The War between the Sexes"; Gorfkle, "Re-Constituting the Feminine"; and Maroto Camino, "María de Zayas and Ana Caro."

16. "[S]upuesto que el alma es toda una en varón y en la hembra, no se me da más ser hombre que mujer; que las almas no son hombres ni mujeres, y el verdadero amor en el alma está, que no en el cuerpo; y el que amare el cuerpo con el cuerpo, no puede decir que es amor, sino apetito" (*Desengaños*, p. 317). Relevant research on the trope cross-dressing includes Bravo-Villasante, *La mujer vestida de hombre*; Bullough and Bullough. *Cross Dressing, Sex, and Gender*; Garber, *Vested Interests*; and McKendrick, *Women and Society*.

17. DiGangi, *Homoerotics of Early Modern Drama*, pp. 6–23.

18. Gossy, "Skirting the Question," p. 26.

19. See, for example, Herrera Puga, *Sociedad y delincuencia*, pp. 246–69; and Perry, "The 'Nefarious' Sin." In *Crime and Society in Early Modern Seville*, Perry notes that in Seville: "Lesbians were also severely punished in the [royal] prison. According to Chaves, the women in prison spoke the same tough language as underworld men. . . . Some made artificial male genitalia; those who were discovered were given 200 lashes and permanently exiled from Seville" (p. 84). For more on early modern homoeroticism, see Goldberg, *Queering the Renaissance* and *Sodometries*; and Sinfield, *Cultural Politics, Queer Readings*.

20. "No había llegado a su noticia qué era amar, ni ser amada" (*Desengaños*, p. 296).

21. "¿Quién ha visto que una dama se enamore de otra?" (*Desengaños*, p. 320).

22. "[E]lla y todas lo juzgaban a locura, antes les servía de entretenimiento y motivo de risa, siempre que la veían hacer extremos y finezas de amante, llorar celos y sentir desdenes, admirando que una mujer estuviese enamorada de otra, sin llegar a su imaginación que pudiese ser lo contrario" (*Desengaños*, p. 309).

23. "Más te quiero yo mujer que no hombre" (ibid.).

24. "Cada uno busca y desea lo que ha menester" (ibid.).

25. "Ya le pesara que fuera Estefanía y no don Esteban" (*Desengaños*, p. 322).

26. Kaminsky, "María de Zayas," p. 491.

27. Armon, "Mariana de Caravajal's *Navidades*," p. 244. Armon takes up female friendship in Zayas, Carvajal, and Meneses in *Picking Wedlock* (pp. 81–88).

28. Carvajal, in Valis, "Mariana de Carvajal," p. 273; hereafter Valis's translations are cited in the text as "Carvajal." "[Q]uedó tan disgustada que, por vengar su enfado, los trataba con rigurosos desdenes" (Carvajal, *Navidades de Madrid*, p. 120, hereafter cited as *Navidades*).

29. "[A]mada de todas" and "Preciábase de ser tan cortés y afable con las mujeres como cruel con los hombres" (*Navidades*, p. 121).

30. DiGangi, *Homoerotics of Early Modern Drama*, p. 10.

31. Valis, "Mariana de Carvajal," p. 262.

32. Kaminsky has pointed out that marriage represents the disorder of patriarchy in *The Disenchantments of Love*, as evidenced by the number of wives victimized by their spouses in the volume (personal correspondence, July 2003).

33. Armon, "The Romance of Courtesy," p. 241.

34. "Pues no te espantes, . . . que si nací libre de amor, no lo estoy de haber nacido mujer" (*Navidades*, p. 122).

35. DiGangi, *Homoerotics of Early Modern Drama*, pp. 26, 92. Male bonding, including male homoeroticism, has received far more critical attention than any aspect of women's sociality or eroticism. See, among others, Cruz, "'Homo ex machina'?"; Donnell, "Between Night and Day"; Heiple, "Lope de Vega"; and Vélez-Quiñones, *Monstrous Displays*). Traub's *Renaissance of Lesbianism* is one of the most complete studies of historical female homoeroticism to date. Also see Castle, *The Apparitional Lesbian*; and Velasco, *The Lieutenant Nun*.

36. Similarly, contemporary philosophers such as Judith Butler and Elizabeth Grosz have suggested that rather than look for signs of sexual identity, we should question the nature of one's allegiances and investments (see Butler, *Bodies that Matter* and "Imitation and Gender Subordination"; and Grosz, *Space, Time, Perversion*). Teresa DeLauretis considers similar ideas in *The Practice of Love*.

37. The following have commented on rivalry in Zayas: Cruz, "Feminism," p. 43; Profeti, "Los parentescos ficticios," p. 241; and Gorfkle, "Seduction and Hysteria." Carvajal's representations of women's homosociality have been mentioned by several critics (see Armon, "The Romance of Courtesy," pp. 243–44; Profeti, "Los parentescos ficticios," p. 244; J. Jiménez, "Doña Mariana de Carvajal y Saavedra," pp. 18–21; Valis, "Mariana de Carvajal," p. 261; and Walliser, "Recuperación panorámica," pp. 331–32). In "Beyond Entertainment," Nancy Cushing-Daniels emphasizes Carvajal's depiction of domesticity as a stabilizing force (p. 72). Also see Soriano (xv–xviii).

38. For discussions of femininity and solidarity in Zayas and Carvajal, see Kaminsky, "Dress and Redress" and "María de Zayas," pp. 487–509; Cushing-Daniels, "Beyond Entertainment"; Ordóñez, "Woman and Her Text"; Romero-Díaz, *Nueva nobleza, nueva novela*; and Vollendorf, *Reclaiming the Body* (especially pp. 197–215).

39. Kaminsky, "María de Zayas," p. 497.

CHAPTER 4

1. On literacy, see note 7 in the introduction.

2. For editions of the female-authored plays discussed in this chapter, see Zayas, *La traición en la amistad*; and Soufas, *Women's Acts*. Innovative studies on women and theater include Daniels, "Re-Visioning Gender"; Soufas, *Dramas of Distinction*; and Hegstrom and Williamsen, *Engendering the Early Modern Stage* (particularly Williamsen, "Charting Our Course: Gender, the Canon, and Early Modern Theater," pp. 1–16).

3. Cascardi, *Ideologies of History*, pp. 17–46.

4. Soufas, *Dramas of Distinction*, p. 35.

5. These playwrights' texts are available in Soufas, *Women's Acts*, in which Soufas

cites the one known reference to Caro and Zayas's association in Madrid (p. 133).

6. None of these plays has a date of composition assigned yet. Azevedo probably wrote during her time of service to Queen Isabel (1621–44); Caro was active as a writer in the 1630s and 1640s; and Zayas might have written her play between 1630 and 1635 (see Soufas, *Women's Acts*). Nothing is known about Caro after 1653, or about Zayas after the publication of *The Disenchantments of Love* in 1647.

7. Soufas also groups Azevedo, Zayas, and Caro in *Dramas of Distinction*.

8. D. Smith, Introduction, p. 26.

9. Ibid.

10. As William Blue suggests: "The fundamental differences among these plays can be marked by looking at the paths rather than the preordained destinations" (*Spanish Comedies and Historical Contexts*, p. 27).

11. Roof, *Come as You Are*, p. 7.

12. Ibid., p. 16.

13. O'Driscoll, "Outlaw Readings," p. 41. Likewise, Marilyn Farwell focuses on textual instability in *Heterosexual Plots and Lesbian Narratives* (p. 3).

14. For an overview of Azevedo's life, see Soufas, *Women's Acts*, pp. 1–3.

15. *Dicha y desdicha del juego y devoción de la Virgen* and *La margarita del Tajo que dio nombre a Santarén* both appear in ibid., pp. 4–90.

16. Beatriz says: "[S]iempre obligan más / que la sangre amantes veras" (ll. 1200–1201) ("true lovers always oblige more than mere blood"). Quotes from Azevedo and Caro are taken from Soufas's *Women's Acts*. Spanish and English quotes from Zayas come from Hegstrom and Larson's critical bilingual edition. All other translations are my own.

17. "[M]uchos casan por amores" (Azevedo, *El muerto disimulado*, l. 2002).

18. Rodrigo sees Jacinta as deceptive, when in fact she is loyal to her lover (ll. 2046–48). Alvaro wrongly asserts that Beatriz has no preferences of her own (ll. 3056–57).

19. Zayas, *Traición en la amistad*, ll. 39–43, hereafter cited as *Traición*.

20. "[G]uerra de amor" (*Traición*, l. 37).

21. "[C]ayó la amistad en tierra / y amor victoria apellida" (*Traición*, ll. 173–74).

22. Larson, "Reforming the Golden Age," p. 122.

23. Larson, "Gender, Reading, and Intertextuality," p. 134.

24. "¿No sale, prima, el aurora / con tan grande presunción?" (*Traición*, ll. 891–92).

25. "[E]s vuestro talle extremado; / me ha turbado, y casi estoy / muerta de amores en veros" (*Traición*, ll. 900–903). I have followed Soufas's punctuation here.

26. "No hay más bien / que ver, cuando viendo estoy / tal belleza. ¡El cielo os dé / la ventura cual la cara!" (*Traición*, ll. 915–18).

27. "Soy vuestra servidora, / y a fe que desde esta hora, / cautiváis mi voluntad" (*Traición*, ll. 938–40).

28. "[S]i hombre fuera, yo empleara / en vuestra afición mi fe" (*Traición*, ll. 919–20).
29. Soufas, *Dramas of Distinction*, p. 143.
30. "[E]l amor en el sentido de amistad" (Paun de García, "*Traición en la amistad*," p. 387).
31. "Señores míos, Fenisa, / cual ven sin amantes queda. / Si alguno la quiere, avise / para que su casa sepa" (*Traición*, ll. 2911–94).
32. Wilkins's "Subversion through Comedy?" and Stroud's "Love, Friendship, and Deceit" discuss Fenisa's exclusion. Soufas suggests that Zayas uses Fenisa to demonstrate the lack of tolerance for independent women in theater ("María de Zayas's [Un]Conventional Play," p. 51). Similarly, Hegstrom Oakey has suggested that the ending posits a challenge to convention by putting women in charge of the marriage matches and exploding the myth that only men are active and women are passive ("The Fallacy of False Dichotomy," p. 60). Larson examines these two types of readings, in which Fenisa is seen as punished and as a defiant female literary figure, and declares that both are feasible, for the play has an uncertain closure that defies a single interpretation ("Gender, Reading, and Intertextuality," pp. 133–37).
33. "Yo soy quien soy. / Engañaste si imaginas, / Ribete, que soy mujer; / mi agravio mudó mi ser" (Caro, *Valor, agravio y mujer*, ll. 507–10, hereafter cited as *Valor*).
34. "How well you know how to persuade!" ("¡Qué bien sabéis persuadir!" [*Valor*, l. 1073]).
35. Soufas, *Dramas of Distinction*, p. 120.
36. Ibid.
37. "Leonardo fui, mas ya vuelvo / a ser Leonor" (*Valor*, ll. 2723–24).
38. "'Leonardo, ¿así me engañabas?' / 'Fue fuerza, Estela'" (*Valor*, ll. 2730–31).
39. "Quedemos / hermanas, Leonor hermosa" (*Valor*, ll. 2732–33).
40. Sidney Donnell pinpoints one of the obstacles to writing about same-sex pairings: Such an ending "would require a renegotiation of patriarchal relations because women would no longer be a necessary site of exchange between men" ("Between Night and Day," p. 453). On questions of marriage and exchange, see Friedman, "'Girl Gets Boy?'"
41. For the early modern context, Valerie Traub describes in "The (In)Significance of Lesbian Desire" (p. 72) the tendency to represent female-female eroticism as fleeting: "Female homoeroticism is thus figurable not only in terms of the always already lost, but the always about to be betrayed." Terry Castle's study of post-Enlightenment lesbianism, *The Apparitional Lesbian*, traces the association between ghosts and lesbians since the eighteenth century (p. 60).
42. Traub has suggested that highly charged interactions between women were possible on the English stage "precisely because they did not signify" ("The (In)Significance of Lesbian Desire," p. 80).

CHAPTER 5

1. See, for instance, the work of Electa Arenal, Sonja Herpoel, Asunción Lavrin, Kathryn McKnight, Stephanie Merrim, Kathleen Myers, Isabelle Poutrin, Amanda Powell, Stacey Schlau, Elissa Weaver, and Alison Weber.

2. On conversion houses, see Perry, "Magdalens and Jezebels." For a discussion of the increase in religious men and women in the seventeenth century, see Hillgarth, *The Mirror of Spain*, pp. 148–52; and Sánchez Lora, *Mujeres*, pp. 107–13. Lavrin has shown that, at least in colonial Mexico, the expense of placing a daughter in a convent was comparable to that of marrying her off ("Unlike Sor Juana?" p. 62).

3. See Arenal and Schlau, *Untold Sisters*, pp. 1–17; and Burns, "Nuns, Kurakas, and Credit," pp. 55–59.

4. Sánchez Lora gives the example of a woman who, upon professing as a Poor Claire, sold a slave and the slave's daughter to raise the cash to pay her convent dowry (*Mujeres*, p. 129). For more on the class structures of convents, see Schlau, "Following Saint Teresa," pp. 286–90; Weber, "Spiritual Administration"; and Baernstein, *A Convent Tale*, pp. 1–26.

5. Schlau, "Following Saint Teresa," p. 287.

6. The particularities of religious orders are dealt with in detail in Rapley, *The Dévotes*; and DeMolen, *Religious Orders*. Also see Herpoel for a study of autobiographical writing by women.

7. See Ahlgren, *Teresa of Avila*, for more on two of the most prolific and important letter writers, Saint Teresa and María de Agreda.

8. In *Teatro breve de mujeres*, research director Fernando Doménech Rico notes that Sor Francisca's play contains nothing to indicate it was written by a nun for a convent audience (p. 44). The play appears in Doménech, pp. 49–64.

9. Stephanie Merrim, in *Early Modern Women's Writing*, points out the difficulties of placing Sor Juana in a comparative context, particularly given "a relative lack of subjects [i.e., authors] for comparison, especially in terms of women writing on secular subjects" (p. xiii). Subsequently published editions of women's writing have introduced more secular-themed texts to modern audiences (e.g., Whitenack and Campbell, *Zayas and Her Sisters, 1*; and Soufas, *Women's Acts*).

10. For more on Azevedo, see Soufas, *Dramas of Distinction*, pp. 70–104. On hagiographical drama by women, see Soufas et al., "Playing with Saint Isabel," pp. 123–41. Souza's play, housed at the Biblioteca Nacional in Madrid, has no publication information and no date.

11. See Arenal and Schlau, *Untold Sisters*, pp. 1–17; Myers and Powell, *A Wild Country*; and Poska and Lehfeldt, "Redefining Expectations," pp. 21–42. Elissa Weaver has analyzed Tuscan nuns' views on the convent wall as a source of fantasy in "The Convent Wall."

12. On the complexities of writing on command, see Weber's *Teresa de Avila*. In conjunction with Weber's book, Jean Franco's *Plotting Women* also has been influential in helping scholars interpret religious women's writing.

13. I include Portuguese-born Sor Violante because she wrote both in Castilian and Portuguese and because she lived during the period of Spain's annexation of Portugal.

14. "Belisa, el amistad es un tesoro / tan digno de estimarse eternamente, / que a su valor no es paga suficiente / de Arabia, y Potosí la plata y oro. / Es la amistad un lícito decoro / que se guarda en lo ausente y lo presente, / y con que de un amigo el otro siente / la tristeza, el pesar, la risa, el lloro. / No se llama amistad la que es violenta, / si no la que es conforme simpatía, / de quien lealtad hasta la muerte ostenta: / Esta la amistad es que hallar querría, / ésta la que entre amigas se sustenta, / y ésta, Belisa, en fin, la amistad mía" (Olivares and Boyce, *Tras el espejo la musa escribe*, p. 271). The translation is mine. The dedication to Ferreira remains likely, but unconfirmed.

15. Electa Arenal notes that, of the four or five full manuscripts Sor Marcela completed, all but one were burned at the request of a confessor ("Vida y teatro conventual," p. 212). See Alisa Joanne Tigchelaar, "Instruction and Self-Identification," for more on the dramatic tradition in Teresian convents.

16. Excellent work on Sor Marcela has been done by Arenal and Schlau (*Untold Sisters*), Arenal and Sabat de Rivers (editors of Sor Marcela de San Félix's complete works, *Literatura conventual*), and Susan Manell Smith ("The Colloquies of Sor Marcela"). As every scholarly work on Sor Marcela discusses at length, she was the illegitimate daughter of the actress Micaela de Luján and the playwright Lope de Vega. See, for example, Arenal, "Vida y teatro conventual," pp. 211–14; Sor Marcela de San Félix, *Literatura conventual*, p. 18; S. Smith, "The Colloquies of Sor Marcela," p. 1; and Tigchelaar, "Instruction and Self-Identification," pp. 158–65. Another nun who might have been included in this analysis of convent theater is Sor María de San Alberto, who wrote short dramatic texts intended for performance during Christmas. See Schlau, *Viva al Siglo*, pp. 49–92.

17. Arenal and Schlau, *Untold Sisters*, p. 243.

18. Arenal and Sabat de Rivers cite Jean Louis Flecniakoska's calculation that *Muerte del apetito* would have taken two and a half hours to perform, whereas the other coloquios are approximately half as long (Marcela de San Félix, *Literatura conventual femenina*, p. 38; Flecniakoska, *La loa*, p. 12).

19. Schlau and Arenal, "Not Only Her Father's Daughter," pp. 222–23.

20. Marcela de San Félix, *Literatura conventual femenina*, p. 159, ll. 1454–61, hereafter cited as *Literatura*. All Spanish quotations of Sor Marcela are taken from this source, edited by Arenal and Sabat de Rivers. English quotations are from Powell's translation of most of the play (Marcela de San Félix, "The Death of Desire").

21. Desire speaks of the stinginess of the women in charge of dispensing food, for example (ll. 1389–92), and the character Lies in "In Praise of Religion" ("Estimación de la religión") complains about the bad food, lack of drink, hard beds, and lack of food (*Literatura*, p. 202–4, ll. 1277–1348). Joy in "The Nativity" ("El nacimiento") also discusses food constantly.

22. "Leave the poor crazy people with their misfortune and misery, which without

a doubt will increase in company such as this"; "Dejad a los pobres locos / con su desgracia y miserias, / que sin duda crecerá / en compañía como ésta" (*Literatura*, p. 336, ll. 736–39).

23. Susan Smith interprets the arrival of the mute men as an inscription of "effective convent administration" ("The Colloquies of Sor Marcela," p. 199).

24. "Enseñada me parece / que quedo con tus palabras" (*Literatura*, p. 135, ll.546–47).

25. "[M]ás que al fuego" (*Literatura*, p. 140, ll.715).

26. In "In Praise of Religion," Truth describes Lies as "hija del Demonio" and Soul finally comes to agree that she is a "vil mujer" (*Literatura*, p. 171, ll. 95, 104).

27. "Yo quisiera amar de suerte / y tan desnudo a mi Dios, / que sólo su ser divino / fuera blanco de mi amor, / de suerte que ni el criarme, / ni el redimirme en rigor, / ni el conservarme tampoco / fomentara mi afición, / sino tan sólo el ser quién es / en sí mismo y sin ficción" (*Literatura*, p. 232, ll. 657–66).

28. "[E]l santo y divino esposo / ardiendo en fuego de amor" (*Literatura*, p. 237, ll. 847–48).

29. Arenal notes the hybrid nature of Sor Marcela's work, attributing it to her innovative adaptation of secular theater to her religious purposes ("Vida y teatro conventual," p. 214).

30. "[P]or quererte yo tanto / te doy amorosas quejas" (*Literatura*, p. 248, ll. 45–46). Later, Tepidity insists she has been deceived (p. 249, l. 97).

31. "Since she has, finally, raised me and she loves me so much, I cannot find good enough reason to dismiss her"; "Como ella, en fin / me ha criado / y me tiene tanto amor, / no puedo hallar ocasión / tan grande que la despida" (*Literatura*, p. 255, ll. 318–21).

32. "Oración: Al Amor quiero llamar. / Alma, por Dios, no te escondas, / y mira que le respondas / con más agrado que a mí./ Alma: Como yo le vea aquí, / ten por cierto que soy tuya. / Oración: Procuro que seas suya, / que yo soy el medio no más" (*Literatura*, p. 257, ll. 381–84).

33. In "In Praise of Religion," Lies accuses an evil force of speaking badly of her, and notes that because of the envy others feel toward her, such gossip was predictable (*Literatura*, p. 175, ll. 231–50). Soul says that she wants to please the negative characters (Lies and the World) and, later, the positive characters (Religion and Truth). Similarly, in "The Death of Desire" she vacillates between Desire and the supportive, virtuous sisters.

34. "Y perdonad nuestras faltas, / que Amor, que nos hizo hacerlas, / también puede perdonarlas" (*Literatura*, p. 267, ll. 789–91).

35. For an excellent overview of the querelle des femmes, see King and Rabil, "The Other Voice in Early Modern Europe," which appears in all books in the University of Chicago series of the same name, including in Fonte, *The Worth of Women*, pp. vii–xvii. Also see chapter 2 in Merrim, *Early Modern Women's Writing*, pp. 38–91.

36. María de los Angeles Campo Guiral discusses Abarca's literary ties at length in her biography, *Doña Ana Francisca Abarca de Bolea*, pp. 59–95.

37. Campo Guiral suggests in the preface to her edition of Abarca's *Vigilia y octa-*

vario that Abarca's niece, Francisca Bernarda Abarca y Vilanova, played a key role in preparing the manuscript and trying to get it published (p. xxxviii).

38. "Este libro sepultado / muchos años le ha tenido / el sepulcro del olvido," (Abarca de Bolea, *Vigilia y octavario* [1679], p. xxvii). With the exception of this prefatory material, all quotes from Abarca are from Campo Guiral's 1994 edition of *Vigilia y octavario*, hereafter cited as *Vigilia*. English translations are mine.

39. Campo Guiral dates some of the poems from *Vigilia* to 1650–69 (*Vigilia*, p. xlv).

40. See Campo Guiral's explanation of the biographical reference (*Vigilia*, p. 60n.155).

41. "[D]e muchas mujeres que por sus escritos y bien empleado tiempo fueron celebradas de historiadores y hombres insignes" (*Vigilia*, p. 65).

42. "[P]orque apenas hay hombre que no guste de oír hablar mal de las mujeres" (*Vigilia*, p. 67).

43. "[D]eben desentender lo que las solicita pesadumbre" (ibid.).

44. "[F]uria más fiera y ponzoñosa / es la ira de mujer esquiva" (*Vigilia*, p. 259).

45. "[A]unque los lucimientos de las mujeres muchas veces los obscurecen la incredulidad y emulación" (*Vigilia*, p. 122).

46. "[T]an ajustadas décimas y, más, por ser de mujer" (*Vigilia*, p. 413).

47. Whitenack, "Internalized Misogyny," p. 253.

48. "[C]ruelísimos azotes con unas correas muy anchas" (*Vigilia*, p. 102).

49. "[A]gradado de su cara y apacible trato y sabida su buena sangre y pobreza, le contó su calidad y la dijo que si quería ayudarle a cobrar sus joyas se casaría con ella, llevándola a su patria" (*Vigilia*, p. 103).

50. Whitenack, "Internalized Misogyny," pp. 256–57.

51. "[G]rito, que lo ponía en el cielo y penetraba todas las cuadras" (*Vigilia*, p. 103).

52. "[P]ara escarmiento general de mujeres que, con sus estafas, disminuyen las haciendas ajenas" (*Vigilia*, p. 105).

53. "[L]a crueldad de una loca mujer" (*Vigilia*, p. 339).

54. "[V]ivía de estafas y hacer burlas a los forasteros" (*Vigilia*, p. 336).

55. With the exception of mentioning convents and making one comment about nuns having to live with the "the leftovers and crumbs from their parents' estates," Abarca rarely refers to convent life or women's friendship ("desperdicios y migajas de las casas de sus padres" [*Vigilia*, p. 344]).

CHAPTER 6

1. Arenal and Schlau describe the writers Ana de San Bartolomé and María de San José as "two of Saint Teresa's most beloved Daughters and direct inheritors of her vision" (*Untold Sisters*, p. 19).

2. Exploring the imbalance between *vidas* with male and female subjects, Kathryn Joy McKnight has found that the few men who wrote spiritual autobiographies

did not reflect the self-doubt seen in women's texts. Instead, they articulated confidence, self-affirmation, and a sense of righteousness about the undertaking (*The Mystic of Tunja*, pp. 55–56).

3. For an overview of rhetorical strategies employed in spiritual women's writing, see Weber, *Teresa of Avila*; Arenal and Schlau, *Untold Sisters*; Herpoel, *A la zaga de Santa Teresa*; chapter 2 ("Gender, Tradition, and Autobiographical Spiritual Writings") in Myers and Powell, *A Wild Country*, pp. 298–340; and Schlau, *Spanish American Women's Use of the Word*.

4. Elizabeth Alvilda Petroff has discussed the overdetermined quality of women's life stories in terms of the need for hagiographers to justify the behavior of women who did not conform to gender expectations (i.e., by rejecting marriage, learning to read, etc.): "Apparently, the hagiographer did not feel it was sufficient simply to present to us what the saint did and then affirm this event as a miracle because it obviously violated the usual order of things. God's will, and not the saint's will, had to be apparent in the event from its very genesis" (*Body and Soul*, p. 166).

5. Ronald Surtz provides a brief overview of this shift between the fifteenth and sixteenth centuries: "Over time, the Inquisition sought to discredit the type of unmediated experience of the divine embodied in mystics and visionaries. Women, in particular, were branded as the victims of a delusion, a move that effectively discredited their extraordinary religious experiences" (*Writing Women*, p. 140).

6. For more on women's spirituality in the period, see Arenal and Schlau, *Untold Sisters*; Giles, *Women in the Inquisition*; Kagan, *Lucrecia's Dreams*; and Márquez, *Los alumbrados*.

7. Recalling the time in which he read the vida of doña María de Pol to his mother, Bernique explains: "[A]dmirando yo el misterio de que un hijo suyo hubiese sido el escritor de las virtudes de su madre, me respondió, que lo mismo había de suceder con su merçed, llamándome con grazejo repetidas veces su historiador" (fol. 2v–3). All citations from Bernique and Sor Catalina are taken from Bernique's biographical text, *Idea de perfección y virtudes*, hereafter cited in text and notes as *Idea*. All punctuation and spelling have been modernized for ease of reading. The prefatory material has folio pagination, while the rest of the text is marked with page numbers. Also see Barbeito Carneiro's chapter on Catalina de Jesús, pp. 86–94 in *Mujeres del Madrid Barroco*, pp. 86–94; Bilinkoff, *Related Lives*; and Herpoel, *A la zaga de Santa Teresa*.

8. Myers and Powell explain that the two common genres of spiritual texts were confessional-autobiographical writings and hagiographic biographies (*A Wild Country*, p. 328). A combined autobiography/biography similar to Bernique's is that of Marie de l'Incarnation, which was written as a private document on the request of her son, who, like Juan Bernique, was a priest; and that of doña María de Pol, mentioned by Catalina herself as a model for her own biography. Jodi Bilinkoff, who is working on Pol, has indicated that the text is housed at the Biblioteca Nacional in Madrid. For more on Marie de l'Incarnation, see Bruneau, *Women Mystics*, and Greenberg, *Baroque Bodies*, pp. 160–208. Col-

laboration in women's vidas usually involved a confessor, but we have another family example in the visionary texts of Elisabeth of Schönau (d. 1164), which were produced with the help of Elisabeth's brother, Eckbert. See Clark, "Holy Woman or Unworthy Vessel?"

9. For discussions of vidas and religion in the Americas, see Mooney, *Gendered Voices*, p. 7. Also see A. Greer and Bilinkoff, *Colonial Saints*; Lavrin, "Sexuality in Colonial Mexico"; and Myers, *Neither Saints nor Sinners*.

10. "Si debe mi madre por mujer fuerte ser aplaudida, lo dirá quien esta vida leyere, que yo aunque hijo suyo, y con la licencia que Salomón me concede, no me atrevo a publicarla con este superlativo, sólo no sufro que sus obras en las sombras del olvido queden sepultadas" (*Idea*, fol. 2v).

11. Bilinkoff, "Confessors," p. 93. Bilinkoff makes reference to the Bernique text as well and is working on the text with a focus on Juan Bernique rather than on Sor Catalina herself (see *Related Lives*).

12. For more on the role of religious men as mediators of women's spirituality, see Coakley, "Friars as Confidants"; Haliczer, *Sexuality in the Confessional*; and Mooney, *Gendered Voices*.

13. "[N]o diré más de aquello [la vida], que fielmente he trasladado de los papeles y cartas originales que rendida a la obediencia escribió, y en mi poder paran" (*Idea*, p. 4). Later in the book Bernique refers to letters (from Catalina to her confessor) that he has in his control (p. 204).

14. In the introduction to the excellent collection *Gendered Voices*, Mooney observes that "customarily no text authored by the female protagonist in question has survived against which we might check the claims of her male scribe or hagiographer" (p. 8). For more on the writing process of convent autobiographies, see Weber, "Three Lives of the *Vida*."

15. "Impedíanla estos designios la obligación precisa de la crianza de sus hijos. . . . Pero se enfervorizó tanto y tomaron tanto cuerpo estos deseos que clandestinamente tuvo dispuesto irse a entrar Religiosa Descalza de Santa Clara como fugitiva de los engaños del mundo, atropellando las obligaciones de acudir a sus hijos" (*Idea*, p. 63).

16. Catalina "gastaba mucho tiempo en leer libros de comedias, novelas y otros semejantes . . . dejándose llevar de la ingeniosidad profana de estos libros" (*Idea*, p. 17). She had an "inclinación nativa" toward chastity and "aborrecía el estado del matrimonio como contrario a sus designios," according to Bernique (pp. 18–19).

17. "Conjuráronse contra mí todas las criaturas y todos los medios que se pueden pensar para que esto [el matrimonio] se consiguiese. Entraba con tal disgusto en el matrimonio y con tanto aborrecimiento, que no puedo decir con verdad de adónde me venía porque los deseos y propósitos que antes tuve de guardar castidad y ser religiosa los tenía muy olvidados. Diéronme unas calenturas no sé si certifiqué fueron de pena" (Catalina, *Idea*, p. 19). Throughout the chapter, I cite the quotations that Bernique attributes to his mother's writings as Catalina, *Idea*.

18. "A la mujer o castillo que la guarde o marido que la cele" (*Idea*, p. 20).

19. "Mucho tiene que disimular el hombre advirtiendo la fragilidad de la mujer; pero si en ésta se junta poco rendimiento, demasiada altivez, apetito a componerse, gastar galas y amiga con exceso de recreos, es insufrible la carga y necesita de notable sufrimiento para guardar la paz tan deseada en este estado" (*Idea*, p. 23).

20. About his father, Bernique concludes: "It doesn't seem that he lacked anything to be perfect" ("no parece le faltó cosa para ser perfecto" [*Idea*, p. 37]).

21. "Frecuentaba, lo que podía, los sacramentos, que le comunicasen valor para tolerar la cruz del matrimonio, de terrible peso para ella" (*Idea*, p. 25). Sor Catalina's maternal obligations are discussed on the same page.

22. "Yo pienso que todos los trabajos que suceden en el mundo hacia esta parte tienen la mayor culpa las mujeres . . . pues con sus trajes, ademanes y ansias de parecer bien dan ocasión y atrevimiento a los hombres para tantas culpas" (Catalina, *Idea*, pp. 28–29).

23. "En el tiempo de casada . . . qué ahogos, qué trabajos no padecí, qué aborrecimiento al marido. . . . Valióme para todas estas ocasiones el natural, que su Magestad me había dado, que aborrecía todo lo que era contrario a la virtud de la castidad" (Catalina, *Idea*, p. 26).

24. "Este era el único medio de evitar culpas y conservarse en honestidad y recato. ¡O qué delicada es la joya de la castidad y el cristal de la pureza!" (*Idea*, p. 32).

25. "Dispuso su Magestad privarla del marido, o para aliviarla del estado para ella tan molesto o para confundir del todo su vanidad, imposibilitándola a seguir del mundo las locuras" (*Idea*, p. 34).

26. "Santo mío, llevadme a Alcalá" (Catalina, *Idea*, p. 32).

27. "Cumplió el Santo Bendito . . . mi petición tan presto, que dentro de un mes cayó malo mi marido y murió de aquella enfermedad y me vine a Alcalá luego" (Catalina, *Idea*, p. 35).

28. "Hallaron su cuerpo después de trece años, que fueron a enterrar a otro, sin corrupción alguna y un olor que admiraron los presentes, y el hábito entero, como si le acabaran de enterrar" (Catalina, *Idea*, p. 38).

29. "Esto mismo confiesa mi madre, haciendo alarde para confusión suya, de la perfección que experimentó en su esposo, y ahora, después de abrir los ojos a la verdad, fue por ella reconocida" (*Idea*, p. 37). The theme of the incorrupt, lifelike cadaver arises repeatedly in narratives of sanctity. As Thurston's *Physical Phenomenon of Mysticism* suggests, this phenomenon was so closely associated with female saints that, in Bynum's words, "incorruptibility, either of the whole cadaver or of a part, seems a virtual requirement for female sanctity by the early modern period" (*Fragmentation and Redemption*, p. 187).

30. "Son tantos los trabajos que se pasan que me hallo con cortedad para explicarlos y sólo me sirve de confusión conocer son ningunos en su comparación los que se pasan en la vida espiritual, teniendo por norte, guía y objeto a un Dios purísimo y no a un hombre imperfecto y tosco" (Catalina, *Idea*, p. 34).

31. "Viose libre del yugo del matrimonio para ella tan molesto, pero con la pensión de la crianza de sus hijos, que no la brumaba poco" (*Idea*, p. 12).

32. "Peleé con terribles contradicciones y deseé casarme mucho y me acuerdo tuve

este deseo y no sé si se lo pedí a nuestra Señora, entiendo que sí, que me diese un marido casto, y que haciendo voto de castidad, conseguía mis deseos de seguir el mundo y sus vanidades y juntamente lo que tenía natural incinación que éra de guardar castidad" (Catalina, *Idea*, p. 45).

33. Barbeito Carneiro has postulated that Catalina had a phobia of sex (*Mujeres del Madrid Barroco*, p. 86).

34. Among her many fine observations about vidas, Isabelle Poutrin points out that references to Saint Teresa's writings are "omnipresent" in prologues and life writings of contemplative women (p. 79).

35. "Empezó a castigar su cuerpo con extraordinario rigor y aspereza; mas como las acciones reguladas por dictamen propio pocas veces dejan de inclinarse a un extremo" (*Idea*, p. 56).

36. Bernique notes that women "have such little knowledge, too much credulity, and are easily perverted" ("el conocimiento [de las mujeres] es tan corto, la credulidad demasiada y la perversión más fácil" [*Idea*, p. 55]).

37. "Dábame grande pena no poder entrar a ser siquiera lega por los inconvenientes de los hijos" (Catalina, *Idea*, p. 64).

38. "No faltaba a la asistencia de sus hijos, pues el buen ejemplo de la madre es la más eficaz doctrina para su educación y enseñanza" (*Idea*, p. 67).

39. On page 284, Bernique mentions that, at the date of his writing (around 1692–93), the school had been open twenty-two years. Catalina did not have children in the first years of marriage, according to Bernique (*Idea*, p. 22), which means that they were probably born between 1656 and 1661, so they would have been between ten and fifteen when the school opened.

40. Sor Catalina herself is said to have written of being "desocupada de hijos" (p. 72) and Bernique twice refers to her "tan tierna edad" in chapters 1, page 8, and 2, page 1.

41. Bernique explains that his great aunt "amábala tiernamente" (*Idea*, p. 85) and, in response to Catalina's acts of humility: "No sólo la notaba estos actos, sino que como anciana, pues pasaba de ochenta, se dedicó a gruñirlo todo con rara impertinencia" (p. 195).

42. "Tenía mucha repugnancia y aversión a mi Tía, en quien me dio su Magestad un ejercicio, que si lo hubiera llevado bien, era bastante para ser muy santa" (Catalina, *Idea*, p. 196).

43. Catalina's idea of the *colegio* was "conveniente a la educación mujer, que aunque sobran Cátedras para los rudimentos de la mocedad y adquisición de las ciencias, faltan escuelas para la enseñanza de las doncellas" (*Idea*, p. 273).

44. "[P]orque la casa en que vivía con su Tía era muy frequentada de gente de Universidad por causa de tener en ella el arte de la imprenta; y así la primera diligencia en que se empeñó fue desocuparla de este ejercicio porque no podía ser buena escuela de doncellas donde era tan frecuente y cuotidiano el concurso de la gente" (*Idea*, p. 273). The aunt's comments on losing her livelihood appear on p. 274.

45. "[M]uchas personas llevadas de la fama de su santidad la entregaron sus hijas para que educadas con su virtud y ejemplo se criasen" (*Idea*, p. 274).

46. She hated going to the court to request funding, but since the foundation of the *colegio* "fue en suma pobreza y los señores son los condutos [sic] por donde envía el Cielo el socorro a los suyos," she asked for financial help (*Idea*, p. 202).

47. "Being that way, which meant that in every kind of penitence she was very cruel to herself, she was very mild and soft on her daughters, attending with much discretion and good judgment to the bodily capacities of each one" ("Siendo así, que en todo género de penitencias era para sí tan cruel, fue muy blanda y suave para sus hijas, atendiendo con mucha discreción y cordura a las fuerzas corporales de cada una" [*Idea*, p. 86]).

48. "Colgose el niño de mi cuello, y fueron tantas las delicias y deleite que mi alma sentía que no es fácil explicarlo. Echó N[uestra] Señora de sus pechos santísimos un rayo de leche a mis labios; parecióme era para más suficiencia, para escribir lo que me mandaba" (*Idea*, p. 349).

49. "Las caricias que recibió de su piadoso hijo eran superiores a su lengua, pues ni aun en la limitada capacidad de su corazón contenerse podían. Diola para llegar a lo sumo de los favores a gustar de los purísimos nectares de sus virginales y sagrados pechos, o para purificar así sus labios y escribir lo que su confesor la mandaba, como ella afirma, o para que se reconociese adoptada por hija suya, y como criada a expensas de su cuidado, la hacía participante de las soberanas dulzuras de sus bienaventurados pechos" (*Idea*, pp. 349–50).

50. "Tan continua era su asistencia en los hospitales, tan frecuente en las visitas de los menesterosos enfermos de los arrabales, que ganó con su piedad el nombre de madre de los que con tanta caridad asistía" (*Idea*, p. 227).

51. At age five the girl fell into a well, only to be rescued by a daring man who was sustained by Catalina's prayers. Eight years later, Catalina calmed a dog that was attacking the girl (*Idea*, p. 377). Bernique mentions that he could narrate other miracles, but he stops himself "so as not to be bothersome in their narrative" ("por no ser molesto en su narrativa" [p. 378]).

52. Perry, *Gender and Disorder*, p. 102.

53. "[P]adeció muchos pesares de su tía y parientes, con que la humillaban y afeaban esta asistencia, juzgando que en una mujer moza y de buen parecer era más que peligrosa esta piedad; pero aunque éste era el pretexto, la verdad del sentimiento era el peligro de su salud en daño de sus hijos; pero nada de esto podía detener el corriente de sus piedades" (*Idea*, p. 183).

54. "Encerró también consigo a sus dos hijas, a ejemplo del Patriarca Noé, que recogió a sus hijos en el arca que labró para la salvación del linaje humano, pues siendo la primera obligación la de los propios, no era justo cuidase de la crianza de hijos ajenos y dejase olvidados a los suyos" (*Idea*, p. 275).

55. "Veíase obligada a no salir de casa, por acudir a la asistencia de sus hijos, y esto era para ella un terrible martirio, porque cualquier sujeción le era intolerable; pero a todo se rendía a fuerza de la obligación, que era quien más su natural detenía. En medio desta continua violencia, que en el estado de casada experimentó, conservaba siempre los buenos ejercicios, en que se había criado" (*Idea*, p. 24).

56. Mooney, *Gendered Voices*, p. 10. Karen Scott has studied the unusual case of

Catherine of Siena and Raymond of Capua (in which the male- and female-authored texts are available for comparison) and concludes: "Finally, in his desire to foster her canonization, he downplayed or omitted information that would have made her appear too strong a woman to be considered a saint" ("Mystical Death, Bodily Death," p. 143).

57. "No puedo sufrir, cuando veo, se quejan las Religiosas de unas nonadas; si les faltó esto o aquello; si les alteraron las horas; si comieron más tarde o más temprano [. . .] y otras cosas deste género; si estuvieran con la carga del matrimonio, experimentaran como hacían esto y mucho más, y las hicieran obedecer, si no de grado, por fuerza y con menos mérito, y menos consuelo, porque no hay luz de que se hace aquello por Dios" (Catalina, *Idea*, pp. 42–43).

58. "Así lo escribe para consuelo de las que abrazaron el estado más perfecto de la Religión" (*Idea*, pp. 40–41).

59. "¿Qué intolerable cosa es sufrir la carga de los hijos y criarlos? ¿Qué ejercicio tan penoso puede haber en la vida espiritual que llegue a esto? Confieso que se me ha hecho poco cuánto he padecido desde que el Señor me llamó para sí, aspecto de los intolerables trabajos del matrimonio. Solía hacérsele mucho a mi confesor el tiempo que de noche estaba en la oración y dábamelo a entender así, y yo me reía y no sé si se lo decía, ¿cuántas más malas noches pasé yo criando los hijos? Dormía menos y andaba más fatigada y sin los alivios que da el Señor a los que gastan la noche en hacerle compañía" (Catalina, *Idea*, p. 41).

60. Two excellent studies on early modern religious expression and devotion are Certeau, *The Mystic Fable*, and Weber, *Teresa de Avila*.

61. "Son tantos los trabajos que se pasan que me hallo con cortedad para explicarlos" (Catalina, *Idea*, p. 34).

62. For example, *Idea*, pp. 128–29, 133.

63. "En una ocasión me vino una complacencia que me dejó toda bañada en vanidad mirándome a los pies" (Catalina, *Idea*, p. 129). And, later: "Reconozco de mí no he hecho cosa" (p. 132).

64. "[C]astigando la más leve falta" (*Idea*, p. 130).

65. Women want "hablar con todos y a todas horas de materias espirituales" (*Idea*, p. 133).

66. "Y esta razón tiene más lugar en el sexo femíneo [sic], donde por la mucha fragilidad y debilidad de la naturaleza es más fácil esta commoción" (*Idea*, p. 139).

67. "De aquí se originó el desazón grande con que vivió en el estado del matrimonio, porque cualquier yugo de sujeción y rendimiento era para ella intolerable" (*Idea*, p. 192).

68. "Era la aflicción tan grande que la hizo prorrumpir en estas palabras: acaba Señor con mi vida y no me tengáis con vuestra ausencia y desvío tan atormentada" (*Idea*, p. 163).

69. "Hermana, ¿cuándo la llevan a la Inquisición?" (*Idea*, p. 168).

70. "Decíales; estoy tan lejos de buscar culpa donde no la hay que si la razón me lo saneara, desnudara a mis obras de toda malicia. Tenemos un amo y Señora que no repara en delicadeces, disimula con sus siervos conociendo su nativa fragilidad" (*Idea*, pp. 140–41).

71. "Señor, le decía, no es posible conformarme. Si estuviera sola sin la dependencia de hijos, parientes, y doncellas que tengo a mi cargo, y sin el exterior ornato del hábito de mi Padre San Francisco, me arrojara con sumo gusto a sacrificarme en ella" (*Idea*, p. 169).

72. Quotes attributed to Sor Catalina describe her fear of the Inquisition, including horrible dreams, but provide no details about her encounter with the tribunal. The punishment of beatas surfaces in another incident: A famous beata was forced to parade through town, and the next day, Catalina's confessor made her do the same in an exercise of humility. Although everyone yelled at Catalina, taking her for the "evil" woman, she is said not to have heard anything because she was so absorbed in God (*Idea*, p. 179).

73. Bruneau summarizes the threat posed throughout Europe by such unaffiliated women: "The most vulnerable [women] were those who refused the cloister, thus escaping ecclesiastical supervision, such as the Beguines in the Low Countries, Northern France, and Germany, the beatas in Spain, and the terciary orders in Italy" (*Women Mystics*, p. 19). Also see Kagan, *Lucrecia's Dreams*; Perry, *Gender and Disorder*, pp. 97–117; Poutrin, *Le voile et la plume*, pp. 104–6; and Rapley, *The Dévotes*.

74. "[C]on una cara mirar a Dios y con otra atender al mundo y a sus vanidades" (*Idea*, p. 48).

CHAPTER 7

1. Judith Bennett and Amy Froide use the terms "ever married" and "never married" to discuss single women in Europe in their edited volume *Singlewomen in the European Past*.

2. Convents did offer some protection from the Inquisition but did not always shelter their inhabitants completely. See, for example, Judith Brown's highly readable account of a sixteenth-century nun's ascent to power and subsequent fall from grace in *Immodest Acts*.

3. William Monter, in *Frontiers of Heresy*, refers to witchcraft as the "forgotten offense" and indicates: "The Inquisition prosecuted Renaissance high magic only sporadically" (p. 258).

4. Monter explains that, for the most part, Protestants differed from Catholics in that "theirs became a heresy primarily of speech rather than behavior. By the 1560s the Holy Office had reduced it to seven cardinal errors, or more precisely to seven doctrinal positions which 'Lutherans' opposed" (ibid., p. 240).

5. Mary Giles summarizes the threat that Illuminists posed to the status quo: "Alumbrados encouraged interiorized Christianity in the spirit of medieval *devotio moderna*, the ideas of Erasmus, and Lutheranism" ("Francisca Hernández," p. 78). Also see Márquez's *Los alumbrados*, and, for more on beatas, Perry, "Beatas and the Inquisition."

6. One biographer states that the dough flew "with such strange violence and force that I do not doubt that it was launched by the devil himself" ("con tan extraña

violencia y fuerza que no dudo fue arrojada del demonio") (*Vida de María de Orozco y Luján*, fol. 6; hereafter cited in text and notes as *Vida*).

7. Jodi Bilinkoff, in an article that mentions Catalina de Jesús y San Francisco, notes: "The Inquisition clamped down on women perceived as purveyors of dangerous ideas" ("Confessors," p. 85).

8. Jesús Imirizaldu's *Monjas y beatas embaucadoras* provides samples of sentences, letters, and stories related to women whose spiritual activities were perceived as unorthodox.

9. "[E]l Dem[onio], como se lo tenía amanazado la aporreó, y maltrató en el coro dando grandes bramidos, con que las religiosas se comenzaron a turbar, y parezerles no les convenía tenerla en su compañia" (*Vida*, fol. 3v).

10. The priest wrote: "[C]on fundamento no puedo determinar nada; sólo digo que por esos fundamentos no se puede decir que está endemoniada" (*Vida*, fol. 4v).

11. Orozco was a *hidalga*, meaning that her family had a claim to lineage in the lower ranks of the nobility.

12. Bravo Tamargo, *Vida de la venerable señora*, pp. 2, 8, 11.

13. Ibid., p. 18.

14. Ibid., p. 5.

15. Barbeito Carneiro, *María de Orozco y Luján*, p. 29.

16. "[C]on que quedó muy contenta: mas el estómago se le inquietó de suerte que la hizo vomitar la inmundicia y cuánto había en él," and then the Virgin arrived (Matheo de Jesús María, *Tomo Tercero*, fol. 17v–18).

17. "Logró el enemigo común, y de esta virtuosa doncella particular, el que la echassen de el Atrio de el Señor, que es la Religión: y para que todo el mundo tomasse armas contra ella, la volbió a el siglo despreciable a los ojos de extraños, y propios, por expulsa, por afeada, por ciega y por útil para nada" (Bravo Tamargo, *Vida de la venerable señora*, pp. 48–49).

18. Barbeito Carneiro, *María de Orozco*, p. 26.

19. "Solía responder con gracia a los que la persuadían a que se casase diciendo: 'Por cierto, el que se casara conmigo llevara buena hacienda a su casa, una mujer con cuatro tachas, las peores del mundo: vieja, fea, enferma y pobre'" (Mss. 13425, Biblioteca Nacional, qtd. in ibid., p. 33).

20. On 17 June 1628, Valle wrote that it pleased her that only she and two other women had been deposed. She described the men as "bonísimos y muy cuerdos" (Barbeito Carneiro, *Cárceles y mujeres*, p. 153). Teresa Valle de la Cerda's writing and related materials appear in this source and are hereafter cited as Valle. Also see an analysis of the case in Carlos Puyol y Buil, *Inquisición y política*.

21. "En cuanto a la certeza de que eran demonios los que dijeron las cosas que están referidas, siempre creí, y ahora lo creo, que lo eran, así por las cosas que experimenté en mí como por las que vi en las demás, las cuales es imposible poder a quien las veía dejarle duda ninguna de que lo eran, ni que veinte y dos mujeres de tan diferentes condiciones y naturales pudieran fingir cosas tan ajenas de sus entendimientos y aún de los mayores del mundo" (Valle, p. 171).

22. "[H]abían hecho en él tal efecto y recibido su alma tanta luz que no le había en

su vida movido cosa tanto para de veras servir a Dios como lo que había oído" (Valle, p. 172).

23. "También se verifica claramente no haber tenido este mal su principio en el Convento, sino que fue Dios servido de que mucho antes de que se fundase, en las religiosas que después le padecimos entrasen los demonios" (Valle, p. 173).

24. "Y ansí, los consentí con el Padre fray Francisco, teniéndole en lugar de padre y estando tan segura de su santidad como tengo dicho" (Valle, p. 177). Also see p. 182 on her physical relationships with other clerics.

25. "En muchas, muy grandes sentimientos de que no les hiciera muchas caricias, y parecerles que las hacía a las demás y a ellas no" (Valle, p. 176).

26. "[P]orque cuando voy a decir las cosas me falta la memoria" (Valle, p. 179).

27. "No me acuerdo de otra cosa por ahora" (Valle, p. 184).

28. "¿[Q]uiénes eran las súbditas a quienes quería ganar?" (Valle, p. 235).

29. "[S]i el demonio lo dijo, ¿qué culpa tengo yo?" (Valle, p. 236). For an analysis of group demonic possession in early modern Europe, including a reference to the San Plácido convent of Teresa Valle de la Cerda and the Ursuline convent of Loudun, France, from 1633 to 1640, see Sluhovsky, "The Devil in the Convent."

30. Barbeito Carneiro, *Cárceles y mujeres*, p. 229n.74.

31. Kagan, *Lucrecia's Dreams*, p. 125. Kagan discusses the confraternity on p. 127.

32. Ibid., p. 160.

33. Ibid., pp. 154–56.

34. Ibid., p. 159. For another analysis of a woman's visions and prison experiences, see Rhodes, "'Y Yo Dije, Sí, señor.'"

35. Single women and those between the ages of fifty and seventy represent the highest numbers of all women tried for witchcraft throughout Europe during the centuries of the witch craze. Approximately 80 percent of those tried were women, with the figure at 71 percent for Castile, for example (see Scarre and Callow, *Witchcraft and Magic*). Classic books on witchcraft and gender include Barstow, *Witchcraze*; Ehrenreich and English, *Witches, Midwives, and Nurses*; and Roper, *Oedipus and the Devil*.

36. Ruggiero, *Binding Passions*, p. 21. Ruggiero's *Binding Passions* is an exemplary study of love magic. For magic's connection to sex in Spain, see Sánchez Ortega, "Sorcery and Eroticism." For more on sorcery in the psychic landscape of early modern Europe, see Ruggiero, *Companion*, pp. 475–90.

37. "¿No habrá algún remedio para que mi marido no me destruya?" (Romero, fol. 33). All citations are from the 1702 trial of the two women (Romero and Gómez, Sección Inquisición, hereafter cited as Romero).

38. The women "tienen malas costumbres" and "están en reputación de grandísimas embusteras," according to María Díaz (Romero, fols. 3v–4).

39. See, for example, Romero, fols. 25v and 33. With regard to language, it is interesting to note the euphemisms used for affairs, which are referred to as illicit or sensual communication, friendship, and sensual dependence (*comunicación ilícita, comunicación sensual, amistad, amistad ilícita, and dependiencia* [sic] *sen-*

sual [see Romero, fol. 2v, 9, 10, 24, 30v, etc.]). Renato Barahona provides an overview of such language in *Sex Crimes*, pp. 62–69.

40. "[P]or no poder tolerarle por lo fuerte de su natural" (Romero, fols. 35v).

41. "Dionisio ha jurado a la cruz de su espada me ha de dar un castigo que me acuerde de él toda mi vida" (Romero, fol. 12v).

42. For a related discussion, see Quezada, "The Inquisition's Repression of *Curanderos.*"

43. "[C]on demasiada pesadumbre" (Romero, fol. 12v).

44. The letter from the Hospital de la Caridad in Talavera states that the Inquisition's intentions are being frustrated because Romero "está poco menos que baldada de ambos brazos, es forastera y sin ningunos medios para su alimento, incapaz de ganar por su trabajo para él" (Romero, fol. 130).

CHAPTER 8

1. Helen Nader, editor of *Power and Gender in Renaissance Spain*, commented at the Society for Spanish and Portuguese Historical Studies in Madrid, 2003, that the Mendoza women had high levels of education, but that nobody knows who provided them with that education. Also see the previously quoted reference to Sara Nalle's literacy statistics (*God in La Mancha*, p. 69).

2. For women in converso culture, see Melammed, "Crypto-Jewish Women." On the representation of mothers in family chronicles, biographies, and religious women's writing, see Schlau, *Viva al Siglo*, pp. 11–27.

3. On Hispano-Arabic writing by women, see Rubiera Mata, *Poesía femenina hispanoárabe.*

4. Kaminsky provides an excellent overview of women's literary tradition and English translations of texts by nineteen women in *Water Lilies.*

5. For more on Spanish women in the 1500s, see Bel Bravo, *Mujeres españolas*; Cruz, "Willing Desire"; Navarro, *Antología poética*, pp. 7–63; and Vollendorf, "Women Writers in Sixteenth-Century Spain."

6. For more on women's access to education in twentieth-century Spain, see the following essays in Vollendorf, *Recovering Spain's Feminist Tradition*: introduction, pp. 1–27; Josebe Martínez-Gutiérrez, "Feminist and Political Praxis during the Spanish Civil War," pp. 278–92; and Margaret Jones, "*Vindicación Feminista* and the Feminist Community in Post-Franco Spain," pp. 311–36.

7. See Bergmann, "The Exclusion of the Feminine," and Stephanie Merrim's chapter, "The New Prometheus: Women's Education, Autodidacticism, and the Will to Signature," in Merrim, *Early Modern Women's Writing*, pp. 191–248. See Aldecoa, *Historia de una maestra*, and Martín Gaite, *Usos amorosos de la postguerra*, for more on women and education in the Franco period. For a basic, if somewhat dated, history of women's education, see Stock, *Better than Rubies.*

8. Tenorio Gómez, *Las madrileñas de mil seiscientos*, p. 23. Information about moralists and their ideologies can be found in ibid., pp. 11–28; Ríos Izquierdo, *Mujer y sociedad*; and Vigil, *La vida de las mujeres.*

9. Merrim, *Early Modern Women's Writing*, p. 197.

10. Merrim's erudite discussion of the querelle explores its potential for feminist expression as well as the reality that it "sometimes degenerat[ed] into mere exercises in logic." She praises French writer Marie de Gournay (1565–1645) and Sor Juana Inés de la Cruz as being among those who "maximize[d] the potential of the debate" (ibid., pp. xv–xvii).

11. As Elizabeth Rapley has shown in *The Dévotes* (pp. 42–73), women in France extended formal instruction by creating what came to be known as "teaching congregations."

12. Margaret L. King's classic study *Women of the Renaissance* discusses Wolley, Astell, and other women in the context of the early modern period.

13. Sor Teresa de Jesús María, *Trata de una breve relación*, pp. 45–46. This is a beautiful text with no title page.

14. See, for example, María de San Alberto's corpus of poems to Saint Teresa in Schlau, *Viva al Siglo*, pp. 93–214.

15. Madre Hipólita refers to her *maestra* as the person "[a] la que tenía en lugar de madre" (Madre Hipólita de Jesús y Rocaberti, *Libro primero*, p. 6).

16. Even as she details the ill treatment she received from her mother, Sor Estefanía repeatedly describes her mother as someone she dearly loved (Estefanía de la Encarnacion, *La vida*, fols. 11v–12, 14v–15). For more on Sor Estefanía, see Barbeito Carneiro, "Una madrileña polifacética."

17. Sor Estefanía writes that she had a teacher, but that her mother also gave her instruction. She discusses her role as a teacher to Beatriz de Villena on folio 27a, indicating that she took on the task because her mother felt obligated to comply with Villena's request. Estefanía had discovered her artistic talent some time earlier, and her uncle had given her art classes. It seems that he also sexually assaulted her: "Cobróme el marido de mi tía tan grande afición que hacía excesos conmigo" ("My aunt's husband took such a great interest in me that he took liberties with me") (fol. 24v).

18. Schlau, *Viva al Siglo*, p. 11.

19. See ibid., pp. 1–47; and Arenal and Schlau, *Untold Sisters*, pp. 131–89.

20. Melammed lays out the role of women in the maintenance of Jewish culture in "Crypto-Jewish Women." Also see Starr-LeBeau, *In the Shadow of the Virgin*. For similar research on Moriscas's involvement in the perpetuation of Moorish culture, see Perry, "Moriscas."

21. "[P]orque la nueva lectura engendra nuevos pensamientos, y apaga la devoción del alma" (Ossorio, *Huerta del celestial esposo*, p. 165). Although Ossorio's book was published after her death, the manuscript likely circulated among her sisters during her lifetime.

22. "Y también es cosa muy indecente, que la Religiosa esté toda entregada al sueño, como las bestias, echada con las manos apartadas . . . que por eso nos mandan acostar vestidas, porque no podamos tocar con las manos al cuerpo desnudo" (ibid., p. 122).

23. In the prologue, Pinelo adopts a typically humble attitude, describing herself as "poco escrituraria [sic]" and claiming to know "poco más que nada." The pages

in the prologue to *Libro de las alabanzas* are not numbered, but this appears on what would be folio 4.

24. Pinelo speaks of raising children in convents on folios 356v–357. In the prologue, she notes that she was raised in the convent "almost since I was born" ("casi desde que nací" [Pinelo, *Libro de las alabanzas*, fol. 5v]).

25. "[P]lantas chiquitas en estos jardines de Dios" (ibid., fol. 357).

26. "[T]oda nuestra vida sobre la tierra es una guerra continua, la cual se experimenta, no sólo en la vida temporal, sino también, y aún con más viveza, en la vida de perfección" (Angela María de la Concepción, *Riego espiritual para nuevas plantas*, p. 6). I do not know Sor Angela's birth and death dates.

27. "Y pues somos nuevas plantas, sea muy nuevo en todo nuestro fervor para tomar las armas domando nuestras pasiones, y abrazando las virtudes, que con eso alcanzaremos el triunfo, y presentaremos a nuestro Divino Esposo la victoria" (ibid., p. 10).

28. "[C]arísimas mías, amadas siervas del Señor" (ibid., p. 10), "carísimas" (p. 20), "carísimas hermanas" (p. 39), and "hijas carísimas" (p. 57).

29. Arenal and Schlau, *Untold Sisters*, p. 20. See chapter 1 of *Untold Sisters*, "More than One Teresa: A Movement of Religious Women," for more on María de San José. Also see the nun's *Book for the Hour of Recreation*.

30. "De tres condiciones y suertes de personas se pueblan los conventos," some have "naturales perfectos," others "no son malos ni buenos," and others are "de inclinaciones perversas y de naturales indómitos" (María de San José, *Instrucción de novicias*, p. 412). Women of "humor y natural melancólico" should not be nuns and should be sent home (p. 432). Sagrada Familia's edition of Madre María's *Escritos espirituales* includes other texts by the Carmelite as well.

31. Arenal and Schlau, *Untold Sisters*, p. 20.

32. "[T]emía por sus pecados" (María de San José, *Instrucción de novicias*, p. 437).

33. Alisa Joanne Tigchelaar has studied Madre María's convent drama in "Instruction and Self-Identification."

34. See Sánchez, *The Empress*, for an overview of the strategies used by Habsburg women to influence the monarch. As mentioned previously, the noblewomen of the Mendoza family are the subjects of Nader, *Power and Gender*.

35. Padilla, *Lágrimas de la nobleza*, pp. 190–222.

36. "Sirven las sentencias de recuerdos a los entendidos, a los ignorantes dan luz" (Padilla, *Idea de nobles*, p. vi).

37. Ibid., pp. v–vi.

38. Chapter 1 discusses "la malicia, la envidia, y la avaricia" of the court (Guevara, *Desengaños de la corte*, p. 3). "Muchos andan perdidos y echan a perder a sus mujeres con enfermedades sucias, con que pierden la sucesión, y al que la tiene nacen los hijos tan enfermos que al primer aire que les da se les mueren" (p. 7).

39. "Es sin duda que si algunas mujeres que se conocen de ánimo y valor las entraran en los consejos y juntas los dieran tan buenos como los más acertados consejeros" (ibid., p. 14).

40. "[E]l que no lo toma es loco" (ibid., p. 26). Also see Guerara's *Warnings to the Kings*.

41. As Barbeito Carneiro points out in her edition of Madre Magdalena's text, *Cárceles y mujeres*, the nun based her ideas on Cristóbal Pérez de Herrera's essay "Discursos del amparo de los legítimos pobres y reducción de los fingidos" ("Discourses on the Aid to the Legitimately Poor and on the Reduction of Those Who Fake Their Poverty"). Little is known about Madre Magdalena's life (Barbeito Carneiro, *Cárceles y mujeres*, pp. 37–42), but her text begs a comparison with the nineteenth-century writer Concepción Arenal (1823–93), who worked in prisons and wrote about penal reform (see Charnon-Deutsch, "Concepción Arenal").

42. People saw the proposed *galera* as having "demasiado rigor y severidad, particularmente siendo inventada por mujer contra mujeres" (Magdalena de San Jerónimo, *Razón y forma*, p. 66).

43. "[L]as mujeres vagantes, ladronas, hechiceras, alcahuetas y otras semejantes" (ibid., pp. 68–69).

44. "[E]stas miserables mujeres enemigas de Dios y contaminadoras de la república" create a domino effect of sin (ibid., p. 75).

45. Ibid., p. 94.

46. In the introduction to *Cárceles y mujeres* (p. 57), Barbeito Carneiro cites a description of a *galera* written by Luis Cabrera de Córdoba, *Relaciones de las cosas sucedidas en la Corte de España*, p. 343).

47. Constance Sullivan provides an overview of eighteenth-century gender ideology in "Constructing Her Own Tradition." Also see T. Smith, *The Emerging Female Citizen*.

WORKS CITED

Note: Inquisition trials are listed under the defendants' names.

Abarca de Bolea, Ana Francisca. *Vigilia y octavario de San Juan Baptista.* Zaragoza: Pascual Bueno, 1679. Edited and with an introduction by María de los Angeles Campo Guiral. Zaragoza: Instituto de Estudios Altoaragoneses, 1994.

Ahlgren, Gillian. "Francisca de los Apóstoles: A Visionary Voice for Reform in Sixteenth-Century Toledo." In Giles, *Women in the Inquisition*, pp. 119–33.

Aldecoa, Josefina. *Historia de una maestra.* Barcelona: Anagrama, 1990.

———. *Teresa of Avila and the Politics of Sanctity.* Ithaca, N.Y.: Cornell University Press, 1996.

Amezúa, Agustín de. "Formación y elementos de la novela cortesana." In *Opúsculos histórico-literarios.* Vol. 1. Madrid: Real Academia Española, 1951, pp. 194–279.

Angela María de la Concepción (Sor). *Riego espiritual para nuevas plantas: Sacado y recogido de la doctrina de los Padres de la iglesia y Doctores Místicos.* Madrid: Melchor Alvarez, 1691.

Arenal, Electa. "Vida y teatro conventual: Sor Marcela de San Félix." In Monika Bosse, Barbara Potthast, and André Stoll, eds., *La creatividad femenina en el mundo del barroco hispánico. María de Zayas, Isabel Rebeca Correa, Sor Juana Inés de la Cruz.* Vol. 1. Kassel: Ed. Reichenberger, 1999, pp. 209–19.

———, and Georgina Sabat de Rivers, eds. *Literatura conventual femenina: Sor Marcela de San Félix, hija de Lope de Vega: Obras completas.* Ed. Electa Arenal and Sabat de Rivers. Barcelona: PPU, 1988.

———, and Stacey Schlau, eds. and intro. *Untold Sisters: Hispanic Nuns in their Own Works.* Trans. Amanda Powell. Albuquerque: University of New Mexico Press, 1989. [Includes numerous nuns' work in English and Spanish.]

Armon, Shifra. "Mariana de Caravajal's *Navidades de Madrid y noches entretenidas:* An Anatomy of Courtesy." Ph.D. diss., Johns Hopkins University, 1993.

———. *Picking Wedlock: Women and the Courtship Novel in Spain.* Lanham, Md.: Rowman and Littlefield, 2002.

———. "The Romance of Courtesy: Mariana de Carvajal's *Navidades de Madrid y noches entretenidas.*" *Revista canadiense de estudios hispánicos* 19.2 (Winter 1995): 241–61.

Autoras en la historia del teatro español (1500–1994). Dir. Juan Antonio Hormigón. Madrid: Asociación de Directores de Escena de España, 1996.

Azevedo, Angela de. *Dicha y desdicha del juego y devoción de la virgen.* In Soufas, *Women's Acts,* pp. 4–44.

————. *El muerto disimulado.* In Soufas, *Women's Acts,* pp. 91–132.

————. *La margarita del Tajo que dio nombre a Santarén.* In Soufas, *Women's Acts,* pp. 45–90.

Baernstein, P. Renée. *A Convent Tale: A Century of Sisterhood in Spanish Milan.* New York and London: Routledge, 2002.

Barahona, Renato. *Sex Crimes, Honour, and the Law in Early Modern Spain: Vizcaya, 1578–1735.* Toronto: University of Toronto Press, 2003.

Barbazza, Marie-Catherine. "Un caso de subversión social: El proceso de Elena de Céspedes (1587–89)." *Criticón* 26 (1984): 17–40.

Barbeito Carneiro, Isabel, ed. and intro. *Cárceles y mujeres en el siglo XVII.* Madrid: Castalia, 1991.

————. *Escritoras madrileñas del siglo XVII: Estudio bibliográfico-crítico.* Madrid: Editorial de la Universidad Complutense, 1986.

————. "Una madrileña polifacética en Santa Clara de Lerma: Estefanía de la Encarnación." *Anales del Instituto de Estudios Madrileños* 24 (1987): 151–63.

————. *María de Orozco y Luján (1635–1709).* Madrid: Ed. del Orto, 1997.

————. *Mujeres del Madrid Barroco: Voces Testimoniales.* Madrid: horas y HORAS, 1992.

Barstow, Anne L. *Witchcraze: A New History of the European Witch Hunts.* San Francisco: Pandora, 1994.

Beinart, Haim. *Los conversos ante el tribunal de la Inquisición.* Trans. José Manuel Alvarez and Angela Pérez. Barcelona: Riopiedras, 1983.

Bel Bravo, María Antonia. *Mujeres españolas en la Historia Moderna.* Madrid: Sílez, 2002.

Bennett, Judith, and Amy Froide, eds. *Singlewomen in the European Past: 1250–1800.* Philadelphia: University of Pennsylvania Press, 1999.

Bergmann, Emilie. "The Exclusion of the Feminine in the Cultural Discourse of the Golden Age: Juan Luis Vives and Fray Luis de León." In Alain Saint-Saëns, ed., *Religion, Body, and Gender in Early Modern Spain.* San Francisco: Mellen Research University Press, 1991, pp. 124–36.

Bernique, Juan de. *Idea de perfección y virtudes: Vida de la V.M. y sierva de Dios Catalina de Jesús y San Francisco. Hija de su tercera orden y fundadora del Colegio de las doncellas pobres de Santa Clara de la Ciudad de Alcalá de Henares.* Alcalá: Con licencia de Francisco García Fernández, Impresor de la Universidad, 1693.

Biersack, Aletta, and Lynn A. Hunt, eds. *The New Cultural History.* Berkeley: University of California Press, 1989.

Bilinkoff, Jodi. "Confessors, Penitents, and the Construction of Identities." In Barbara B. Diefendorf and Carla Hesse, eds., *Culture and Identity in Early Modern Europe (1500–1800).* Ann Arbor: University of Michigan Press, 1993, pp. 83–100.

————. *Related Lives: Confessors and Their Female Penitents, 1450–1750.* Ithaca, N.Y.: Cornell University Press, 2005.

Blázquez Miguel, Juan. *Madrid: Judíos, herejes y brujas. El Tribunal de Corte (1650–1820).* Toledo: Arcano, 1990.

Blue, William R. *Spanish Comedies and Historical Contexts in the 1620s.* University Park: Pennsylvania State University Press, 1996.

Bourland, Caroline. "Aspectos de la vida del hogar en el siglo XVII según las novelas de Doña Mariana de Carabajal y Saavedra." In *Homenaje ofrecido a Menéndez Pidal.* Vol. 2. Madrid: Librería y Casa Editorial Hernando, 1925, pp. 331–68.

Boyer, H. Patsy. "The War between the Sexes and the Ritualization of Violence in Zayas's *Disenchantments.*" In Alain Saint-Saëns, ed., *Sex and Love in Golden Age Spain.* New Orleans: University Press of the South, 1996, pp. 123–45.

Bravo Tamargo, Francisco. *Vida de la venerable señora Doña María Orozco y Luján.* Madrid: N.p., 1719.

Bravo-Villasante, Carmen. *La mujer vestida de hombre en el teatro español (Siglos XVI–XVII).* Madrid: Revista de Occidente, 1955.

Brown, Joan L., and Crista Johnson. "Required Reading: The Canon in Spanish and Spanish American Literature." *Hispania* 81.1 (March 1998): 1–19.

Brown, Judith. *Immodest Acts: The Life of a Lesbian Nun in Renaissance Italy.* Oxford: Oxford University Press, 1986.

Brown, Kathleen M. *Good Wives, Nasty Wenches, and Anxious Patriarchs: Gender, Race, and Power in Colonial Virginia.* Chapel Hill and London: University of North Carolina Press for the Institute of Early American History and Culture in Williamsburg, Va., 1996.

Brownlee, Marina S. *The Cultural Labyrinth of María de Zayas.* Philadelphia: University of Pennsylvania Press, 2000.

Bruneau, Marie-Florine. *Women Mystics Confront the Modern World: Marie de l'Incarnation (1599–1672) and Madame Guyon (1648–1717).* Albany: SUNY Press, 1997.

Buestein, John. "Jewish Male Menstruation in Seventeenth-Century Spain." *Bulletin of the History of Medicine* 73.3 (1999): 447–56.

Bullough, Vern L., and Bonnie Bullough. *Cross Dressing, Sex, and Gender.* Philadelphia: University of Pennsylvania Press, 1993.

Burns, Kathryn. "Nuns, Kurakas, and Credit: The Spiritual Economy of Seventeenth-Century Cuzco." In Dinan and Meyers, *Women and Religion,* pp. 43–67.

Burshatin, Israel. "Elena alias Eleno: Genders, Sexualities, and Race in the Mirror of Natural History in Sixteenth-Century Spain." In Sabrina Petra Ramet, ed., *Gender Reversals and Gender Cultures: Anthropological and Historical Perspectives.* New York: Routledge, 1996, pp. 105–22.

———. "Interrogating Hermaphroditism in Sixteenth-Century Spain." In Sylvia Molloy and Robert McKee Irwin, eds., *Hispanisms and Homosexualities.* Durham, N.C., and London: Duke University Press, 1998, pp. 3–18.

———. "Written on the Body: Slave or Hermaphrodite in Sixteenth-Century Spain?" In Josiah Blackmore and Gregory S. Hutcheson, eds., *Queer Iberia: Sexualities, Cultures, and Crossings from the Middle Ages to the Renaissance.* Durham, N.C., and London: Duke University Press, 1999, pp. 420–56.

Butler, Judith. *Bodies That Matter: On the Discursive Limits of "Sex."* New York: Routledge, 1993.

————. "Imitation and Gender Insubordination." In Diana Fuss, ed., *Inside/Out*. New York: Routledge, 1991, pp. 13–31.

Bynum, Caroline Walker. *Fragmentation and Redemption: Essays on Gender and the Human Body in Medieval Religion*. New York: Zone, 1991.

Cabrera de Córdoba, Luis. *Relaciones de las cosas sucedidas en la Corte de España: Desde 1599 hasta 1614*. Madrid: Imprenta de J. Martín Alegría, 1847.

Cabrillana, Nicolás. *La almería morisca*. Granada: Universidad de Granada, 1982.

Cammarata, Joan, ed. *Women in the Discourse of Early Modern Spain*. Gainesville: University of Florida Press, 2003.

Campo Guiral, María de los Angeles. *Doña Ana Francisca Abarca de Bolea*. Zaragoza: Departamento de Cultura y Educación, 1993.

Caro Mallén de Soto, Ana. *El Conde Partinuplés*. In Soufas, *Women's Acts*, pp. 137–62.

————. *Valor, agravio y mujer*. In Soufas, *Women's Acts*, pp. 163–94.

Carvajal, Mariana de. *Navidades de Madrid*. Ed. and intro. Catherine Soriano. Madrid: Comunidad de Madrid, 1993.

Cascardi, Anthony J. *Ideologies of History in the Spanish Golden Age*. University Park: Pennsylvania State University Press, 1997.

Casey, James. *Early Modern Spain: A Social History*. New York and London: Routledge, 1999.

Castle, Terry. *The Apparitional Lesbian*. New York: Columbia University Press, 1993.

Catalina de Jesús y San Francisco. See Bernique, Juan de.

Cátedra, Pedro M., and Anastasio Rojo. *Bibliotecas y lecturas de mujeres. Siglo XVI*. Salamanca: Instituto del Libro y de la Lectura, 2004.

Cerda, Juan de la. *Vida política de todos los estados de las mujeres*. Alcalá de Henares: N.p., 1599.

Certeau, Michel de. *The Mystic Fable*. Vol. 1. *The Sixteenth and Seventeenth Centuries*. Trans. Michael B. Smith. Chicago: University of Chicago Press, 1995.

Céspedes, Elena/Eleno de. Inquisition Trial. Sección Inquisición, Leg. 234, Exp. 24, Archivo Histórico Nacional, Madrid.

Charnon-Deutsch, Lou. "Concepción Arenal and the Nineteenth-Century Debates about Women's Sphere and Education." In Vollendorf, *Recovering Spain's Feminist Tradition*, pp. 198–216.

Chaytor, Miranda. "Husband(ry): Narratives of Rape in the Seventeenth Century." *Gender and History* 7.3 (November 1995): 378–407.

Clark, Anne L. "Holy Woman or Unworthy Vessel? The Representations of Elisabeth of Schönau." In Mooney, *Gendered Voices*, pp. 35–51.

Coakley, John. "Friars as Confidants of Holy Women in Medieval Dominican Hagiography." In Renate Blumenfeld-Kosinski and Timea Szell, eds., *Images of Sainthood in Early Medieval Europe*. Ithaca, N.Y.: Cornell University Press, 1991, pp. 222–46.

Cohen, Jeffrey Jerome, ed. *Monster Theory: Reading Culture*. Minneapolis: University of Minnesota Press, 1996.

Colahan, Clark. "María de Jesús de Agreda: The Sweetheart of the Holy Office." In Giles, *Women in the Inquisition*, pp. 155–70.

Contreras, Jaime. "Family and Patronage: The Judeo-Converso Minority in Spain." In Perry and Cruz, *Cultural Encounters*, pp. 127–45.

_____. *El Santo Oficio de la Inquisición de Galicia, 1560–1700. Poder, sociedad y cultura.* Madrid: Akal, 1982.

Cooperman, Bernard Dov, ed. *In Iberia and Beyond: Hispanic Jews between Cultures.* Newark: University of Delaware Press, 1998.

Costa Fontes, Manuel Da. "Four Portuguese Crypto-Jewish Prayers and Their 'Inquisitorial' Counterparts." In Alexander Borg and Marcel Erdal, eds., *Modern Language Review 6–7 (1990–93).* Wiesbaden: Harrassowitz Verlag, 1993, pp. 67–104.

Cruz, Anne J. "Feminism, Psychoanalysis, and the Search for the M/Other in Early Modern Spain." *Indiana Journal of Hispanic Literature* 8 (Spring 1996): 31–54.

_____. "'Homo ex machina?': Male Bonding in Calderón's *A secreto agravio, secreta venganza.*" *Forum for Modern Language Studies* 25.2 (1989): 154–66.

_____. "Willing Desire: Luisa de Carvajal y Mendoza and Female Subjectivity." In Nader, *Power and Gender in Renaissance Spain*, pp. 177–94.

Cruz, Anne J., and Mary Elizabeth Perry. Introduction to *Culture and Control in Counter Reformation Spain.* Minneapolis: University of Minnesota Press, 1992, pp. i–xxiii.

_____, eds. *Culture and Control in Counter Reformation Spain.* Minneapolis: University of Minnesota Press, 1992.

Cueva y Silva, Leonor de la. *La firmeza en la ausencia.* In Soufas, *Women's Acts*, pp. 198–224.

Cushing-Daniels, Nancy. "Beyond Entertainment: The Story behind the Walls of Mariana de Carvajal's *Navidades de Madrid y noches entretenidas.*" *Monographic Review / Revista Monográfica* 13 (1997): 64–72.

Daniels, Mary Blythe. "Re-Visioning Gender on the Seventeenth-Century Spanish Stage: A Study of Actresses and Autoras." Ph.D. diss., University of Kentucky, 1998.

Daston, Lorraine, and Katherine Park. "The Hermaphrodite and the Orders of Nature: Sexual Ambiguity in Early Modern France." In Louise Fradenburg and Carla Freccero, eds., *Premodern Sexualities.* New York and London: Routledge, 1996, pp. 117–36.

Davis, Natalie Zemon. *Fiction in the Archives.* Stanford, Calif.: Stanford University Press, 1987.

_____. *Society and Culture in Early Modern France.* Stanford, Calif.: Stanford University Press, 1975.

DeDieu, Jean Pierre. "The Archives of the Holy Office of Toledo as a Source for Historical Anthropology." In Gustav Henningsen and John Tedeschi, eds., in association with Charles Amiel, *The Inquisition in Early Modern Europe: Studies on Sources and Methods.* Dekalb: Northern Illinois University Press, 1996, pp. 158–89.

DeLauretis, Teresa. *The Practice of Love: Lesbian Sexuality and Perverse Desire.* Bloomington: Indiana University Press, 1994.

Delgado, María José, and Alain Saint-Saëns, eds. *Lesbianism and Homosexuality in*

Spanish Golden Age Literature and Society. New Orleans: University Press of the South, 2000.

DeMolen, Richard, ed. *Religious Orders of the Catholic Reformation: In Honor of John C. Olin on His Seventy-Fifth Birthday*. New York: Fordham University Press, 1994.

DiGangi, Mario. *The Homoerotics of Early Modern Drama*. London: Cambridge University Press, 1997.

Dinan, Susan E., and Debra Meyers, eds. and intro. *Women and Religion in Old and New Worlds*. New York and London: Routledge, 2001.

Dolan, Frances E. *Dangerous Familiars: Representations of Domestic Crime in England, 1550–1700*. Ithaca, N.Y.: Cornell University Press, 1994.

Doménech Rico, Fernando, ed. *Teatro breve de mujeres (Siglos XVII–XX)*. Madrid: Asociación de Directores de Escena de España, 1996.

Domínguez Ortiz, Antonio. *Los judeoconversos en la España moderna*. Madrid: MAPFRE, 1991.

————. *Política y hacienda de Felipe IV*. Madrid: Editorial de Derecho Financiero, 1960.

Donnell, Sidney. "Between Night and Day: Aurora or the Transvestite Achilles in Monroy y Silva's *El caballero dama*." *Romance Language Annual* 7 (1995): 450–55.

Dopico-Black, Georgina. *Perfect Wives, Other Women: Adultery and Inquisition in Early Modern Spain*. Durham, N.C.: Duke University Press, 2001.

Dreger, Alice Domurat. *Hermaphrodites and the Medical Invention of Sex*. Cambridge: Harvard University Press, 1998.

Ehrenreich, Barbara, and Deirdre English. *Witches, Midwives, and Nurses: A History of Women Healers*. Old Westbury, N.Y.: Feminist Press, 1973.

Elliott, J. H. *The Count-Duke of Olivares: The Statesman in an Age of Decline*. New Haven and London: Yale University Press, 1986.

————. *Spain and Its World: 1500–1700*. New Haven and London: Yale University Press, 1989.

Enríquez de Guzmán, Feliciana. *Segunda parte de la Tragicomedia los jardines y campos sabeos*. In Soufas, *Women's Acts*, pp. 229–258.

Epstein, Julia, and Kristina Straub. "Introduction: The Guarded Body," in *Body Guards: The Cultural Politics of Gender Ambiguity*. New York and London: Routledge 1991, pp. 1–28.

————, eds. *Body Guards: The Cultural Politics of Gender Ambiguity*. New York and London: Routledge 1991.

Erauso, Catalina de. *Memoir of a Basque Lieutenant Nun: Transvestite in the New World*. Trans. Michele Stepto and Gabriel Stepto. Foreword by Marjorie Garber. Boston: Beacon, 1996.

Escamilla, Michèle. "A propos d'un dossier inquisitorial des environs de 1590: Les étranges amours d'un hermaphrodite." In Augustin Redondo, ed., *Amours légitimes amours illégitimes en Espagne (XVIᵉ–XVIIᵉ siècles)*. Paris: Publications de la Sorbonne, 1985, pp. 167–82.

Escritoras españolas (1500–1900), Microfiche catalogue. Part I: 1500–1800. Part II: 1800–1900. Madrid: Chadwyck-Healey España, 1992–93.

Espinosa, Juan de. *Diálogo en laude de las mugeres.* [1580]. Ed. and intro. José López Romero. Granada: A. Ubago, 1990.

Estefanía de la Encarnación (Sor). *La vida de Soror Estephania de la Encarnacion, Monja Profesa en el Monasterio de Religiosas Franciscas de Nuestra Madre Santa Clara en esta Villa de Lerma.* 1631. Mss. 7459, Biblioteca Nacional, Madrid.

Farr, James R. *Authority and Sexuality in Early Modern Burgundy (1550–1730).* New York and Oxford: Oxford University Press, 1995.

Farwell, Marilyn. *Heterosexual Plots and Lesbian Narratives.* New York: New York University Press, 1996.

Flecniakoska, Jean Louis. *La loa.* Madrid: Sociedad general española de librerías, 1975.

Folch Jou, Guillermo, and María del Sagrario Muñoz. "Un pretendido caso de hermafroditismo en el siglo XVI." *Boletín de la Sociedad Española de Historia de la Farmacia* 93 (1973): 20–33.

Foner, Eric. *Who Owns History?* New York: Hill and Wang, 2001.

"Forum: Letters on 'Inflecting the *Converso* Voice.'" *La Corónica* 25.2 (Spring 1997): 159–205.

Foucault, Michel, ed. *I, Pierre Rivière, having slaughtered my mother, my sister, and my brother . . . A Case of Parricide in the 19th Century.* Trans. Frank Jellinek. New York: Pantheon, 1975.

Francisca de Santa Teresa (Sor). "Entremés del estudiante y la sorda." In Doménech Rico, pp. 49–64.

Franco, Jean. *Plotting Women: Gender and Representation in Mexico.* New York: Columbia University Press, 1989.

Friedman, Edward. "'Girl Gets Boy?': A Note on the Value of Exchange in the *Comedia.*" *Bulletin of the Comediantes* 39.1 (Summer 1987): 75–83.

Garber, Marjorie. *Vested Interests: Cross Dressing and Cultural Anxiety.* New York: Routledge, 1992. Reprint, New York: HarperPerennial, 1993.

Garrido, Elisa, ed., with Pilar Folguera, Margarita Ortega, and Cristina Segura. *Historia de las mujeres de España.* Madrid: Sintesis, 1997.

Gil, Juan. *Los conversos y la Inquisición sevillana.* 8 vols. Seville: Universidad de Sevilla y La Fundación El Monte, 2000.

Giles, Mary E. "Francisca Hernández and the Sexuality of Religious Dissent." In Giles, *Women in the Inquisition,* pp. 75–97.

_____, ed. *Women in the Inquisition: Spain and the New World.* Baltimore, Md., and London: Johns Hopkins University Press, 1999.

Ginzburg, Carlo. *The Cheese and the Worms: The Cosmos of a Sixteenth-Century Miller.* Trans. John and Anne Tedeschi. Baltimore, Md., and London: Johns Hopkins University Press, 1986.

Goldberg, Jonathan, ed. *Queering the Renaissance.* Durham, N.C.: Duke University Press, 1994.

_____. *Sodometries: Renaissance Texts, Modern Sexualities.* Stanford, Calif.: Stanford University Press, 1992.

Gorfkle, Laura. "Re-Constituting the Feminine in 'Amar sólo por vencer.'" In Williamsen and Whitenack, *María de Zayas*, pp. 75–89.

_____. "Seduction and Hysteria in María de Zayas's *Desengaños amorosos*." *Hispanófila* 114 (May 1995): 11–28.

Gossy, Mary. "Skirting the Question: Lesbians and María de Zayas." In Sylvia Molloy and Robert McKee Irwin, eds., *Hispanisms and Homosexualities*. Durham, N.C.: Duke University Press, 1998, pp. 19–28.

Goytisolo, Juan. "El mundo erótico de María de Zayas." *Disidencias*. Barcelona: Seix Barral, 1977, pp. 63–115.

Graycar, Regina. "Telling Tales: Legal Stories about Violence against Women." *Cardozo Studies in Law and Literature* 8.2 (Fall/Winter 1996): 297–315.

Greenberg, Mitchell. *Baroque Bodies: Psychoanalysis and the Culture of French Absolutism*. Ithaca, N.Y.: Cornell University Press, 2001.

Greenblatt, Stephen. "Fiction and Friction." In Thomas Heller, Sosna Morton, David Wellbery, Arnold Davidson, Ann Swidler, and Ian Watt, eds., *Reconstructing Individualism: Autonomy, Individuality, and the Self in Western Thought*. Stanford, Calif.: Stanford University Press, 1986, pp. 30–52.

Greer, Allan, and Jodi Bilinkoff, eds. and intro. *Colonial Saints: Discovering the Holy in the Americas, 1500–1800*. New York and London: Routledge, 2003.

Greer, Margaret. *María de Zayas Tells Baroque Tales of Love and the Cruelty of Men*. University Park: Pennsylvania State University Press, 2000.

Grosz, Elizabeth. *Space, Time, Perversion*. New York: Routledge, 1995.

Guevara, María de. (Condesa de Escalante). *Desengaños de la corte, y mujeres valerosas*. 1664. R/4496, Biblioteca Nacional, Madrid.

_____. *Warnings to the Kings: Advice on Restoring Spain*. Ed. and trans. Nieves Romero-Díaz. Chicago: University of Chicago Press, forthcoming 2006.

Halavais, Mary. *Like Wheat to the Miller: Community, Convivencia, and the Construction of Morisco Identity in Sixteenth-Century Aragon*. New York: Columbia University Press, 2002.

Haliczer, Stephen. "The First Holocaust: The Inquisition and the Converted Jews of Spain and Portugal." In Haliczer, *Inquisition and Society in Early Modern Europe*, pp. 7–18.

_____, ed. and trans. *Inquisition and Society in Early Modern Europe*. Totowa, N.J.: Barnes and Noble, 1987.

_____. *Inquisition and Society in the Kingdom of Valencia, 1478–1834*. Berkeley: University of California Press, 1990.

_____. *Sexuality in the Confessional: A Sacrament Profaned*. New York: Oxford University Press, 1996.

Hegstrom (Oakey), Valerie. "The Fallacy of False Dichotomy in María de Zayas's *Traición en la amistad*." *Bulletin of the Comediantes* 46.1 (Summer 1994): 59–70.

Hegstrom (Oakey), Valerie, and Amy R. Williamsen, eds. *Engendering the Early Modern Stage: Women Playwrights in the Spanish Empire*. New Orleans: University Press of the South, 1999.

Heiple, Daniel. "Lope de Vega Explores Homoerotic Desire." In Joseph Ricapito, ed.,

Selected Proceedings: Louisiana Conference on Hispanic Languages and Literatures. Baton Rouge: Louisiana State University Press, 1994, pp. 121–31.

Heller, Scott. "Rediscovering the Racy Fiction of a Seventeenth-Century Spanish Woman." *Chronicle of Higher Education,* 2 February 2001, p. 15

Herpoel, Sonja. *A la zaga de Santa Teresa: Autobiografías per mandato.* Amsterdam and Atlanta: Rodopi, 1999.

Herrera de Salcedo, Antonio. *Espejo de la perfecta casada.* Madrid: N.p., 1637.

Herrera Puga, Pedro. *Sociedad y delincuencia en el siglo de oro.* Madrid: Editorial Católica, 1974.

Hillgarth, J. N. *The Mirror of Spain, 1500–1700: The Formation of a Myth.* Ann Arbor: University of Michigan Press, 2000.

Hillman, David, and Carla Mazzio, eds. *The Body in Parts: Fantasies of Corporeality in Early Modern Europe.* New York: Routledge, 1997.

Hipólita de Jesús y Rocaberti (Madre). *Libro primero de su admirable vida, y doctrina, que escribió de su mano por mandado de sus prelados y confesores.* Sale a luz de orden del ilustríssimo y excelentíssimo señor don Fray Juan Tomas de Rocaberti, su sobrino. Valencia: Francisco Mestre, 1679.

Imirizaldu, Jesús. *Monjas y beatas embaucadoras.* Madrid: Editora Nacional, 1977.

Jiménez, Julio. "Doña Mariana de Carvajal y Saavedra: *Navidades de Madrid y noches entretenidas, en ocho novelas.* Edición crítica y anotada." Ph.D. diss., Northwestern University, 1974.

Jiménez, Lourdes Noemi. "Imágenes costumbristas: Historia y écfrasis en 'Amar sin saber a quién.'" In Whitenack and Campbell, *Zayas and Her Sisters, 2,* pp. 219–33.

Jones, Ann Rosalind, and Peter Stallybrass. "Fetishizing Gender: Constructing the Hermaphrodite in Renaissance Europe." In Epstein and Straub, *Body Guards,* pp. 80–111.

Jones, Margaret. "*Vindicación Feminista* and the Feminist Community in Post-Franco Spain." In Vollendorf, *Recovering Spain's Feminist Tradition,* pp. 311–36.

Jordan, Constance. *Renaissance Feminism: Literary Texts and Political Models.* Ithaca, N.Y.: Cornell University Press, 1990.

Juana Inés de la Cruz (Sor). *The Answer / La respuesta.* Ed. and trans. Electa Arenal and Amanda Powell. New York: Feminist Press, 1994.

———. *Obras completas.* 4 vols. Ed. Alfonso Méndex Plancarte (Vols. 1–3) and Alberto G. Saledo (Vol. 4). Reprint. Mexico City: Fondo de Cultura Económica, 1976.

Kagan, Richard L. *Lucrecia's Dreams: Politics and Prophecy in Sixteenth-Century Spain.* Berkeley: University of California Press, 1989.

Kagan, Richard L., and Abby Dyer, eds. and trans. *Inquisitional Inquiries: The Secret Lives of Jews and Other Heretics.* Baltimore, Md.: Johns Hopkins University Press, 2004.

Kamen, Henry. *Empire: How Spain Became a World Power, 1492–1763.* New York: HarperCollins, 2003.

———. *Inquisition and Society in Spain in the Sixteenth and Seventeenth Centuries.* 2nd ed. Bloomington: Indiana University Press, 1985.

_____. *Spain in the Later Seventeenth Century, 1665–1700*. New York and London: Longman, 1980.

Kaminsky, Amy Katz. "Dress and Redress: Clothing in the *Desengaños amorosos* of María de Zayas y Sotomayor." *Romanic Review* 79.2 (1988): 377–91.

_____. "María de Zayas and the Invention of a Women's Writing Community." *Revista de Estudios Hispánicos* 35 (2001): 487–509.

_____, ed. and intro. *Water Lilies / Flores del agua: An Anthology of Spanish Women Writers from the Fifteenth through the Nineteenth Century*. Minneapolis: University of Minnesota Press, 1996. [Includes women's texts from four centuries, in English and Spanish.]

Kelly, Joan. "Did Women Have a Renaissance?" In *Women, History, and Theory: The Essays of Joan Kelly*. Chicago: University of Chicago Press, 1984, pp. 19–50.

Kessler, Suzanne J. *Lessons from the Intersexed*. New Brunswick, N.J., and London: Rutgers University Press, 1998.

King, Margaret L. *Women of the Renaissance*. Chicago: University of Chicago Press, 1991.

King, Margaret L., and Albert Rabil Jr. "The Other Voice in Early Modern Europe: Introduction to the Series." In *The Worth of Women*, by Moderata Fonte. Ed. and trans. Virginia Cox. Chicago: University of Chicago Press, 1997, pp. vii–xxvi.

Laqueur, Thomas. *Making Sex: Body and Gender from the Greeks to Freud*. Cambridge: Harvard University Press, 1990.

Larson, Catherine. "Gender, Reading, and Intertextuality: Don Juan's Legacy in María de Zayas's *La traición en la amistad*." *Inti: Revista de literatura hispánica* 40–41 (Fall 1994–Spring 1995): 129–38.

_____. "Reforming the Golden Age Dramatic Canon: Women's Writing, Women's Voice, and the Question of Value." *Gestos* 7.14 (November 1992): 117–25.

Lavrin, Asunción. "Sexuality in Colonial Mexico: A Church Dilemma." In Asunción Lavrin, ed., *Sexuality and Marriage in Colonial Latin America*. Lincoln: University of Nebraska Press, 1989, pp. 47–95.

_____. "Unlike Sor Juana? The Model Nun in the Religious Literature of Colonial Mexico." In Stephanie Merrim, ed., *Feminist Perspectives on Sor Juana Inés de la Cruz*. Detroit: Wayne State University Press, 1991, pp. 61–85.

Luis de León (Fray). *La perfecta casada*. [1583]. Ed. Javier San José Lera. Madrid: Espasa Calpe, 1992.

Magdalena de San Jerónimo (Madre). *Razón y forma de la galera y la casa real, que el rey nuestro señor manda hacer en estos reinos para castigo de las mujeres vagantes, ladronas, alcahuetas y otros semejantes*. [Valladolid: Francisco Fernández de Córdova, 1608.] In Barbeito Carneiro, *Cárceles y mujeres en el siglo XVII*, pp. 61–96.

Manuel, Bernarda. Inquisition Trial. Sección Inquisición, Leg. 164, Exp. 7, Archivo Histórico Nacional, Madrid.

Maravall, José Antonio. *La literatura picaresca desde la historia social: Siglos XVI y XVII*. Madrid: Taurus, 1986.

Marcela de San Félix (Sor). *Literatura conventual femenina: Sor Marcela de San Félix, hija de Lope de Vega: Obras completas.* Ed. Electa Arenal and Sabat de Rivers. Barcelona: PPU, 1988.

————. "The Death of Desire." Trans. Amanda Powell. In Arenal and Schlau, pp. 250–68.

María de Jesús de Agreda (Madre). *Correspondencia con Felipe IV: Religión y razón de estado.* Ed. Consolación Baranda. Madrid: Ed. Castalia, Instituto de la mujer, 2001.

María de San Alberto (Madre). *Viva al Siglo, Muerta al Mundo. Selected Works / Obras escogidas by / de María de San Alberto (1568–1640).* Ed, intro., and trans. Stacey Schlau. New Orleans: University Press of the South, 1998.

María de San José (Madre). *Instrucción de novicias: Diálogo entre dos religiosas que Gracia y Justa se llaman sobre la oración y mortificación con que se deben criar las novicias.* [1602]. Ed. Simeón de la Sagrada Familia's edition of Madre María's *Escritos espirituales.* 2nd ed. Rome: Postulación General, 1979.

Maroto Camino, Mercedes. "María de Zayas and Ana Caro: The Space of Woman's Solidarity in the Spanish Golden Age." *Hispanic Review* 67.1 (Winter 1999): 1–16.

————. *Book for the Hour of Recreation.* Ed. Alison Weber. Trans. Amanda Powell. Chicago: University of Chicago Press, 2003.

Márquez, Antonio. *Los alumbrados: Orígenes y filosofía (1525–1559).* 2nd ed. Madrid: Taurus, 1980.

Márquez Villanueva, Francisco. *El problema morisco (desde otras laderas).* Madrid: Prodhufi, 1991.

Marshall, Sherrin, ed. *Women in Reformation and Counter-Reformation Europe.* Bloomington: Indiana University Press, 1989.

Martín Gaite, Carmen. *Usos amorosos de la postguerra.* Barcelona: Anagrama, 1987.

Martínez-Gutiérrez, Josebe. "Feminist and Political Praxis during the Spanish Civil War." In Vollendorf, *Recovering Spain's Feminist Tradition,* pp. 278–92.

Masten, Jeffrey. *Textual Intercourse: Collaboration, Authorship, and Sexualities in Renaissance Drama.* Cambridge: Cambridge University Press, 1997.

Matheo de Jesús María (Fray). *Tomo Tercero: Apuntamientos originales de N. P. Fr. Matheo de Jesús María a la Vida de la V[enerable] S[anta] D[oña] María Orozco, desde el año de 1690 hasta el de 1709 en que murió.* Mss. 6995, Biblioteca Nacional, Madrid.

McKendrick, Melveena. *Women and Society in the Spanish Drama of the Golden Age: A Study of the Mujer Varonil.* London: Cambridge University Press, 1974.

McKnight, Kathryn Joy. *The Mystic of Tunja: The Writings of Madre Castillo, 1671–1742.* Amherst: University of Massachusetts Press, 1997.

Melammed, Renée Levine. "Crypto-Jewish Women Facing the Spanish Inquisition: Transmitting Religious Practices, Beliefs, and Attitudes." In Meyerson and English, *Christians, Muslims, and Jews,* pp. 197–219.

————. *Heretics or Daughters of Israel? The Crypto-Jewish Women of Castile.* New York and Oxford: Oxford University Press, 1999.

————. "Judaizers and Prayer in Sixteenth-Century Alcázar." In Cooperman, pp. 273–95.

Meneses, Leonor de. *El desdeñado más firme, primera parte.* Ed. Judith Whitenack and Gwyn Campbell. Potomac, Md.: Scripta Humanistica, 1994.

Merrim, Stephanie. *Early Modern Women's Writing and Sor Juana Inés de la Cruz.* Nashville: Vanderbilt University Press, 1999.

Meyerson, Mark D., and Edward D. English, eds. *Christians, Muslims, and Jews in Medieval and Early Modern Spain: Interaction and Cultural Change.* Notre Dame, Ind.: University of Notre Dame Press, 1999.

Monter, William. *Frontiers of Heresy: The Spanish Inquisition from the Basque Lands to Sicily.* Cambridge: Cambridge University Press, 1990.

Mooney, Catherine, ed. and intro. *Gendered Voices: Medieval Saints and Their Interpreters.* Philadelphia: University of Pennsylvania Press, 1999.

Mujica, Bárbara. *Sophia's Daughters: Women Writers of Early Modern Spain.* New Haven: Yale University Press, 2004. [Textual selections of thirteen women authors in Spanish.]

Myers, Kathleen Ann. *Neither Saints nor Sinners: Writing the Lives of Spanish American Women.* New York: Oxford University Press, 2002.

Myers, Kathleen Ann, and Amanda Powell. *A Wild Country out in the Garden: The Spiritual Journals of a Mexican Nun.* Bloomington: Indiana University Press, 2001.

Nader, Helen, ed. *Power and Gender in Renaissance Spain: Eight Women of the Mendoza Family, 1450–1650.* Urbana: University of Illinois Press, 2004.

Nalle, Sara. *God in La Mancha: Religious Reform and the People of Cuenca, 1500–1650.* Baltimore, Md.: Johns Hopkins University Press, 1992.

———. "Literacy and Culture in Early Modern Castile." *Past and Present* 125 (November 1989): 65–96.

Navarro, Ana, ed. and intro. *Antología poética de escritoras de los siglos XVI y XVII.* Madrid: Castalia, Instituto de la mujer, 1989.

Netanyahu, Benzion. *Toward the Inquisition: Essays on Jewish and Converso History in Late Medieval Spain.* Ithaca, N.Y.: Cornell University Press, 1997.

Nirenberg, David. *Communities of Violence: Persecution of Minorities in the Middle Ages.* Princeton: Princeton University Press, 1996.

———. "Conversion, Sex, and Segregation: Jews and Christians in Medieval Spain." *American Historical Review* 107.4 (October 2002): 1065–93.

Norton, Mary Beth. *Founding Mothers and Fathers: Gendered Power and the Forming of American Society.* New York: Knopf, 1996.

O'Driscoll, Sally. "Outlaw Readings: Beyond Queer Theory." *Signs* 22.1 (Fall 1996): 30–51.

Olivares, Julián, and Elizabeth Boyce, eds. *Tras el espejo la musa escribe: lírica femenina de los Siglos de Oro.* Madrid: Siglo Veintiuno, 1993.

Ordóñez, Elizabeth. "Woman and Her Text in the Works of María de Zayas and Ana Caro." *Revista de Estudios Hispánicos* 19 (1986): 3–13.

Ossorio, Constanza. *Huerta del celestial esposo, fundado sobre el opúsculo de N. P. S. Bernardo, que comienza: Ad quid venisti?* Sevilla: Thomas López de Haro, 1686.

Padilla Manrique, Luisa María de. (Condesa de Aranda). *Idea de nobles y sus desem-*

peños en aforismos. *Parte cuarta de Nobleza Virtuosa.* Zaragoza: Hospital Real y General de Nuestra Señora de Gracia, 1644.

———. *Lágrimas de la nobleza: Parte tercera de Nobleza Virtuosa.* Zaragoza: Pedro Lanaja y Lamarca, 1639.

Park, Katharine. "The Rediscovery of the Clitoris: French Medicine and the Tribade, 1570–1620." In Hillman and Mazzio, *The Body in Parts*, pp. 171–93.

Paun de García, Susan. "*Traición en la amistad* de María de Zayas." *Anales de literatura española* 6 (1988): 377–90.

Pérez de Herrera, Cristóbal. "Discursos del amparo de los legítimos pobres y reducción de los fingidos." Madrid: Luis Sánchez, 1598.

Pérez Molina, Isabel. "Las mujeres y el matrimonio en el derecho catalán moderno." In Isabel Pérez Molina, et al., *Las mujeres en el antiguo régimen: Imagen y realidad.* Barcelona: ICARIA, 1994, pp. 21–56.

Pérez Villanueva, Joaquín. "Felipe IV y la Inquisición y espiritualidad de su tiempo: su figura desde tres espistolarios." In Angel Alcalá et al., eds., *Inquisición española y mentalidad inquisitorial: Ponencias del Simposio Internacional sobre Inquisición. Nueva York, abril de 1983.* Barcelona: Ariel, 1984, pp. 434–60.

Perry, Mary Elizabeth. "Beatas and the Inquisition in Early Modern Seville." In Haliczer, *Inquisition and Society in Early Modern Europe,* pp. 147–68.

———. *Crime and Society in Early Modern Seville.* Hanover, N.H.: University of Press of New England, 1980.

———. *Gender and Disorder in Early Modern Seville.* Princeton: Princeton University Press, 1990.

———. *The Handless Maiden: Moriscos and the Politics of Religion in Early Modern Spain.* Princeton: Princeton University Press, 2004.

———. "Magdalens and Jezebels in Counter Reformation Spain." In Cruz and Perry, *Culture and Control in Counter Reformation Spain,* pp. 124–44.

———. "Moriscas and the Limits of Assimilation." In Meyerson and English, *Christians, Muslims, and Jews,* pp. 274–89.

———. "The 'Nefarious' Sin in Early Modern Seville." *Journal of Homosexuality* 16.1–2 (1988): 67–90.

Perry, Mary Elizabeth, and Anne J. Cruz, eds. and intro. *Cultural Encounters: The Impact of the Inquisition in Spain and the New World.* Berkeley: University of California Press, 1991.

Petroff, Elizabeth Alvilda. *Body and Soul: Essays on Medieval Women and Mysticism.* Oxford: Oxford University Press, 1994.

Pike, Ruth. *Aristocrats and Traders: Sevillian Society in the Sixteenth Century.* Ithaca, N.Y.: Cornell University Press, 1972.

Pinelo, Valentina. *Libro de las alabanzas y excelencias de la gloriosa Santa Ana.* Sevilla: Clemente Hidalgo, 1601.

Poska, Allyson. *Regulating the People: The Catholic Reformation in Seventeenth-Century Spain.* Boston and Leiden: Brill, 1998.

Poska, Allyson, and Elizabeth Lehfeldt. "Redefining Expectations: Women and the Church in Early Modern Spain." In Dinan and Meyers, *Women and Religion,* pp. 21–42.

Poutrin, Isabelle. *Le voile et la plume: Autobiographie et sainteté fémenine dans l'Espagne moderne.* Madrid: Casa de Velázquez, 1995.

Profeti, Maria Grazia. "Los parentescos ficticios desde una perspectiva femenina: María de Zayas y Mariana de Carvajal." In Augustin Redondo, ed., *Les parentés fictives en Espagne.* Paris: Publications de la Sorbonne, 1988, pp. 223–46.

Puyol y Buil, Carlos. *Inquisición y política en el reinado de Felipe IV: Los procesos de Jerónimo de Villanueva y las monjas de San Plácido, 1628–1660.* Madrid: Consejo Superior de Investigaciones Científicas, 1993.

Quezada, Noemí. "The Inquisition's Repression of *Curanderos.*" In Perry and Cruz, *Cultural Encounters,* pp. 37–57.

Rapley, Elizabeth. *The Dévotes: Women and Church in Seventeenth-Century France.* Montreal and Kingston, London, Buffalo: McGill–Queen's University Press, 1990.

Rhodes, Elizabeth. "'Y Yo Dije, Sí, señor': Ana Domenge and the Barcelona Inquisition." In Giles, *Women in the Inquisition,* pp. 134–54.

Ríos Izquierdo, Pilar. *Mujer y sociedad en el siglo XVII a través de los avisos de Barrionuevo.* Madrid: horas y HORAS, 1994.

Rodríguez Cuadros, Evangelina, ed. and intro. *Novelas amorosas de diversos ingenios del siglo XVII.* Madrid: Castalia, 1987.

Romero, María, and Juana Gómez. Sección Inquisición, Leg. 95, Exp. 1, Archivo Histórico Nacional, Madrid.

Romero-Díaz, Nieves. *Nueva nobleza, nueva novela: Reescribiendo la cultura urbana del barroco.* Newark: Juan de la Cuesta, 2002.

Roof, Judith. *Come as You Are.* New York: Routledge, 1996.

Root, Deborah. "Speaking Christian: Orthodoxy and Difference in Sixteenth-Century Spain." *Representations* 23 (1988): 118–34.

Roper, Lyndal. *Oedipus and the Devil: Witchcraft, Sexuality, and Religion in Early Modern Europe.* London and New York: Routledge, 1994.

Roth, Norman. *Conversos, Inquisition, and the Expulsion of the Jews from Spain.* Madison: University of Wisconsin Press, 1995.

Rubiera Mata, María Jesús, ed. and intro. *Poesía femenina hispanoárabe.* Madrid: Instituto de la mujer, Castalia, 1999.

Ruggiero, Guido. *Binding Passions: Tales of Magic, Marriage, and Power at the End of the Renaissance.* New York and Oxford: Oxford University Press, 1993.

———. *A Companion to the Worlds of the Renaissance.* Malden, Mass.: Blackwell, 2002.

Ruiz, Teofilo. *Spanish Society (1400–1600).* Harlow, Eng., and New York: Longman, 2000.

Sacristán, María Cristina. *Locura e Inquisición en Nueva España, 1571–1760.* México, D.F.: Fondo de Cultura Económica, 1992.

Sánchez, Magdalena. *The Empress, the Queen, and the Nun: Women and Power at the Court of Philip III of Spain.* Baltimore, Md., and London: Johns Hopkins University Press, 1998.

Sánchez Lora, José. *Mujeres, conventos y formas de la religiosidad barroca.* Madrid: Fundación Universitaria Española, 1988.

Sánchez Ortega, María Helena. *Ese viejo diablo llamado el amor: La magia amorosa en la España moderna.* Madrid: UNED, 2004.

_____. *La mujer y la sexualidad en el antiguo régimen.* Madrid: Ed. Akal, 1992.

_____. "Sorcery and Eroticism in Love and Magic." In Perry and Cruz, *Cultural Encounters,* pp. 58–92.

Scarre, Geoffrey, and John Callow. *Witchcraft and Magic in Sixteenth- and Seventeenth-Century Europe.* Houndmills, Basingstoke, Hampshire: Palgrave, 2001.

Schlau, Stacey. "Following Saint Teresa: Early Modern Women and Religious Authority." *Modern Language Notes* 117.2 (2002): 286–309.

_____. *Spanish American Women's Use of the Word: Colonial through Contemporary Narratives.* Tucson: University of Arizona Press, 2001.

_____, ed., intro., and trans. *Viva al Siglo, Muerta al Mundo. Selected Works / Obras escogidas by / de María de San Alberto (1568–1640).* New Orleans: University Press of the South, 1998.

Schlau, Stacey, and Electa Arenal. "Not Only Her Father's Daughter: Sor Marcela de San Félix Stages a Nun's Profession." In Hegstrom and Williamsen, *Engendering the Early Modern Stage,* pp. 221–38.

Schutte, Anne Jacobson. "Inquisition and Female Autobiography: The Case of Cecilia Ferrazzi." In Craig Monson, ed., *The Crannied Wall: Women, Religion, and the Arts in Early Modern Europe.* Ann Arbor: University of Michigan Press, 1992, pp. 105–18.

Scott, Karen. "Mystical Death, Bodily Death: Catherine of Siena and Raymond of Capua on the Mystic's Encounter with God." In Mooney, *Gendered Voices,* pp. 136–67.

Seidenspinner-Núñez, Dayle. "Inflecting the *Converso* Voice: A Commentary on Recent Theories." *La Corónica* 25.1 (Fall 1996): 6–18.

Serrano y Sanz, Manuel. "Carvajal y Saavedra (Doña Mariana de). *Apuntes para una biblioteca de escritoras españolas desde el año 1401 al 1833.* Vol. 1. Madrid: Sucesores de Rivadeneyra, 1903, pp. 236–44.

Sinfield, Alan. *Cultural Politics, Queer Readings.* Philadelphia: University of Pennsylvania Press, 1994.

Sluhovsky, Moshe. "The Devil in the Convent." *American Historical Review* 107.5 (December 2002): 1379–1411.

Smith, Bruce R. *Homosexual Desire in Shakespeare's England.* Chicago: University of Chicago Press, 1991.

_____. "Premodern Sexualities." *PMLA* 115.3 (May 2000): 318–29.

Smith, Dawn. "Introduction: The Perception of Women in the Spanish *Comedia.*" In Anita Stoll and Dawn Smith, eds., *The Perception of Women in Spanish Theater of the Golden Age.* Lewisburg, Pa.: Bucknell University Press, 1991, pp. 17–29.

Smith, Susan Manell. "The Colloquies of Sor Marcela de San Félix and the Tradition of Sacred Allegorical Drama." Ph.D. diss., University of Virginia, 1998.

Smith, Theresa A. *The Emerging Female Citizen: Gender and Enlightenment in Spain.* Berkeley: University of California Press, forthcoming.

Soriano, Catherine. "Introducción." In Carvajal, *Navidades de Madrid,* pp. ix–xxi.

Soufas, Teresa Scott. *Dramas of Distinction: A Study of Plays by Golden Age Women.* Lexington: University of Kentucky Press, 1997.

————. "María de Zayas's (Un)Conventional Play, *La traición en la amistad.*" In Charles Ganelin and Howard Mancing, eds., *The Golden Age Comedia: Text, Theory, and Performance.* West Lafayette, Ind.: Purdue University Press, 1994, pp. 148–64.

————, ed. *Women's Acts: Plays by Women Dramatists of Spain's Golden Age.* Lexington: University of Kentucky Press, 1997.

Soufas, Teresa Scott, with Dixon Abreu, Laura Barbas, Isabel Crespo, Angeles Farmer, Daniela Flesler, Shani Moser, Roberto Ortiz, Marcie Rinka, Christina Sisk, Paulina Vaca, Juping Wang, and Nancy Whitlock. "Playing with Saint Isabel: Drama from the Pen of an Unknown Adolescent." In Vollendorf, *Recovering Spain's Feminist Tradition,* pp. 123–41.

Souza, Joana Theodora de. *El gran prodigio.* N.p., n.d. R/12199, Biblioteca Nacional, Madrid.

Spanier, Bonnie B. "Lessons from 'Nature': Gender Ideology and Sexual Ambiguity in Biology." In Epstein and Straub, *Body Guards,* pp. 329–50.

Starr-LeBeau, Gretchen. *In the Shadow of the Virgin: Inquisitors, Friars, and Conversos in Guadalupe, Spain.* Princeton: Princeton University Press, 2003.

Stock, Phyllis. *Better Than Rubies: A History of Women's Education.* New York: G. P. Putnam's Sons, 1978.

Stroud, Matthew. "Love, Friendship, and Deceit in *La traición en la amistad* by María de Zayas." *Neophilologus* 69 (1985): 539–47.

Sullivan, Constance. "Constructing Her Own Tradition: Ideological Selectivity in Josefa Amar y Borbón's Representation of Female Models." In Vollendorf, *Recovering Spain's Feminist Tradition,* pp. 142–59.

Surtz, Ron. *Writing Women in Late Medieval and Early Modern Spain.* Philadelphia: University of Pennsylvania Press, 1995.

Tenorio Gómez, Pilar. *Las madrileñas de mil seiscientos: Imagen y realidad.* Madrid: horas y HORAS, 1993.

Teresa de Jesús María (Sor). *Trata de una breve relación de la vida que qunta una monja descalça.* N.p., 1633. Mss. 8482, Biblioteca Nacional, Madrid.

Teresa of Jesus. *The Complete Works of St. Teresa of Jesus.* Ed. and trans. E. Allison Peers. 3 vols. London: Sheed, 1978.

Thurston, Herbert. *The Physical Phenomenon of Mysticism.* Ed. J. H. Crehan. London: Burns, Oates, 1952.

Tigchelaar, Alisa Joanne. "Instruction and Self-Identification on the Cloistered Stage: Dramatic Production in the Seventeenth-Century Spanish Convent." Ph.D. diss., Indiana University, 1999.

Torres, Fray Agustín de. "Relación verdadera de una carta (1617)." Con licencia del santo provisor don Francisco de Lederma. Impreso en Granada por Juan Muñoz, n.d. Mss. 2058, Biblioteca Nacional, Madrid.

Traub, Valerie. "The (In)Significance of Lesbian Desire." In Goldberg, *Queering the Renaissance,* pp. 62–83.

———. *The Renaissance of Lesbianism in Early Modern England.* Cambridge: Cambridge University Press, 2002.

———. "The Rewards of Lesbian History." *Feminist Studies* 25.2 (Summer 1999): 363–94.

Traub, Valerie, M. Lindsey Kaplan, and Dympna Callaghan, eds. *Feminist Readings of Early Modern Culture: Emerging Subjects.* Cambridge: Cambridge University Press, 1996.

Trumbach, Randolph. "London's Sapphists: From Three Sexes to Four Genders in the Making of Modern Culture." In Epstein and Straub, *Body Guards,* pp. 112–41.

Tueller, James. *Good and Faithful Christians: Moriscos and Catholicism in Early Modern Spain.* New Orleans: University Press of the South, 2002.

Valis, Noël M. "Mariana de Carvajal: The Spanish Storyteller." In Katharina M. Wilson and Frank J. Warnke, eds., *Women Writers of the Seventeenth Century.* Athens and London: University of Georgia Press, 1989, pp. 251–82.

Valle de la Cerda, Teresa. In Barbeito Carneiro, *Cárceles y mujeres,* pp. 125–265.

Velasco, Sherry. *The Lieutenant Nun: Transgenderism, Lesbian Desire, and Catalina de Erauso.* Austin: University of Texas Press, 2000.

———. "Reconsidering Romance in Mariana de Carvajal's 'La venus de Ferrara.'" In Whitenack and Campbell, *Zayas and Her Sisters, 2,* pp. 189–201.

Vélez-Quiñones, Harry. *Monstrous Displays: Representation and Perversion in Spanish Literature.* New Orleans: University Press of the South, 1999.

Vida de María de Orozco y Luján. Mss. 6625, Biblioteca Nacional, Madrid.

Vigil, Mariló. *La vida de las mujeres en los siglos XVI y XVII.* Madrid: Siglo Veintiuno, 1986.

Vives, Juan Luis. *The Instruction of a Christian Woman. [1524].* Ed. Charles Fantazzi. Chicago: University of Chicago Press, 2000.

Vollendorf, Lisa. "The Future of Early Modern Women's Studies: The Case of Same-Sex Friendship and Desire in Zayas and Carvajal." *Arizona Journal of Cultural Studies* 4 (2000): 265–84.

———. *Reclaiming the Body: María de Zayas's Early Modern Feminism.* Chapel Hill: University of North Carolina Press, 2001.

———, ed. and intro. *Recovering Spain's Feminist Tradition.* New York: Modern Language Association of America, 2001.

———. "Women Writers in Sixteenth-Century Spain." In Gregory Kaplan, ed., *Dictionary of Literary Biography: Sixteenth-Century Spain.* Westport, Conn.: Greenwood Press, 2005.

Walker, Garthine. "Rereading Rape and Sexual Violence in Early Modern England." *Gender and History* 10.1 (April 1998): 1–25.

Walker, Lenore. *The Battered Woman.* New York: HarperCollins, 1980.

Walliser, Marta. "Recuperación panorámica de la literatura laica femenina en lengua castellana (hasta el siglo XVII)." Ph.D. diss., Boston College, 1996.

Weaver, Elissa. "The Convent Wall in Tuscan Convent Drama." In Craig A. Monson, ed., *The Crannied Wall: Women, Religion, and the Arts in Early Modern Europe.* Ann Arbor: University of Michigan Press, 1992, pp. 73–86.

Weber, Alison. "Spiritual Administration: Gender and Discernment in the Carmelite Reform." *Sixteenth Century Journal* 31.1 (2000): 123–46.

_____. *Teresa de Avila and the Rhetoric of Femininity*. Princeton: Princeton University Press, 1989.

_____. "The Three Lives of the *Vida*: The Uses of Convent Autobiography." In Marta V. Vicente and Luis R. Corteguera, eds., *Women, Texts, and Authority in the Early Modern Spanish World*. Aldershot, Eng., and Burlington, Vt.: Ashgate, 2003, pp. 107–25.

Welles, Marcia. *Persephone's Girdle: Narratives of Rape in Seventeenth-Century Spanish Literature*. Nashville: Vanderbilt University Press, 2000.

Whitenack, Judith A. "Internalized Misogyny: A Study of Two Tales by Ana Abarca de Bolea." In Whitenack and Campbell, *Zayas and Her Sisters*, 2, pp. 253–70.

_____. Introduction to *María de Zayas*, ed. Williamsen and Whitenack, pp. 1–10.

Whitenack, Judith A., and Gwyn Campbell, eds. *El desdeñado más firme, primera parte*, by Leonor de Meneses. Potomac, Md.: Scripta Humanistica, 1994.

_____, eds. *Zayas and Her Sisters, 1: Novelas by Seventeenth-Century Spanish Women*. Asheville, N.C.: Pegasus, 2000.

_____, eds. *Zayas and Her Sisters, 2: Essays on Novelas by Seventeenth-Century Spanish Women*. Binghamton, N.Y.: Global Publications–Binghamton University, 2001.

Wiesner, Merry. *Women and Gender in Early Modern Europe*. Cambridge: Cambridge University Press, 1993.

Wilkins, Constance. "Subversion through Comedy? Two Plays by Sor Juana Inés de la Cruz and María de Zayas." In Anita Stoll and Dawn Smith, eds., *The Perception of Women in Spanish Theater of the Golden Age*. Lewisburg, Pa.: Bucknell University Press, 1991, pp. 107–20.

Williamsen, Amy R. "Charting Our Course: Gender, the Canon, and Early Modern Theater." In Hegstrom and Williamsen, *Engendering the Early Modern Stage*, pp. 1–16.

Williamsen, Amy R., and Judith A. Whitenack, eds. and intro. *María de Zayas: The Dynamics of Discourse*. Madison, N.J.: Fairleigh Dickinson University Press, 1995.

Yllera, Alicia, ed. Introducción to Zayas, *Desengaños amorosos*, pp. 11–110.

Zayas y Sotomayor, María de. *Desengaños amorosos*. 2nd ed. Ed. Alicia Yllera. Madrid: Cátedra, 1993.

_____. *The Disenchantments of Love*. Trans. H. Patsy Boyer. Binghamton: SUNY Binghamton Press, 1997.

_____. *The Enchantments of Love*. Trans. H. Patsy Boyer. Berkeley: University of California Press, 1990.

_____. *Novelas amorosas y ejemplares*. Ed. Julián Olivares. Madrid: Cátedra, 2000.

_____. *La traición en la amistad*. In Soufas, *Women's Acts*, pp. 277–308.

_____. *La traición en la amistad / Friendship Betrayed*. Ed. Valerie Hegstrom. Trans. Catherine Larson. Lewisburg, Pa.: Bucknell University Press, 1999.

INDEX